COMMANDMENT
AND
COMMUNITY

SUNY Series in Jewish Philosophy
Kenneth Seeskin, Editor

COMMANDMENT AND COMMUNITY

New Essays in Jewish Legal and Political Philosophy

edited by

DANIEL H. FRANK

State University
of New York
Press

Published by
State University of New York Press, Albany

© 1995 State University of New York

Production by Susan Geraghty
Marketing by Bernadette LaManna

Printed in the United States of America

For information, address State University of New York Press, State University
Plaza, Albany, N.Y., 12246

Library of Congress Cataloging-in-Publication Data

Commandment and community : new essays in Jewish legal and political
    philosophy / edited by Daniel H. Frank.
        p. cm.—(SUNY series in Jewish philosophy)
    Includes bibliographical references and index.
    ISBN 0-7914-2429-4.—ISBN 0-7914-2430-8 (pbk).
    1. Judaism and politics—Congresses. 2. Jewish law—Philosophy-
-Congresses. 3. Philosophy, Jewish—Congresses. I. Frank, Daniel
H., 1950- . II. Series.
BM645.P64C66 1995
296.3'877—dc20   94-18406
                                                          CIP

10 9 8 7 6 5 4 3 2 1

296.3877
C734

CONTENTS

INTRODUCTION

Despite a vigorous debate commenced in medieval times concerning the nature, number, and scope of Jewish foundational principles ("roots"), to understand Judaism as a set of doctrines and beliefs that Jews hold is not a particularly Jewish notion; it assimilates Judaism to a philosophical sect or a political party. Although this may have been part of the intent of those intellectuals engaged in dogmatics, it is certainly the case that for the much greater part of its history Judaism has been construed by Jews and non-Jews alike as a *way of life.* This is of course not to say that the way of life that is Judaism is lacking in "theory," in cognitive content and philosophical presuppositions. Nor is it to suggest that Jews are unreflective or insensitive as they go about their business. This latter has historically been a particularly popular charge leveled against Jews and Judaism, the impetus being to pay off the "materiality" or "carnality" or "legalism" of Judaism against the "spirituality" or morality of, say, Christianity. But to grant Jews qua Jews a spiritual life and a set of doctrines and beliefs that undergird their religious outlook is to overlook, or to pay too little attention to, the supreme importance of *practice* in Judaism. Perhaps even to put it thus is too dichotomous. Perhaps Judaism is pragmatic in the classical sense, as a mode of living that manifests the *unity* of thought and action. The commandments are commandments to *act* or not to act in certain ways, to celebrate the Sabbath, not to eat milk with meat, and so forth. And even those commandments that enjoin certain beliefs, such as in the unity and perfection of God, are commandments whose meaning at least in part requires a certain "materialization." So, for example, the weekly Sabbath celebration underscores and gives meaning to a certain belief, the perfection and beneficence of the creator. More globally, if, as Maimonides inter alios suggests, the primary purpose of the commandments is to expunge idolatry, then the rectification of belief is inextricably linked to and made manifest by action.

Such "materialization" of belief does not desacralize Judaism or render it less spiritual. Indeed, Judaism can well be conceived of as a way of life established for the purpose of sanctifying the mundane, of living for the sake of ennobling the created order. To live thus is to attach one's life to a project of redemption.

Redemption literally means "to buy back." To redeem an item pawned or stolen, to ransom it, requires both love and effort (work). And in redeeming the item one restores it to its natural place. From this angle, Judaism may be seen as a way of life devoted to restoration and renewal, to bringing about *dignified* change, change that demands a supreme sensitivity to the nature of the object involved. For Jews, God created everything in its place and in so doing deemed it good. Our goal as divine agents requires the same normative constraint. The irony, of course, is that the goodness of the created order is not entirely perspicuous, and therefore we must muddle about and ponder the extent to which the world is created *for us.*

Judaism is for Jews, not vice-versa. It is the (constitutive) means whereby Jews achieve the summum bonum, the highest good. Given our foregoing analysis, the summum bonum is perforce political. It is political in the broadest sense because it entails praxis, practical-political activity pursued for the sake of engendering goodness, a goodness and fulfillment with a dignity commensurate with the object in question. This is the thrust of Lenn Goodman's chapter, "Toward a Jewish Philosophy of Justice." Goodman develops a theory of justice based explicitly upon classical Jewish sources, both biblical and rabbinic. His theory is a normative one, indeed this very fact is mandated by its being based upon traditional sources. The tradition demands, as we might put it, theory for the sake of practice, and a metaethical theory is perforce ruled out. Goodman's normative theory of justice is based upon deserts. The deserts are resultant upon the claims that beings make, and these claims are grounded ontologically, in the way the world is. The divinely created world is good, has value; and for Goodman, this ontological given provides the grounding for a nonconventionalist, specifically non-Hobbesian, theory of justice. Goodman's "naturalist" theory blends Aristotelian and Kantian elements, philosophical anthropology and deontology. For Goodman, a Jewish philosophy of justice, based squarely upon traditional texts, must be at once sensitive to the dignity and intrinsic worth of beings, especially persons, *and* to their various attempts to achieve perfection. Only by keeping both aspects in mind can a Jewish theory of justice give due credit to duty and to reward, to the categorical nature of commandments and to the purposes for which they are instituted.

Oliver Leaman, in "Is a Jewish Practical Philosophy Possible?" asks whether a project such as Goodman's can succeed. Can a *philosophical* project be grounded in *religious* sources, given that religious and philosophical language are so very different from each other? Leaman illustrates his thesis by showing how flexible and open-ended our interpretations of religious language and stories are, so flexible in fact that they can be made to agree or disagree with a vast variety of philosophical positions. For Leaman, we (philosophers) require a theory of "translation" between philosophical and religious language *before* we can bring them together to construct a Jewish practical philosophy. The reader will note that Leaman's brief is itself open-ended, not dogmatically asserting that, say, a Jewish theory of justice cannot succeed, but rather suggesting that in lieu of a fully worked out theory of translation the philosopher exercise caution before claiming credit for a theory based upon Jewish sources. All too often, Leaman implies, the interpretation of text and the theory "based upon" it are question-begging. In its own way, Leaman's chapter appears to point in the direction of an antifoundational pluralism. The reader will want to tease out the hermeneutical implications of Leaman's position relative to traditional source interpretation.

My chapter, "Reason in Action: The 'Practicality' of Maimonides's *Guide*," attempts to show that Maimonides's *Guide*, too often presented piecemeal, as a patchwork of independent (theoretical) mini-treatises on creation, negative theology, and so on, can be interpreted along the lines of Aristotelian *practical* philosophy. The *Guide* is, after all, a guide for one perplexed about the meaning and intelligibility of his life. Joseph, the addressee of the *Guide*, like the auditors of Aristotle's *Ethics*, is perplexed about the goal and meaning of his life; and Maimonides, like Aristotle, takes it to be his charge to enlighten and, importantly, to *motivate* his student toward the requisite end. The *Guide* itself, whose explicit subject is the science of the law, is overarchingly concerned with showing the perplexed student that his accustomed way of life, a life lived in accord with traditional (halakhic) norms, is philosophically intelligible. And I argue that this point is *not* a theoretical point, but a practical one that has direct application to the overcoming of the initial perplexity and thereby to the achievement of ultimate felicity. The *Guide*, thus interpreted, is a paradigm of political praxis and practical philosophy, concerned with helping a future communal leader establish his way of life on a firm philosophical foundation and thereby position himself as a reflective member of his community.

The first part of the volume concludes with a notable instantiation of Jewish political praxis. With specific reference to current (1993–1994) national debates concerning health care reform, Elliot Dorff's "Jewish Tradition and National Policy" presents both the constitutional and the theological grounding for his own, and by implication general Jewish, involvement in the current political discussion. Despite the constitutional separation of church and state embodied in the first amendment, Dorff nevertheless finds grounds in American legal history for vigorous religious participation in public debate. And, despite the assumption of some Jewish sources and groups that only Judaism can embody God's will and that therefore Jews should remain aloof from (secular) political discourse and debate, Dorff finds historical, philosophical, and theological grounds for Jews *as Jews* to engage in American political debate. The entire discussion thus argues for a closer relationship between religion and the shaping of public policy than strict separationists, religious or secular, would allow.

The second set of chapters addresses certain aspects of Jewish legal theory and the history of Jewish political thought. Some of the chapters make clear the interplay between halakha and politics, between commandment and community, which, as just noted, is pronounced throughout the tradition. The classical codifiers of the law were communal leaders. Wherever and whenever Judaism is defined by reference to halakhic norms, Jewish political life is carried on against the backdrop of those very norms. Until the modern period, halakhic norms grounded moral and political life and were construed as enabling the achievement of communal and personal felicity. And today, as the exchange between Noam Zohar and David Bleich makes abundantly clear, halakhic discussion is hardly bereft of political implications. Correlatively, Jewish political thought never was and is not now a wholly secular enterprise, however much Greek political philosophy or contemporary liberal theory undergirds it. Maimonides, Abravanel, and contemporary Zionist thinkers such as Kook, Leibowitz, and Hartman present their arguments as the best readings of the tradition, biblical and rabbinic. In sum, political innovation or retrenchment, indeed the ebb and flow of Jewish political life, continues to be in large measure internally generated by the open-endedness of halakhic interpretation.

Aryeh Botwinick, in "Underdetermination of Meaning by the Talmudic Text," addresses this issue of interpretive open-endedness. For Botwinick, the underdetermination of meaning by text is a pervasive feature of talmudic argument. Such underdetermination or open-endedness of meaning animates many of the specific insights into and justification of talmudic argument. It also goes a long way in accounting for how innovation and change take place within Jewish law and communal practice. Decontextualizing previously received biblical, tannaitic, and early amoraic texts enables one to reconstitute and reinterpret them in a way which makes them relevant to new circumstances. Further, such interpretive open-endedness tends to subvert a strictly historical, contextual approach to the favored texts, an approach that lends itself to a hermeneutic rigidification. For Botwinick, there is an ineradicably aggadic element in even the most austerely halakhic discussion, and he illustrates this with reference to halakhic discussions concerning divorce and sin offerings.

In "Nachmanides's Conception of *Ta'amei Mitzvot* and Its Maimonidean Background," Josef Stern presents Nachmanides's account of the reasons or explanation for the Mosaic law and the interpretive principles expressive of them. Nachmanides's position is clarified with reference to Maimonides's. The latter's famous discussion in the third book of the *Guide* grounds the law in both social-political and suprapolitical goals, goals expressed by, what Stern calls, the *external* and the *internal* meanings of parables in the relevant texts. In addition to their parabolic (allegoric) meanings, the parables have a nonparabolic (literal) signification for Maimonides, and must to allow access to truth to the nonphilosophical masses. It is in their respective attitudes toward nonparabolic, literal signification that, according to Stern, Maimonides and Nachmanides differ. Nachmanides, unlike Maimonides, does not view the literal meaning of parabolic text as obfuscatory and sometimes even false; for Nachmanides, the *peshat*, the nonpara-bolic, literal meaning of the text is just that: part of the *meaning* of the text, the product of a bona fide authorial intention and not merely a disingenuous sop to the masses. Perhaps the non-Maimonidean position here presented is expressive of Nachman-ides's general hesitation about the elitist implications of Mai-monides's philosophical (Aristotelian) interpretation of Scripture. The reader will want to ponder the possible implications of Mai-monides's and Nachmanides's differing hermeneutic methodologies.

Abraham Melamed's "The Attitude Toward Democracy in Medieval Jewish Philosophy" and Reuven Kimelman's "Abravanel and the Jewish Republican Ethos" are nicely congruent. Melamed's chapter reveals the essentially monarchist and antidemocratic outlook of medieval Jewish political philosophy. From Maimon-ides through the Tibbonids (Samuel and Moses) to Samuel ben Judah of Marseilles in the fourteenth century, medieval Jewish political philosophers based their political theorizing on both halakhic norms and Platonic and Platonically inspired Farabian and Averroist political thought. Given the latter, it is hardly sur-prising that a strong monarchic, antidemocratic sensibility is mani-fest. Kimelman picks up the story where Melamed ends, with the republican, antimonarchism of Abravanel in the fifteenth century. But Kimelman's chapter emphasizes that we are quite misguided to think that the republican tradition which Abravanel represents is deviant, a *new* and late development in Jewish political thought. For Kimelman, an authentic republican or at least antimonarchic position can be elicited from biblical, rabbinic, and even medieval sources. Kimelman, therefore, calls into question the linear devel-opment of Jewish political philosophizing, from a monarchic, anti-republican position to a republican, antimonarchic one. Melamed's and Kimelman's chapters differ about what counts as traditional, normative, Jewish political philosophy, but the reader will note that there is no disagreement that, whatever the regnant tradition or traditions, Jewish political philosophizing, however much in-debted to Plato and others, is firmly grounded in canonical texts, biblical and rabbinic.

Even Spinoza, arguably the first modern Jew, despite, or per-haps on account of, his excommunication, grounds his critique of the tradition in canonical text. As David Novak, in "Spinoza's Challenge to the Doctrine of Election," makes clear, the philosophically inspired inversion of the traditional Jewish doctrine of election that Spinoza offers in his *Tractatus Theologico-Politicus* is presented as his (Spinoza's) best reading of the very tradition with which he was at odds. For Spinoza, the traditional theocentrism of the Jewish doctrine of election becomes anthropocentric; Israel chooses God and covenants with him, not vice versa. Further, for Spinoza, in direct contrast to the tradition, the (historical) election at Sinai and the promulgation of the (particularistic) ritual and ceremonial laws are *not* the *completion* of the process begun with the institution of the (universal) Noachide laws; rather, the choosing of God is a historically contingent *means* to a universal, moral end. As Novak presents the case, Spinoza emerges as paradigmatically representative of the modern, cosmopolitan, liberal, assimilationist trend in Jewish life and thought; but, again, this new tradition envisions itself as "traditional," congruent with the intensions of the foundational texts.

Spinoza's critique of halakhic Judaism from the standpoint of a universal morality informs the lively debate between Noam Zohar and David Bleich. In "Morality and War: A Critique of Bleich's Oracular Halakha," Zohar takes issue with what he takes to be Bleich's amoral construal of the halakha pertaining to the initiation of war and noncombatant immunity. This is not a debate between an antihalakhist and a halakhist, for Zohar himself argues from *within* the halakhic tradition for an alternative approach to Bleich's. Particulars aside, Zohar's general claim is that halakha is and must be constrained by "common morality." For him, halakha must be congruent with moral norms, lest a certain arbitrariness and license intrude into rabbinic decision making.

In his vigorous response, Bleich takes issue with Zohar's basic premise, that halakha must be evaluated by reference to extra-halakhic, moral norms. For Bleich, the halakha is a self-contained system, creates its own norms, and thus is in no need of extra-halakhic validation. This does not entail for Bleich that the halakha is insulated from moral considerations, but rather that such normative constraints be elicited from *within* the law itself, generally in the form of the supererogatory *lifnim mi-shurat ha-din* ("[acting] beyond the limit of the law.")

If supererogation plays as substantive a role within halakha as Bleich suggests, then the dispute between his position and Zohar's is transformed into a question about whether or not halakha (or any legal system) can generate from within itself a set of regulative moral norms. The reader will be forced to ask: Is law grounded in morality or is morality grounded in law?

This debate on the foundations of halakha, with its obvious contemporary political and moral ramifications, makes clear once again the nexus between law and politics in Jewish political life and thought. Whether developing a theory of justice or pondering the most appropriate form of constitution, whether grounding participation in national policy making or defending a certain military policy, what invigorates all forms of Jewish political and communal life and thought is an ongoing debate with the rich texts of the tradition. Commandment and community enrich each other.

The fourteenth annual conference of the Academy for Jewish Philosophy provided the occasion for the initial presentation of virtually all the chapters in this volume; Abraham Melamed's chapter is reprinted, slightly revised and with permission, from the *Jewish Political Studies Review* (vol. 5, nos. 1–2, Spring 1993). The Academy conference, "Jewish Legal and Political Philosophy," was held June 6–7, 1993 in Evanston, Illinois, at Northwestern University. In light of the discussions at the meetings, the essays first presented there have been revised, and only Melamed's chapter has been published previously.

The editor is grateful to Kenneth Seeskin for his generous support of this project. In addition, all the participants in the conference owe a collective debt of gratitude to Seeskin and to Northwestern for the excellent facilities that were provided.

PART 1

Judaism and Political Praxis

Toward a Jewish Philosophy
of Justice

Lenn E. Goodman

What I want to argue in this chapter is that a Jewish philosophy of justice should be ontological. It should ground the deserts of beings in the very nature of their being. I do not wish to claim that a sound philosophy of justice must be Jewish. There are many ways of anchoring the widely shared ideals that cluster under the idea of justice. Indeed the effort to give grounding to such ideals might seem otiose—an ironic attempt to justify justice itself—were it not for the broad areas of controversy about the footings and the coverage of the idea, controversy that solid grounding for the idea of justice might help to settle, or at least to clarify.

In laying out the grounds of such core ideals as those of rights and obligations, and so helping to work out the anatomy and scope of the claims that such ideas underwrite, the Jewish sources are of inestimable value. But the ontological theory I want to defend, and have defended in *On Justice: An Essay in Jewish Philosophy*,[1] is not uniquely Jewish. It has allies and kin in many of the philosophical and moral traditions of humanity; it would be anomalous and suspect, as a theory of justice, if it had none. Those who think that Jewish ideas must be uniquely Jewish to be authentically or interestingly Jewish are pursuing a form of chauvinism and not any kind of philosophy. Nor is it my intention to write a natural history of all the notions that can, with varying degrees of credibility, claim Jewish ancestry. Rather, what Jewish philosophy must do, as sharply distinguished from history or even the philosophy of Judaism, is to work out a credible line of argument, working in dialogue with the Jewish sources. This means securing the truth philosophically to the best of one's ability and allowing the sources to inform one's understanding—and one's understanding, even as one reads, to inform one's reading of the sources. The method is not novel. It has been used throughout the many epochs in which Jewish thinkers have had to reconstitute and recapture the ancient insights of their tradition, recasting them in a new idiom, rethinking them in a new age, and so keeping them alive. But the method is decidedly normative. It is never sheerly descriptive.[2]

The Jewish sources do make many unique and distinctive contributions to the articulation of an ongoing conversation about justice that has continued for some three millennia among thinkers, jurists, lawmakers, and statesmen sensitive to that ideal. But it is more important to me that the idea I am enunciating should have a Jewish future than to celebrate its Jewish past. Reversing the familiar pragmatism of conventional rhetoric, I think it is at least as important for it to have a Jewish future as an idea as it is for it to have such a future as practice. For without the idea there is no realization; practice loses its shape, its nerve, and rationale, goes brain dead and too easily dissolves into its opposite: *Im ein Torah ein kemach.*

THE EPICUREAN-HOBBESIAN VIEW

It is a common shibboleth in political thinking that justice is an agreement or convention. This is the view put forth by Plato's brothers Glaucon and Adeimantus, when they speak as devil's advocates in the *Republic.* Glaucon, "always an intrepid, enterprising spirit in everything," argues for "the view of the multitude," that justice is a bother. It has its rewards, to be sure, but not intrinsic worth—and, worse, it interferes with our natural desires. It is tolerated or even sought after only because men have gotten together and agreed that they would rather give up the chance of harming one another than risk each others' constant depredations and attacks. Each one of us, Glaucon argues, would surely rather take advantage of the rest than submit to any rule. But, recognizing the exposure we all would face if force and fraud were universal, ego, never setting aside its egotism, submits to a law. The essence and basis of that law is the understanding that I will not take advantage of you, if you, on pain of punishment, undertake not to take advantage of me. Justice here is a mean between extremes—between ego's preferred course, of aggression with impunity, and the fear of being the butt and victim of everyone. The claim that aggression without risk is indeed ego's absolute preference is backed up with the tale of the ring of Gyges and the spurious means by which the despised Lydian dynasty was founded. The intended outcome of Glaucon's argument is the recognition that justice is a convention.[3]

Epicurus, who held the view mooted by Plato's brother, sums it up perfectly: "Natural justice is a compact of mutual advantage to restrict the parties from harming or being harmed by one another."[4] "For all living things which have not been able to make contracts not to harm or be harmed by one another, there is no justice or injustice. The same holds true of those peoples who have been unable or unwilling to make compacts not to harm or be harmed."[5] "Justice is not anything in itself, it is just a compact among men in their various relations in a particular time and place, mutually undertaking not to harm or be harmed."[6] "Injustice is not an evil in itself but only in the fear arising from the apprehension that one will not escape those appointed to mete out retribution."[7] Nothing is intrinsically wrong in injuring another, then, but there is a prudential reason for avoiding harm to others: to avoid trouble, especially trouble of mind. For friends or family of those injured, or agents appointed for the purpose, will seek out the author of an injury. He will never be sure that some Javert will not hunt him down, for the most venial of offenses: "It is not possible for one who surreptitiously violates the compact not to injure or be injured ever to be confident that he will escape retribution, even if he has done so ten thousand times. Down to his death he will remain uncertain of his escape."[8] So criminals will never enjoy the Epicurean goal, *ataraxia*, peace of mind.

The aim and upshot of this theory, with all its prudential suasions and sometimes wishful warnings, is relativism. Right and wrong become contingent on the efficacy of "those appointed to mete out retribution," and their content becomes a matter of convention: "In general terms justice is the same for all, a kind of mutual advantage in their relations. But in terms of a particular country or circumstances the same thing is not just in every case."[9] "Among the things regarded as just, that which has proved mutually advantageous in human relations is what is just, regardless whether or not it is the same for all. If one makes a law and it does not remain mutually advantageous, then it no longer has the character of justice. But if the advantage in terms of justice should shift and agree with the general notion only for a short time, still, for that time that law was just in the eyes of those who regard the facts and do not confuse themselves with empty sounds."[10] "Unless circumstances have changed, actions which have been considered just but do not accord with the general notion in their actual effects are not just. Where circumstances have changed and actions which were held to be just no longer lead to advantage, then they were just when they promoted the common welfare of citizens in their mutual relations; but when no longer advantageous they were no longer just."[11] Here we see vigorous roots of progressivism, utilitarianism, Deweyan experimentalism, Hobbesian nominalism, Benthamite reformism and hatred of legal fictions—even a precedent for Rawls's appeals to ordinary (civil) notions—much that is wholesome, wise, and refreshing; and much that is misleading.

I want to raise two problems about the Epicurean and later Hobbesian view that justice is a convention. The first is what I call the *skyhook problem:* If justice is by agreement, and agreements are conventions, how can any law be binding? I do not mean permanently binding, but binding even for the Epicurean moment of its immediate utility? For the fact that some practice is useful does not in itself entail that any person or institution has authority to impose it—especially not if the utilities are transferred and, like tax revenues, arise in one quarter and alight in another. But even if the prospective benefit is confined to the actor (hardly a typical *social* benefit or a typical demand of law), where does anyone get the right to tell another what goods to pursue or how to pursue them?

If it is argued that individuals have agreed to accept some common authority or rule (and the fiction is maintained that present actors are somehow, by ancestry or patrimony, allegiance, acceptance of goods, or acquiescence in ills, parties to that agreement), we still must ask where societies acquire the authority to bind their members to adhere to their undertakings. Hobbes would have it that it is irrational to break an agreement one has rationally entered into. But that argument violates the basic Epicurean claim, that any norm applies only as long as its benefits continue. How can self-interest bind us to an undertaking no longer seen or believed to be in our interest? And why should even self-interest be heeded—unless there is some intrinsic worth in the individual?

Conventionalists and relativists, of course, want no truck with the idea of intrinsic worth. Hobbes equates worth in general with price, and worthiness with usefulness, as gauged by that most social of all measures, monetary exchange: "The value or worth of a man is, as of all other things, his price, that is to say, so much as would be given for the use of his power; and therefore is not absolute, but a thing dependent on the need and judgment of another. . . . Worthiness . . . consists in a particular power or ability . . . fitness or aptitude." [12] Spinoza criticizes Hobbes on the first of these points, the legerdemain that wants to keep agreements in force beyond their perceived usefulness. Hobbes's efforts here yield the entertaining spectacle of the avowed nominalist trying to work word magic with the fact that promises have been made. Marx attacks the second point, the economic reduction of human value, when he shows that the labor market may drive the replacement cost of human beings below the level of subsistence. But Marx's materialism gives him no words in which to voice the moral abhorrence of such an outcome. The root of the trouble is the false assumption that human worth can be rightly and exhaustively measured in economic terms.

A. E. Taylor comes to Hobbes's defense, charging Spinoza with bad faith for allowing that some pledges can be broken. But the criticism misses the mark. Spinoza exempts us from our undertakings only insofar as they preserve no inherent value. [13] In such a case, he reasons, the contract has been nullified by the misfeasance of one of the parties, and there is no ground for insisting that the other remain bound by it. The Elizabethan sting of the Hobbesian charge that rebels are "forsworn" is blunted by Spinoza's recognition that only worthless or noxious enterprises are rightfully abandoned. When an agreement or convention is sustained by nothing more than the fact that it once was viable, why need there be any compunction in walking away from it? And if only words sustain what has become an unwholesome arrangement, why should one not simply leave it to its fate?

As Mendelssohn makes clear, communities and societies have an inherent value, in virtue of the interests they serve. [14] Crucially, to put the matter in Aristotelian terms, civility and civilization can humanize human life. Yet tyrannies can dehumanize it. History shows us many more instances of both possibilities than the ancients knew. Avoiding what I call the *generic fallacy* (treating genera as though they were species, whose members share the same nature and effects), we can see that it would be wrong to abandon all social engagement. But that fact does not legitimate all modes of government. Hobbes may be right, as apologists of authority before him were often right, in arguing (with concrete cases in mind) that a bad government is better than none at all. But he was wrong in supposing that the only alternative to a bad government is none at all.

Governments *as such* have no authority whatever. The authority of a state must rest on its legitimacy, that is, on what it does, in its particularity, for the interests it was founded to serve, or rather, for the interests in behalf of which its survival is sustained, and those that need its aid. Past or even present acts of consent confer no such authority. To pin authority to consent, as though consent sufficed to legitimate laws, states, or other institutions, is to suspend justice from a skyhook. It legitimates too much, sweeping up into its embrace bad arrangements along with good ones. And it appeals to the putative rationality of choices made under duress (the threat of anarchy) and then seeks to enforce adherence to those choices on the notional grounds that a choice has been made. When the arbitrariness of that appeal is exposed, the positive (as opposed to rational) sanction of authority is unlimbered: the threat of punishment, and behind it, once again, the threat of anarchy, wishfully invoked, like the fanciful avengers of Epicurus's moral fable, or the *ayenbite of inwit* that moralizers hold up as a bogey to threaten an ever less sensitive audience of "pale criminals." But our concern is not with the sanctions of authority but with its basis, not with the likelihood of retribution but with its legitimacy. Here the conventionalism of Hobbes and Epicurus contributes little. For it does not adequately answer the question: On what basis do individuals band together? And it gives no answer at all to the deeper question about the grounds on which they might rightfully expect one another's loyalty or support.

Hobbes's intent is to derive obligations by assuming none and thus to traverse the no man's land that Hume would later demarcate, between the *is* and the *ought*. His strategy is to argue that no one can deny man in a state of nature the right, identical with his power, to defend his life and any interests he might deem conducive to the protection of his life. Fear and vanity, in such a condition of lawlessness, will no doubt motivate many actions. But none of these can be called wrong, because nothing is wrong in itself, and no civil society as yet exists to call any act wrong. But what has not been named wrong is, by Hobbes's standards, done with perfect right. And the proof, apart from appeal to the notion that no one has forbidden anything as yet, lies in the futility of seeking to forbid the intended acts of self-protection that are done, "by a certain impulsion of nature no less than that whereby a stone moves downward."[15] Therefore Hobbes holds that men in a state of nature have rights, or act by right, even though they have, as yet, no obligations.[16] They acquire obligations by their natural desire to protect their rights, or lives, or powers, because reason sees the bootlessness and fruitlessness of continued life in a state of nature, and people enter into civil society, like fish into a trap, reason advising them to give up their powers of aggression and self-defense, in the interest of creating a sovereign, who will use their several powers collectively to exact obedience from each and enforce the protection of all.

The incoherence of this model arises from its equivocation on the idea of right. For to say that no one has yet forbidden (or effectively forbidden!) an act is not to make it justified, and it may well be that I have obligations to others prior to any undertakings I have made in their regard. Indeed, I fail to see how I can have even an obligation to myself, unless I have some worth. The sophistic advocate's plea that no one should be surprised if I take what measures I deem necessary to protect myself amounts not to a justification but only to a prediction. And the notions that plea employs, of self, of measures, of interests, and even of warrant are suspiciously moral in tone, highly parasitic on conceptions made possible through the work, if not of civil society, then at least of some form of community that fosters a sense of personal identity and rational self-interest.[17]

Myths often presuppose what they purport to explain,[18] and the idea of the social contract is no exception. For those who enter civil society, whether on Hobbes's model, or that of Rawls, are somehow expected to know pretty much what the new society will be like. But more troubling from a moral standpoint than that bit of projective thinking, which ignores the immemorial communal character of human life in favor of the notion that in essence those who found a society are proto-Whigs planning a club, or even than the notion that people who acknowledge no responsibility to one another will have a clear conception of their own social wants, is the notion that such wants can somehow be cranked up into a normative program. That can be done, I argue, only by the imputing of deserts. Even Hobbes imports suppositions of desert, sub rosa, into the dialectic of his argument, or it would not work at all. For justice and its demands are not creations of social convention but in some form or another logical prerequisites of the legitimacy of such conventions. It follows that the claims of justice may go much farther than any explicit societal arrangement may acknowledge, and that no such arrangement, no state, nor even any informal communal body like a family, tribe, or nation—groupings that antedate the state and prepare the conditions for its creation—is above moral criticism, dismantling, or reform.

The second difficulty affecting contractual schemes of legitimation is what I call the *exclusion problem:* If societies are collections of individuals who simply covenant together, what is to stop them from arbitrarily excluding certain "others" whose interests thereby simply do not count? If justice is the way we agree to treat one another, then we face not only the problem that we may agree to treat one another unjustly, a real possibility discussed at some length in *On Justice*, but also the problem that we do not seem to have any obligations, on this account, toward others who are not party to our agreement. This is not simply a matter of those who live beyond our boundaries, although in an age of active international trade and global environmental exigencies, they are certainly a morally important class. It is also a matter of those whom the devisers of an agreement may exclude, intentionally, inadvertently, or of necessity. Intentionally, they may exclude the weak, the ignorant, those who cannot "pull their own weight," or have been marked for "ethnic cleansing." Historically all sorts of individuals have been deemed nonpersons: slaves, aliens, persons of other races. But there are also the unborn, the members of future generations, and the large class of persons who for social or intellectual, moral or political reasons, through disability or disadvantage, penal servitude or geographical absence or isolation, are in no position to take part in the lively debate and active deliberative process of a free society, or even the ceremonial consent and declaration of homage, fealty, or allegiance characteristic of history's less participatory societies. Even in a republic there are those whose will is overridden by the majority or outbid by the influential. And democracies are well known in the annals of imperialist adventurism. If the state is a contract, are the nonparticipants not parties to it, and are those who are not parties fair game?

Plainly, nonpersons can be harmed by human agency—species, econiches, monuments of nature, triumphs of art and architecture, institutions, texts, wildernesses, and individual plants and animals. It is contested, in a legalistic sort of way, whether such beings can have interests in a sense relevant to the concerns of justice. For clearly they are not the beings that our American system of law, or the theory on which it was built, was designed to protect. Yet surely at least some of them have worth apart from the social or commercial value that convention may place upon them, and many of them are protected in existing laws—the spotted owl for instance, or the snail darter, which has little social value and perhaps no market price at all. Political contractualists seem to have no basis to consider such beings, except insofar as they become the clients of some economic or political interest—and then the graves of the ancestors or the habitat of the timber wolf suddenly vault from nullity to legal prominence—and we are given the assurance (by contract theory) that right has been done by them when the political process has worked to its conclusion in their regard, quite without reference to their inherent worth or relational impact.

But confining ourselves to persons, are all noncitizens or nonsignatories of a formal civil constitution thereby nonpersons? Are those who are not equal partners in our joint undertakings thereby excluded from the resultant harms, benefits, and responsibilities? This could be called the *Mafia problem*. For the Mafia observes very different standards toward insiders and outsiders. It could also be called the *lifeboat earth problem*, in view of the modest proposals of Garrett Hardin and others to exclude from the human covenant those who seem only to add to the load and the risk of swamping the boat we all share.[19] Does the omnisufficiency of the idea of a social contract serve too well to mask the fact that the human situation, history, and destiny link us together in ways that we may never fully know and that some of us are loath to acknowledge?

Defenders of slavery before the American Civil War professed Lockean standards of liberalism but did not acknowledge their chattel slaves as persons. Their Whiggish creed excluded Tory or feudal notions of variable status. The sharp division of the inalienable rights of persons from the sheer passivity of property exacerbated the polarity and heightened the violence of the American Civil War. Blacks were either persons or property, and if they were property they could not be persons.[20] Biological models were widely invoked, before and long after the Civil War, to show that blacks were less than fully human.[21] Indeed the Smithsonian movement, which led to the founding of physical anthropology, was an offshoot of that invidious campaign. Still worse was reserved for Jews. And, as Uriel Tal showed, the Nazi theorists of race dehumanized their intended victims semeiotically as a prelude to the final solution. Likewise with the fetus, which was treated notionally as a nonperson before its interests were legally undermined or negated.

Yet having interests that deserve regard does not require being party to an agreement. Otherwise, the agreement of gang members to rape or kill or rob some passerby would be perfectly legitimate. Or, if its legitimacy came into conflict with that of other entities, the gang's agreement might have as much standing morally as the decisions and determinations of, say, the state, the neighborhood, the police, in whose deliberations the gang members took no part —or in which they took part with the mental reservation that their participation was in no way prejudicial to their gang dealings and agreements.[22] Consider Japan's imposition of enforced prostitution on women from Korea during World War II. Korea was a subject state and had no effective government. Japan was a modern nation state, whose duly appointed officers decided the fate of the Korean women in the supposed interest of the morale of the Japanese troops and the vital state interests those troops were pledged to serve. What standing do consent theories give the Korean women? Can the notion that justice is an agreement among contracting parties even find the words to describe the enormity that one Japanese government committed and that another concealed for decades after the fact?

The exclusion problem works telling damage on that variety of contractual theory that rests on the notion of passive consent. I hold that consent to a social, political, or economic arrangement is a critical index of the legitimacy of that arrangement. For in normal circumstances there is no better judge of individual interests than those whose interests are affected; and in normal circumstances there is no more reliable standard of an arrangement's legitimacy than its likelihood of serving the interests of the parties. But not all circumstances are normal. Covenantors may be shortsighted about their own interests and morally myopic about those of others. And not all those affected by an agreement are (or even can be) full parties to it. So we must recognize that consent is neither a necessary nor a sufficient condition of justice.

The notion of passive consent arises when it is recognized that even the active and participatory citizenry of a commonwealth are not parties to its full panoply of laws and institutions. They were not present at the creation, and they cannot agree to or even know all the laws and regulations enacted in their name, implemented and enforced by duly constituted authorities. Even in a representative democracy, there will be rules or provisions to which individuals might take exception; and even where consent was freely given item by item, as in a referendum, it might be argued after the fact that some of those consenting did not fully understand the impact of what they had agreed to until damage was done to their interests, or until it was too late to dismantle the now rejected institutions, or to slow their momentum and halt or reverse their effects. There is tacit recognition of such facts as these when champions of the idea that states and their actions are legitimated by consent argue that those who find themselves dissatisfied sufficiently always have the right, at least in a free society, of departing. Their continued presence, it is argued, is sufficient warrant of their consent, showing that they themselves deem their engagement with the society to bring more benefit than harm to the interests they cherish.

I call this appeal to acquiescence an argument *from passive consent* because it substitutes the absence of an effectuated decision to emigrate for the active, but always ambiguous, affirmation of allegiance that traditionally signified consent. The appeal to passive consent, which is a common feature of discussions and debates about political legitimacy ("If they don't like it, they can always leave"), weakens the claim that agreement is a sufficient ground for the legitimacy of a polity by exposing tellingly the exclusionary character of this conception of political legitimacy. For if departure is necessary to prove any governmental action illegitimate and remaining in place is sufficient to legitimate a government and its actions, then any policy that does not provoke abandonment of a nation by a significant number of its people would appear to be legitimate.

Clearly, by our standard, if consent is an important index of legitimacy, the departure from East Germany of large numbers of its people prior to reunification and the desperate flight of much smaller numbers prior to the opening of the borders provide overwhelming evidence of the illegitimacy of the government of the German Democratic Republic. But the refugees' choice of a nation other than their homeland does not clearly show the legitimacy of every state in any land to which the escapees might flee. Desperate people can jump out of the frying pan into the fire. More important, if we take remaining in place as sufficient proof of governmental legitimacy, then we can clearly envision a policy in which a government might rid itself of a minority of "undesirables" or nonconformists, simply by imposing some form of discrimination upon them, such as differential taxation or restrictions on education or reproductive opportunities. Then the argument might be made—if it were assumed that a government is as just as its people think it is—that a discriminatory government is only marginally unjust, or not unjust at all, as long as it allows free egress to its victims or dissenters.

Advocates for human rights (among whom I would hope to be numbered) might object to the idea that any arbitrarily invidious policy can be just. But if second-class citizens, excluded minorities, or dissenters are given free rights of egress and do not leave— because they fear they might lose more by leaving than by staying, or because of normal human inertia or social ties, or through human hope—the advocates of the idea that passive consent is a sufficient condition of our labeling a social arrangement *just* would be in the embarrassing position of defending the view that a state (or any group) might justly impose any disability upon some community or individual, up to the limit of the tolerance of those invidiously treated or oppressed, without injustice, because the continued presence of these victims is clear proof that they find their conditions acceptable and the alternatives freely open to them unacceptable or less acceptable than acquiescence or silent suffering.

The forms of discrimination and oppression that might be tolerated by some or all the members of a group are limited only by human imagination and the stoical or spiritual capabilities of human endurance. Yet it would seem strange to make the justice of some proposed policy contingent on the risk averseness of the members of the target class or the severity of the alternatives available to them elsewhere—allowing legislators or tyrants to make unjust or unhappy conditions elsewhere their accomplices and allies, not only to assure the continued presence of those they plan, say, to exploit, but also to reassure their own conscience as to the rightness of a vicious policy, on the grounds that its victims seem to find submission to it less undesirable than the alternatives accessible to them. Clearly, then, the passive consent mode of legitimation—although it has its proper uses in rhetoric and in scaling to reality the extent of the sufferings or disabilities about which persons may feel moved to complain and although it harbors more verisimilitude than the notion of a mythic moment of consent or the notion that some ritual affirmation can bind allegiance rather than merely signal it—is fatally holed below the waterline. It is no sufficient foundation of political legitimacy. For it will legitimate an almost unlimited array of (tolerated) tortures and depredations. One can even envision circumstances in which the excluded are deceived and kept under the illusion that they or their children might one day join the ranks of those who profit from their exclusion and expropriation. In such a case, the vision of glittering rewards held up by exploiters (and extracted by exploitation) would heighten the tolerance of the exploited and, by the standards of passive consent, heighten the levels of oppression that could be imposed, legitimately, if passive consent is tantamount to legitimation.

I do not think that the instantiation of this last possibility should be sought too breathlessly in our own society. This is not what America has done—certainly not all we have done. But the possibility of such legitimation under theories of passive consent is sufficient grounds for their rejection. The practical moral is that states and their patriots should not take too much pride or comfort in the continued presence within their borders of the people whom they govern. For there are many reasons that might induce long-term residence, not least among them, the hope that the oppressed may nurture of overthrowing a hated oppressor.

Attempts to legitimate the rule of law, or any sort of authority, by appeal to agreement, then, rest on a fiction, dissolving into stories about the past or thought experiments about what certain imaginary persons might have agreed to. Passive consent theories are not theories at all but rhetorical challenges and dares. They seem better designed to justify disabilities than to legitimate civil authority. All appeals to convention, covenant, or consent as the foundation of political legitimacy suspend from nowhere the power of an individual or a group to make an agreement with the expectation that it will be fulfilled. They do not explain how consent can bind the self, let alone another. And they systematically, if sometimes unwittingly, exclude from the scope and sentence of the law all who are not somehow party to an agreement they may never have heard of and might gladly see destroyed.

A FOUNDATION FOR JUSTICE

As an alternative to conventionalist views, I have argued that societies do not create justice. Rather, justice creates societies. Justice is the imparting to all beings of what they deserve. Its recipients need not be human. They need not even be persons. All beings, I argue, have deserts, insofar as they are beings. Prima facie, those deserts are coextensive with the claims that constitute each being. My view that beings are constituted by their claims is related to the existentialist idea that a being is its project, and to Spinoza's equation of the essence of each thing with its conatus, its striving to preserve and promote its own reality. A being is not the mere sum of its history or amalgam of the facts about its static self-identity. Rather, a being is the agency that stakes out for itself a project and an identity grounded in a system of interests. All beings are dynamic in some measure. All affirm, as it were, a certain character, which is their own and which they define in the very act of affirmation that is their history. The interests of a being, prima facie, lie in the consummation of its project. But any dynamic claim is implicitly or potentially infinite in some respect. Wisdom in regard to claims demands recognition of the limitations inherent in all claims made by finite beings. Justice calls for the equilibration of the claims that beings make, subordinating some, coordinating others, optimizing the practical recognition of desert.

This ontological account of justice fosters an objectivist conception of justice rather than the conceptual incoherencies of relativism or subjectivism. And it allows, indeed requires, a general, rather than a restrictive assignment of deserts. Far from confining attention to the interests of some consensual body, it extends consideration to all beings, subjects and nonsubjects, animate and inanimate, natural and artificial. It finds deserts in animals and plants as well as humans; in mountains, rivers, species, and eco-systems as well as sentient beings; in works of art, practices, institutions, memories, sciences, and ideas, as well as planets and galaxies. I do not pretend that the deserts of all these are equal. To predicate desert upon being and identify prima facie desert with being itself (and being with claims) is to recognize hierarchies of value. Personhood, for example, in whatever form it discovers itself, is never to be subordinated wholly to some lesser order of being. But not all value depends on the value of persons or on the values assigned by persons. For claims may deserve to be recog-nized even if they are not our own. Indeed our ability to recognize claims other than our own is part of what gives precedence to human claims.

To spell this out just a little further, what a general theory of deserts entails is that utility to us is not the sole basis of worth. Recognition of this is essential in doing justice to those persons who are not explicitly or implicitly in league with us. And it means, inter alia, that if the rain forest proves to contain no cure for cancer and will never be enjoyed or appreciated as wilderness by the great majority of urban dwellers, it is of no less value intrinsi-cally for that. For the worth of things does not depend exclusively on their use or appreciation. Utility and aesthetic value themselves rest on the intrinsic worth of human subjects—which is anchored axiologically in a general assignment of worth to beings, based on what they are. Such a theory is not only reasonable but useful, for it obviates the need to cloak our impulse, say, to save the rain forest, in appeals to its utility as an oxygen producer (which might be technologically replaced and then overridden by the com-mercial value of its lumber), or, more embarrassing, to cloak the same impulse in appeals to an Epicurean anxiety fable—say, that we may never know whether the cure for AIDS or cancer does not lurk in the jungle, its discovery somehow dependent on that jungle's preservation.

The theory I have proposed is a form of naturalism,[23] but it avoids the reductionism prominent in the most familiar forms of naturalism and for that reason it avoids the naturalistic fallacy. It is naturalistic in that it equates being with value in the classic way that regards being as a perfection and, in the case of creatures, that is, finite, contingent beings, as a gift. Again, it is naturalistic in equating interests with claims and claims with prima facie deserts. One can even say that value is the object of any interest. But here *interest* is more broadly construed than is often customary, and its sense is objective rather than subjective. Value need not be instrumental, because interest need not be external. It need not belong to someone else. A being can have interests, and so deserts, even if no one cares about it. And its worth is not proportioned to the extent and intensity of subjective concerns for it—let alone, desires to consume or possess it.

Relativists equate every state of affairs with what ought to be. This is radically at variance with their critical mode, which sharply distinguishes what is from what ought to be. Hume, for example, not only sunders the discourse of *is* from that of *ought*, but also seeks to rationalize human moral sentiments, epistemic practices, habits of the mind, and even prejudices, on the grounds of their facticity. And Moore, similarly, not only pinions the naturalistic fallacy, but also commits it, for example, in his attempted refutation of idealism, where he assumes the legitimacy of our penchant to presume the reality of the bodies we perceive.

But the naturalism I have proposed, which I think lies at the core of the biblical idea of the worth of beings, avoids the naturalistic fallacy, because it does not equate any mere fact about a thing with what constitutes its value. Still less does it entail that whatever exists should exist. Rather the thesis is that the claims of beings deserve recognition, prima facie, simply because they are the claims of beings: Beings deserve recognition *insofar as* they are beings. It follows that recognition of claims should be scaled to the magnitude of the claims. I do not possess some algorithm for adjudicating all conflicts among claims or some divining rod for discovering all the complementarities that might arise among the claims that beings make. The "art of measurement" capable of assaying ontic claims, adjudicating among them and discovering their complementarities, will be no mere Benthamite calculus but a broad appreciation of the open-ended potentialities of nature in general, and human nature in particular. The open-ended aspirations, voiced and unvoiced, in the projects and activities of all beings make me confident that the naturalism I am broaching is nonreductive. If being is so variously realizable and is always dynamic and creative, as I have suggested, there is no danger of its being confused with mere facticity.

I find value in all beings and argue that if value does not reside in beings *there is nowhere else* in which it could be located. The legitimate criticism of the naturalistic fallacy by Hume, Moore, and others shows that facticity does not entail or amount to legitimacy. But being is more than facticity. To assume that reality is a bare or neutral fact, devoid of value, is to beg that question and in a direction belied by every natural achievement. For to deny the identity of being and value is to deny that being is an achievement. Further it is to deny that anything has any real worth—a position that cannot be sustained, because it is refuted by every act we make, including every speech act. For one who speaks implicitly affirms the value of his or her speaking. Even when one takes a breath, implicitly one affirms the value of life, denying it perhaps in words, but affirming it again as one inhales.

What I *am* arguing is that the existence of something is better than the nonexistence of everything. Certainly there are many things that the world might be better without. But I do not think that any reality is purely evil. For as the evil in a thing increases, so does its incapacity to sustain itself. Evil tends to self-destruct, partly because of its destructiveness to the milieu on which any being must depend. As a result, evil disappears long before it can reach totality. Beings are sustained only by the perfections they attain. The things that we picture as evil are such by virtue of their destructiveness to other things; but what preserves them is their small measure of good. So a universe could not survive, let alone come to be, if it contained only evil. A universe of beings whose perfection is only partial and relative, however, can exist and does sustain itself. That, I believe, is the sort of universe we live in.

The weakness of my position is that it is metaphysical. That is unavoidable. One cannot answer the relativism of the claim that values are real only notionally without saying something about what values really are and so about what is real. I can argue dialectically that one who thinks values are purely notional is as committed to metaphysics as I am. Such a person too has very general notions about what there is and how reality and goodness are related. Yet siting the metaphysic of morals in metaphysics and not in morals does not entail that argument suddenly dries up, as if, when one turns to such very basic questions, one opinion were not better than another—so that the person who holds right and wrong to be matters of convention or opinion has no lesser grounds for that view than any adversary. The dialectical arguments are compelling, and they are not neutral on this question. I find highly relevant and compelling what Kenneth Seeskin argued some years ago (1978) in defense of a related thesis of Leibniz: "If a metaphysician cannot express preferences *qua* metaphysician, then he cannot disapprove of universes suffering from the most severe forms of impoverishment when he is acting in an official capacity. He would have to be able to reflect on any of the infinite number of possible worlds with complete equanimity. A universe containing nothing but a whiff of smoke or a taste of cheese, for example, could not be rejected in favor of a universe as luxurious as the one we inhabit."

I think what has fostered conventionalism about values from the beginning is neither argument nor skepticism but a powerful alliance of marketing and minimalism: marketing, because attorneys and those who train them (originally, sophists) have a product to sell under the slogan "Who's right and who's wrong depends on whose ox is gored"; minimalism, because diversity in moral outlooks is not a new invention but an ancient fact, and conventionalism purports to offer a common ground for a modus vivendi that does not demand ultimate agreement about values, the gods, lifestyles, or any matters other than certain procedural protocols, rules of the game, canons of etiquette, or terms of trade. The market appeal of conventionalism, I grant. But the minimalist pretension, I deny. For conventionalism can be smothering, all-encompassing, and highly demanding of conformity in all sorts of ways: intellectual, moral, spiritual—above all stylistic. Its liberal and pluralistic posture proves a sham, if conventions are to have any force at all, *as conventions*, and then the outlook becomes oppressive and dogmatic. In addition, I do not believe that style is inessential to substance. For, in nature in general and in the human case in particular, style often marks or makes the difference between conflict and accommodation.[24]

But to the argument; one who actually thought being itself devoid of value would be committed to the view that the universe at large might just as well not exist. Such a person could not enunciate, or affirm, or even *hold* the view consistently. For to do so one must act and thus implicitly affirm the worth of acting, the preferability of this act to its alternatives. I too cannot refute the position I reject without appealing to some value. So there might appear to be an impasse, unless I beg the question, because the value of anything at all is in dispute. But the position is not so symmetrical as might seem, for it was not I who denied that there is value in anything. If I assume what my adversary denies, at least I do not assume the contrary of what I hold, as my adversary must do, to maintain anything at all.

Dialectically, I can say that the putative nihilist imagined to deny that there is value in anything at all would have no grounds for staying the hand of some nuclear or ecological terrorist bent on destroying the universe. If there were a doomsday machine (a possibility far more readily envisioned than a real person who found no value in anything), and if some maniac had his finger on the button, the nihilist would have no reason to make the slightest effort to prevent the maniac from pushing the button. But I do not rest my affirmation of the value of beings on such negative and dialectical considerations but on an open appreciation of reality as we find it. In such an appreciation, scientific understanding, aesthetic awe, and religious celebration all respond to the same underlying givens.

The Jewish sources are of help here, for they confirm the value of beings and invite our appreciation of it. When God surveys the world he has created and sees that it is good, he might appear to be making a redundant judgment. Was he not the almighty author of it all, who made exactly what he wanted? Who was present, or even qualified, to judge his work? Yet, like an artisan who has made a table or a cabinet, God assays his creation and judges that it meets his expectation and intent. And more, that it is a good thing, good in itself, a thing that ought to exist, that deserves to exist, for the beauties it now bears, for its value, not to God, who stands in need of nothing, but in itself, as a work of art might be valuable, not because it can be sold or put to some use, but intrinsically. For although the world holds many utilities, they serve no function beyond it, but are perfections relative to *its* purpose, which is the sustenance and flourishing of all sorts of beings. All of these, in their diverse ways and to their diverse degrees, exist for their own sakes and plot their own projects. Maimonides writes:

According to our doctrine of the creation of the entire world out of nothing, the search for a final cause of all existence might well seem necessary. Thus it might be supposed that the end of all existence is simply that the human species should exist to worship God and that all things are done solely for man's sake, even the heavens turning solely for his benefit and in order to bring his needs into being. . . . If this view is examined critically, however, as intelligent men ought to examine views, the fallacy in it is exposed. For the advocate of this belief has only to be asked, "This end, the existence of man—is God able to bring this about without all these preliminaries, or is it the case that man cannot be brought into being until all these things have been done?" If he replies that it is possible, that God is able to give being to man without, say, creating the heavens, then it must be asked, "What is the utility to man of all these things which were not themselves the object but which exist 'for the sake of' something that could have existed without any of them?" Even if the universe does exist for man, and man's end, as has been said, is to serve God, the question remains: What is the object of man's serving God? For His perfection would not be augmented by the worship of all things that He created, not even if they all apprehended Him as He truly is. Nor would He lack anything if nothing but Him existed at all. . . .

For this reason, the correct view, in my judgment, in keeping with religious belief and in consonance with the theories of reason, is that all beings should not be believed to exist for the sake of man's existence. Rather all other beings too were intended to exist for their own sakes, not for the sake of something else. . . . We say that all parts of the world were brought into being by God's will, intended either for their own sake or for the sake of something else intended for its own sake. . . . This view too is stated in the prophetic books: The Lord made each thing le-ma'ano" (Proverbs 16:4). The reference might be to the object [each thing] but if the antecedent is the subject [the Lord], the sense is 'for Himself,' i.e., His will, which is His Identity . . . also called His glory . . . Thus His words, "All that are called by My name and created for My glory, I created, yes and made" (Exodus 33:18). . . .

If you study the book which guides all who seek guidance toward what it true and is therefore called the Torah, this idea will be evident to you from the account of creation to the end. For it never states in any way that any of the things mentioned was for the sake of something else. Rather, of every single part of the world, it is said that He created it, and its being agreed with His purpose. This is the meaning of its saying, "God saw that it was good" (Genesis 1:4). For you have learned what we have explained on how "Torah speaks according to human language" (*Baba Metzia* 31b, cited in *Guide* 1.26; cf. 1.46, citing *Genesis Rabbah* 27). 'Good,' for us, refers to what agrees with our purpose.[25]

In saying that God created all things by his own will and intent, then, Scripture, as the Rambam explains, is saying that God created them for their own sake and only secondarily for the uses they may afford one another. If we judge things anthropocentrically, we shall inevitably find many whose "purposes," in terms of utility to us, baffle us; many will seem to have no purpose at all or to be "detrimental." Yet all serve God's purpose, which is their existence. That is what is meant by their existing for his glory: God's glory is found in the creation of all things for their own sakes. Maimonides is aided to this view by the Neoplatonic response to Stoic anthropocentrism.[26] But the thesis, which he aims at the occasionalists and anthropomorphizers of providence in his own day,[27] is clearly biblical. His reading of "God saw that it was good" is borne out in Isaiah's vision (6:3) of the complementarity of God's transcendence ("Holy, Holy, Holy") with his immanence: "The fill of all the earth is His glory."

God's judgment that the world is good becomes normative when his creatures are commanded to flourish, to be fruitful and multiply, making the earth abound and the sea teem with life. The imperative becomes yet more explicit and directive when God tells his human creatures: "Choose life!" This is not just a slogan on an anti-abortion T-shirt, although it is not irrelevant there. It is an affirmation of value and a counsel against defeatism, the seductive appeal that the Hebrew prophets discover and combat in ancient Egyptian culture, that death is somehow morally or spiritually the matter of ultimate concern. Biblically, light and life are what is blessed—good in themselves and good in what they will achieve. The transcendence of the holy is linked not with death but with life, love, and generosity. Far from being a static facticity, existence here is a good that points beyond itself to the absolute. Through the goodness of finitude, Mosaic naturalism glimpses the timeless, infinite goodness of its source.

Monotheism is based on recognition of the goodness of being.[28] We do not hold that being is good because it is what God made, but that in the goodness of being we see the act and grace of God. God is the absolute goodness in terms of which relative goodness is recognized, gauged, celebrated, and acknowledged. Just as Plato, in his task of uniting all values by acknowledging their complementarity, recognized that what is fairest and best must be most real, so the Torah discovers that what is most real, what is divine, must be not only absolute but fair and good. Accordingly, when Abraham confronts God he equates divine power with unswerving justice, asking rhetorically, "Will not the judge of all the earth do justice?" (Genesis 18:25).

Saadiah makes the underlying reasoning explicit: God rules *because* he is just; the combination of rule with caprice would be possible, he argues, only through a power struggle.[29] But God did not come to power in some pagan theomachy, through a struggle for domination. He rules eternally. Goodness is constitutive in the very idea of God. Thus, when we read in the Psalms that God's throne is firm and everlasting (Psalms 45:7, cf. 9:5, 8, 47:9), we understand not only God's ontic stability but his legitimacy, the stability that only justice brings (see Psalms 93). Here God stands at the summit of a series in which goodness and reality go hand in hand.

One strength of this classical approach is that it does not regard goodness as a property, which we then must deem natural or "nonnatural." The being of things is their nature. But that is no static and neutral fact but the telic groping of all things, in their own ways, toward perfection. The perfection that beings seek is unitary at its source, but not in its particularity. It is not a preordained end, but an end that the actions of beings define and redefine creatively, an open-ended goal—as is clear in any creative work, whether that of the artist or poet, or that of biological or cosmic evolution. If we ask, in Plato's terms, why eternity needs a "moving image" or, in scholastic terms, why time exists at all, the answer, clearly, is that the work of creativity is not over but just begun when creatures reach the shores of existence. Just as a novel does not have an end until it is written, and a portrait does not have an expression until it is completed, so no being is finished with its work until it has played its part. This is what we mean by saying that creatures play a role in their own creation.

The Torah rarely speaks in purely metaphysical language—although there is the remarkable exception in which God names himself *I am that I am*. Yet we can discern a metaphysical foundation in the morals that the Torah teaches, and to do so enables us clearly to thematize the Torah's legislative intent and to mark the nisus of its prescriptions, as elaborated in the prophetic and rabbinic tradition and in the work of philosophers sensitive to that tradition from Philo and Saadiah to Maimonides, Spinoza, and beyond. It is here that we trace the outlines of our idea of desert. It is grounded in the Mosaic conception of the goodness of creation and the metaphysics of the idea of reality as perfection. The good or worth or value of any thing is its being, where being is construed individually and conatively. Beings make claims, and these constitute their essence, their identity or nature, their prima facie interests and deserts. The morally explicit concept here is *zekhut*, desert. If desert is the very reality of things, then it is universal and positive in all beings—although, of course, beings may overstep, and the equilibration of deserts in a multifarious universe will never simply serve the unqualified or unreflective claims of crude conatus.

Consider the universal desert bespoken in the biblical assignment of positive deserts to the trees of a besieged city (Deuteronomy 20:19), to the land that needs *its* sabbaths, to lie fallow (Leviticus 25:8, 26:34, 43; 2 Chronicles 36:21; Jeremiah 25:11), to the ass in the story of Balaam (Numbers 22:28), to the human person, and even the human form, that must not be desecrated or exposed even in the case of an executed criminal (Deuteronomy 21:23) nor mutilated even in the service of God (Leviticus 21:5). These norms, which model the contours of desert, are taken up in the Midrash, where Moses is considerate of his strayed lamb. They are systematized in the Mishnah's broad rule against wanton destructiveness (*bal tashchit*) and in the phased measures taken against a *rodef* or aggressor in hot pursuit, and accordingly in the phased measures taken against a fetus in those rare cases where it becomes a *rodef*, but still merits recognition as a being on the threshold of human life—if not as a person, then, as Philo puts it, as a work of art.[30]

The same humanism, mounted in the same fabric of love of life and being, provides the grand thematic of the Gemara, where the principle of *pikuach nefesh* is anchored in the reasoning that the

Sabbath is created for us, not we for the Sabbath—and so, with all the commandments: "You shall live by them"—by them, not for them (*Yoma* 82a–85b). Life is the aim, but a certain kind of life, not any sort at all costs. Life is good, being is good, worthy of being sustained, capable of being fostered and perfected; and that is our task.

There is evil as well as good in being; there is ugliness, and there is violence and hatred. But being is never evil, and evil is never a being. Evils are parasitic upon the good:[31] Evil is evil only because it mars or violates, destroys or hampers the expression or fulfillment of reality. Again the Tanach helps us to voice the intuitions that can guide metaphysics. For when Ecclesiastes confronts metaphysical moodiness or despair, which the Midrash associates with the cynicism of middle age, all that is criticized is found wanting by comparison to some reality or ideal upheld as its alternative. So evil is exposed as negation, and we are brought to the realization (without the use of much abstraction) that the global condemnation of reality voiced in the preacher's opening lines of metaphysical despond, "Vanity of vanities. All things are vanity," is incoherent. For we can negate only by way of a prior affirmation.

The world contains a great variety of beings, each actively affirming its own identity, setting out its own project and interests. If there were nothing to contradict such interests, their affirmation might warrant their legitimacy. But in a world of multiple particulars, interests will collide. They may also harmonize or complement one another. Because interests can conflict, however, we cannot simply equate deserts with claims. Interests are prima facie deserts. To find the legitimate deserts of all beings we must attend to their specific and particular projects, consult the conflicts and the potentials for complementarity. Ecology and the economy of the garden are valuable models here—but models, not oracles. They yield no trivial or automatic resolutions to all conflicts.

To map the hierarchy of deserts in detail is not a necessary part of the philosophical theory of justice, and efforts to do so might seem to appeal, circularly, only to familiar notions of the relative worth of beings. The normative task of regulating our practical and notional responses to claims of all sorts is a task of culture in general and of law and religion in particular; indeed, it is chief among their tasks. Philosophy cannot successfully usurp it, but it can observe and thematize the criteria in use and criticize intellectually and morally the outcomes of various systematizations.

What we can say philosophically is that the interests of a being are its project or conatus, the very essence of that being as it expresses itself in the world. Sensation, sensibility, considerateness, and consideration are strengths, not weaknesses, in conatus. For they enable a subject to know its limitations without first being brought up short by them. Sentient beings are adept at discovering complementarities that will optimize the realization of deserts. Conscious beings can uncover or create intellectual realms in which even infinite claims are not invidious or self-undermining. And self-conscious beings, that is, persons, can expand their individual identities to accept as their own the interests of other beings. But, for all beings, legitimate deserts are grounded in each being's claims—identical with them if those claims are evaluated contextually. Justice, then, is the recognition of each being's deserts, as equilibrated against those of all others. For there is no reason for one being's deserts to count more than the equivalent claims of another.

Not all claims are equivalent. Because beings vary in ontic worth, their deserts must be scaled to their reality. Claims vary in merit, and their equilibration is not easy. Yet even without a recipe for assaying the relative worth of all rival claims, I can say with confidence that justice cannot be achieved, or understood, if we do not assign deserts to beings; and it will never be complete or universal if we confine deserts to ourselves. The primary rule of the general theory of deserts is that all beings should be treated in accordance with what they are. We can compare this demand for a proper response to the claims all beings make with the recognition called for by facticity in the case of cognitive judgments: Just as facts demand acknowledgment, deserts claim moral recognition. In both cases we have an obligation to respond to things' being as they are. In neither case have we a tautology. For the according of recognition goes beyond the demand for it, although the demand is implicit in the self-affirmation of a being (or a fact). Otherwise the recognition sought would not answer the demand made, or the demand would not be needed.

To implement so broad and potentially nebulous a rule as the demand that the reality of things be recognized, two cardinal principles are needed:

1. Deserts are scaled to the reality each being claims. We do not rightly sacrifice a child to a virus as though their claims were on a par—even though the quasi-life of the virus is all it has.
2. The interests of persons take special precedence and make a special claim. Persons need not be human. They do not win their special consideration on the grounds of looking like us but on the grounds of their subjecthood, a precious achievement in nature. Persons invoke special recognition, not simply because they are capable of returning it—for a dog can respond to recognition, and a person often cannot, whether in infancy or incapacity, or simply in ignorance or absence—but because only subjects are capable of giving or receiving moral regard.

Subjects, then, stand on a moral plateau. Even higher subjects, if they exist, may not rightly subordinate or negate the subjecthood of the rest. All subjects deserve a level of consideration that can be called absolute, in the sense that nothing can be traded for it; it has no price or counterpart; it is not measured on a scale commensurate with other interests. Underlying the special regard deserved by subjects is our primary rule, that all beings must be treated in accordance with what they are. For subjects self-consciously construct their own projects and in so doing call upon one another not only for cooperation but for recognition of the intensionality of their aims.

The moral consideration that is the due of nonpersons can be treated as an extension of the model we use in assigning deserts to persons. But that is a political, rhetorical way of stating the case and can foster the error of claiming the status of subjects for nonpersons. In ontic terms, subjects are the special case, and the general rule is to respect beings for what they are, not for their approximation to our image of ourselves. Living organisms, species, ecosystems like the riverbank or the canyon, the mountain or the shore, implicitly claim recognition, as virtual subjects. Persons claim recognition explicitly. The difference is one not of degree but of kind. It is no more simply a matter of language or commerce than it is of appearance and sympathy. Persons genuinely are subjects, whereas nonpersons are analogous to subjects in having projects and thus interests. In both cases recognition is deserved by the reality that is each being. But those realities differ crucially because of the role that consciousness plays. The interests of non-persons deserve consideration, other things being equal. But those of persons are in some sense inviolable, so long as the persons can be treated as such, and not, like the sniper in the tower, as a public menace or a pest.[32]

The ontological theory I have proposed assigns a special status to persons, but it does not confine interests to persons. The relative deserts of animals, plants, species, monuments of nature and art, institutions, and practices make claims upon our consideration. But the legitimacy of such claims never extends as far as the categorical claims of personhood. To underscore this point, I would say, for example, that I think it is an error of moral judgment to compromise the nutritional needs of a child in the interests of vegetarianism, as I have sometimes seen done. But norms of stewardship can be derived from an ontic account of justice. They cannot be derived from a strictly Kantian view; still less, from a consistently contractarian account. And the effort to derive them from Utilitarian precepts is fraught with paradox and inconsistency. Appeals to sentience like those of Bentham or Tom Regan transform an emotive appeal for the "rights" of sentient beings into an undermining of the very notions upon which the idea of rights depends and still fail to regard the claims made by trees and other nonsentient forms of life—let alone species and ecosystems, institutions, practices, cultures, and ethnicities.

An ontic theory can and should acknowledge a hierarchy of deserts, in which personhood makes special claims. Some moral programs romantically deny such hierarchies, perhaps in part because their exponents overlook the element of ritual necessary in setting out any value system as a practical moral scheme.[33] But to attempt to exclude hierarchies of value is as much to negate deserts as is a denial of all value in things. Once the special claims of personhood are submerged, made commensurable with those of lesser beings, the principle of ontic recognition is violated, and no sound basis for the allocation of recognition remains. The same is true even if deserts that are lesser only in degree are placed on a par with others that exceed them, as, for example, when a whole ecosystem, say, a forest, is placed at risk by the protection in it of some feral species or invading weed. And in general, recognition must be pared and extended to meet the contours of beings' claims, just as nourishment must be shaped to the needs of living beings.

Efforts to "extend" the rights of persons to other sorts of beings, then, are not just inappropriate (since animals cannot vote and plants cannot enjoy an art museum) but misguided. The effect is not the extension of rights (as though plants were now given the vote) but the spread of the relativity of deserts into the realm where deserts are properly conceived as rights and are not relative at all. The outcome is not the announced expansion of the moral franchise but the debasement of its meaning. Animals and plants, species and econiches deserve protection, for what they are as well as for what they may mean to us. But persons have dignity as well as the value that each being attains in its own way. Persons are holy. Genesis expresses this by saying that humans are created in God's image. The reference is not to form but to subjecthood.[34] In humanity we see fulfilled the self-creative project that is present to varying degrees in every form of life.[35] We cannot consistently give moral regard to any project without assigning special regard to the human project.

Does the dignity of persons entail the inevitability of tragedy? Popular thinking may suspect it does, because popular thinking is the playground of sophists and dramatists, who are fond of the idea of conflicts among absolutes—dramatists, because of the emotive energies sparking from the clash of values; sophists, because of an impatience with absolute claims, and even more, with the idea of reconciliation. But most conflicts of principle can be reconciled by reference to a higher principle. This fact is obscured only by the need for nonlinear thinking in discovering that principle and by the interest of some professionals in denying our access to higher principles. We are not helpless, however. Whenever we make value judgments we make reference to the absolute and compare incommensurables.

Several gifts restrain the absoluteness of dignity from inevitably provoking irreconcilable conflicts. The first is language. We can communicate; life need not be so prickly as a minefield. The second is cooperation. As Spinoza noted, we are useful to each other; nothing is more useful to us than each other's aid.[36] The third is modesty. We are capable of consideration and reserve, of according as well as demanding privacy, of consulting each other's interests as well as prosecuting our own. The Talmud expresses the exigencies of the last case negatively when it says that Jerusalem was destroyed because its people pressed for their rights according to the Torah. Any social system depends for its stability not only on ambition but also on accommodation. The ethics of the general recognition of deserts is an ethics of accommodation.

The special recognition deserved by persons is the core value Kant was recognizing when he called upon us to treat humanity in ourselves and others never merely as a means but always also as an intrinsic end. A person, as such, is the projector of individual and shared ends; to respect a person as a person is to respect not necessarily those ends but the freedom and dignity of the self-conscious and self-constructing subject who is their source. The content of Kantian ethics here is not Kant's invention. Kant, like Aristotle and Maimonides, would have thought an ethics without prior history or tradition an anomaly, not an achievement. Humanity has not survived and developed as long as it has without any inkling of the fundamental principles of morals. But Kant's achievement in moral philosophy was to retrieve the Socratic rigor in which logical analysis was first used, for the sake of ethics, and to place it once again in the service of ethics. Specifically, Kant uncovered the inner incoherence Socrates had discovered at the heart of wrongdoing. Kant found a contradiction in any maxim that professes to pursue the good by vicious means. Thus, just as Socrates found incoherence in the idea that courage could be stupid or pigheaded or that piety could be harebrained or unfilial, Kant found a contradiction in the idea of enhancing one's wealth by undermining the security of property, fidelity, or trust or of finding comfort through suicide. Such implicit contradictions become explicit when attempts are made to treat the underlying maxims as matters of principle, that is, as universal laws.

The ethics Kant renders scientific through the rediscovery of Socratic logic is not the ethics of Plato, where the end always justifies the means. Nor is it the virtue ethics of Aristotelian eudaimonism. It is the positive ethics of Scripture, the ethics of love for our fellow human beings and of concrete obligations and prohibitions that give effect to that love. The austere formalism of the Kantian moral law can yield such obligations only by invoking an idea of the good. It was implicit appeal to the good that yielded the contradictions crucial to the Socratic elenchus. And, although Kant's deontology sharply distinguishes the right from the good and excludes the value of ends from moral relevance, making rightness a purely formal matter, Kant does not exclude the good from our maxims but acknowledges it as their core material content. A vicious maxim bears a contradiction because of its implicit appeal to some good, taken as an object of desire.

Many goods might be consistent with the formal demands of the idea of right, but only one will express it, and that is love, regard for being. Here we must supply the missing nexus between Kant's formal and material formulations of the categorical imperative, generalizing the theme Kant voices when he focuses the moral law on its application to humanity and argues that the only material principle capable of becoming a universal moral law is the command to treat humanity in ourselves and others never solely as a means but always at the same time as an end, that is, to regard each person as a subject, and so worthy of respect, a bearer of dignity. In reaching this formulation, Kant's moral formalism, in search of a viable material foundation, has traded places with the usual concreteness of the biblical idiom. For the categorical imperative, when fleshed out in the end-in-itself formulation, demands in concrete and material terms what the Torah prescribes formally in God's commandment to love one another as we love ourselves. What that Golden Rule intends is not that we perform on one another just the behaviors we wish to have performed on ourselves, but that we treat one another with love, esteem for human subjecthood, a deference measured and given content, at least in the first instance, by our self-knowledge and the understanding it gives us of the universal human need for dignity and fulfillment of wholesome desires. What is called for, then, is sympathetic regard for the moral personhood vested in human beings as choosers of their own ends.

The resultant ethics contains clear imperatives and is not confined to "guidelines," although there must be those as well, because ethics will make demands beyond the minimal expectations of its laws. The biblical ethics, whose groundwork Kant laid bare, is not solely and simply an ethics of tendencies, then, as some forms of virtue ethics can be. It is not an uninterpreted "love one another." The Torah tells us concretely *how* to love one another, spelling out the minimal demands of human dignity and painting vivid ethical and ritual pictures of the behaviors it deploys to improve human character and reflectiveness. Thus, the immediate context of the command to love one another as we love ourselves is a tiny, tightly balanced system of obligations regarding reproof.[37]

These cover a range of engagements, from whistle blowing to the subtle dynamics of human tact in sensitive situations of admonition. The Golden Rule is invoked as the general governing principle here. Its scope is hardly confined to these contexts or it could not be invoked a priori, as it is. But the concreteness of its relevance is typified by these applications.

Throughout the Mosaic canon, the biblical idea of justice is founded in the worth of individual beings, seen not as means but as ends in themselves—as subjects or virtual subjects, whose individuality makes claims in behalf of a myriad of projects. Compare the work of Rawls, who tries to derive the liberal principle of respect for subjecthood out of the claim that freedom of choice is the last thing that uncoerced rational agents would give up and the first that they would seek to preserve in founding a society, if they had the choice and did not know in advance what their own roles would be. In *On Justice* I argue that Rawls's argument from the "veil of ignorance" and the "original position" faces a dilemma. To the extent that his claim is meant to be empirical, it is not borne out by experience. Free agents often barter, sacrifice, or debase their freedoms. But, to the extent that his appeal to the virtual choices of hypothetical rational agents is meant strictly as a normative claim, it rests on importing into the concept of rationality a host of culture-bound and historically fleshed-out values that cannot without circularity be drawn from the formal idea of rationality. Virtual consent, the foundation of Rawls's theory of justice, projects what some ideal alter-ego might have determined in ideal conditions. But it carefully tailors the stipulated preconditions and the knowledge and ignorance of the fictive alter-ego to elicit exactly the agreement that the theorist deems appropriate. What Rawls has canonized in the process is not the inviolable dignity of personhood but the relative usefulness of liberty, a usefulness that is invested with an aura of sanctity only by secular traditions and historical associations that Rawls did not initially acknowledge and never openly and explicitly incorporated into the structure of his argument.

JUSTICE AND COMMUNITY

I have argued that society does not create justice. Rather, justice creates society. How so? My argument centers on the notion of community. A community is a group whose members depend on one another for survival or wellbeing. Persons are capable of community in a unique sense. And only through community can their real worth as subjects be acknowledged explicitly, recognized pragmatically, and given scope to flourish. Human beings depend on one another, and on a host of other sorts of beings, for their realization as human beings.

In part my argument is biological. We are a social species. That is what Aristotle meant by the descriptive phrase *zoon politikon*, a civic animal. We live in communities and depend on one another for the character of our existence. From an evolutionary standpoint, communities long antedate any formal social undertakings; they afforded the basis of our humanization, biologically as well as culturally. Consider the obstetric problem of the human head. Human evolution depended on the growth of cranial capacity. But the birth canal can expand only so far, so human beings are born immature compared to other animals. That fact accentuates the importance of the social division of labor, the two-parent family (as in birds, only more so), and the relevance of culture. Hume put it well: "The long and helpless infancy of man requires the combination of parents for the subsistence of their young."[38] The value of culture in turn places yet greater adaptive significance on cranial capacity and further heightens the import of the social division of labor. In this sense we can say with confidence that community antedates not only formal, societal rules and undertakings but the emergence of humanity itself.

A community (*Gemeinschaft*), as distinguished from a societal grouping or organization, is informal. It derives its legitimacy from the goods it serves and may indeed be abandoned if it fails to serve as expected. In this sense it is a voluntary association. But it is not, as other voluntary associations may be, the mere product of a compact, contract, or other formal undertaking. Many communities are natural groups. We might move into a neighborhood, but we are born into a nation, a culture, family, or tribe. And our dependence on our communities is often prior, temporally or ontically, to any choices we may make—as with the gift of language, for example. Our communal obligations stem not from any formal undertaking or equivalence of goods received to services returned or sufferings and risks undergone, but from human interdependence. For we are not atomic isolates and cannot survive as such. Still less can we thrive in isolation, that is, develop or express ourselves in full measure: intellectually, spiritually, culturally, morally—even physically, as, say, the institutions of medical research and practice make abundantly clear. The obligations legitimately imposed by any community stem ultimately from the worth of individuals and from the power of a community to foster their interests and promote the emergence and recognition of subjecthood. That is the heart of the usefulness of any community, and indeed the source not only of its legitimacy but also of its power.

A society (*Gesellschaft*) relies on arrangements and reciprocities that are formal and explicit where communal relations are informal and implicit. The metaphor of a social contract has a different meaning in each case. Societally, it refers to our engagement in a system of relations marked by agreements and overt rules. Communally, it refers to our existential interdependence and interactions, tacit understandings, and bonds of recognition and commitment. We should not be romantic about community. Formal, legal relationships serve in part to regulate the often oppressive or disproportionate demands that communal relationships can make. But we cannot ignore the primacy of the communal to the societal. Communities create societies and survive within them, around them, and above them, as neighborhoods exist within a city, nations embrace a state, and humanity itself senses its rarely exercised but always crucial role as the community above all states and nations. Natural communities like the family, the nation, and humanity are prior to societal institutions like the state, the firm, the union—ontically and in legitimacy. It is they that legitimate our societal undertakings by establishing the bonds of trust, recognition, and extended identity underlying more explicit versions of a social contract. The economic trust that makes trade possible and a monetary system feasible, and the political trust that makes civil life secure and military and police protection possible when that security is threatened are underwritten by bonds of communal cooperation that express our interdependence and thus address the underlying claims of personhood. Even so delicate a modality as courtesy, as I argued in *On Justice*, is not an adornment to more basic social or economic relations but foundational to them, a prerequisite to what superficially might seem the most elementary transactions. It is because we find ourselves in a community, *ab initio*, that we are capable, morally, intellectually, even physically, of making the commitments to one another out of which our societal arrangements arise.

When we consider the biblical idea of a covenant we need to understand that the consent symbolized by the Torah's representation of an oath whose parties are God and a host of persons mostly unborn is not simply an explicit, formal agreement but the explicit articulation of an implicit relationship of shared history, situation, and destiny, upon which the new, formal agreement is predicated. In the same way, beyond the boundaries of neighborhood or peoplehood, where the relationships of interdependency are enacted more impersonally than in a family, yet far more intimately than in a club or firm, humanity at large has a common history, situation, and destiny that link its members with one another in bonds of mutual obligation and legitimate expectation.

When we consider Plato's argument in the *Crito* that the laws are our parents, we must understand not merely that a return of benefits received is asked for and expected by the laws. For that is not in fact what parents ask. And obedience is only in the most tenuous way construable as somehow reciprocating the protections received from law. If all our obligations are formal and conventional, how can there be any legitimate expectation of acknowledgement, let alone return? No promises were made by an infant; and conventionalism finds no norm in nature that would extract such promises or demand their fulfillment. But the underlying reference of Plato's argument is not to promises but to our engagement in a community whose very existence places legitimate demands upon its members, in recognition of the good that is served by human beings' taking one another's interests as their own. Parents and children do make demands on one another, not by virtue of a contract, but by virtue of interdependency. Parents depend on their children to carry forward the project of their lives, and children depend on their parents for the launching of their own project. In any community, what is called for is mutual recognition of worth and dignity, a practical expression of regard that binds us to obligations, even to the point that we may be called upon to risk our lives for one another's safety. The foundations of obligation here are existential, not formal; they are rooted in the worth of human beings.

All relationships, those of a business contract or a simple sale or trade of goods, rest on and presuppose informal relationships of trust, civility, understanding, even the constantly renegotiated significances of language and communication. Language and the conventions it supports in a community of language users ground a complex network of obligations and expectations, without which there would be little scope for formal undertakings, and none at all for law. The explicit type of contract is dependent, then, not just historically but ontically and for its legitimacy, upon the informal and implicit compact that the members of a community (or a community of communities) hold with one another. The foundation of that informal compact in turn is the recognition due to individuals, with persons first, but not alone, among them.

TORAH AND OBLIGATION

We gain insight into the Torah's contribution to the foundations of political, social, and moral philosophy when we consider the polarity between deontological and teleological ethics. Teleology bases its account of ethics on the idea of the good, seeing in ends the justification of all justifiable actions. Deontology finds this account reductionistic and insists on an idea of right and duty irreducible to any other considerations. In *On Justice* I argue at some length[39] that both perspectives are inadequate and incomplete. By trying to set aside as morally indifferent all mere "externals," such as human happiness, welfare, and perfection, and grounding moral worth not in consequences but in intentions, strict deontology in effect abdicates the classic moralist's role of giving guidance and counsel. It refuses the delicate task of establishing priorities among competing and complementary goods: For the deontological purist, every choice is either a matter of principle or morally indifferent. Strict teleology, by contrast, is often committed to a type of naturalism that ignores the element of transcendence presupposed in *any* choice. It thus has difficulty assigning value to anything on *intrinsic* grounds. It may even (as Philippa Foot does[40]) try to avoid anchoring our choices in intrinsic or unconditional values altogether, as though any choice could claim justification merely by its telic link to other choices that themselves have no justification whatever.

The familiar notion of the incompatibility of deontology with teleology is based on overstated versions of both. To be workable, both approaches need supplementation from one another's perspectives. To echo a famous line from Kant's epistemology, where he achieved a better balance between the formal and the material than he did in his ethics: Morality without interests is empty; pragmatism without principles is blind. I find the complementarity needed to give balance to our ethical thinking in the eudaimonism of classical moral sources such as Plato, Aristotle, and Cicero. The well-developed moral approach of the Torah is structurally congruent with these classic formulations. Indeed the Torah's own version of eudaimonism, although not expounded in abstract arguments, is vividly articulated in the prophetic idiom through appeals to experience and vignettes of the good life as projected biblically and elaborated by the rabbinic expositors of the Mosaic law.

Deontology and teleology can be reconciled logically if we open up deontology to its implicit recognition of the moral significance of material values, crucially including the intrinsic value of beings in general and persons in particular. Similarly, we can overcome the ungroundedness of reductive teleologies like pragmatism and utilitarianism, if we expand the range of teleology to include the virtues, as anatomized, say, by Aristotle. Maimonides recognized this when he overcame the dichotomy between virtue ethics and what on the surface might appear a sheer command ethics in Scripture, by interpreting Mosaic ethics as a form of eudaimonism.[41] He reads the rabbinic elaboration of biblical ethics in terms of virtue ethics, when he schematizes the law under the aims it pursues: the establishment of just social and economic relations and civil security, the enhancement of human moral character, and the provision of a symbol system that invites intellectual and spiritual growth (*Guide* 3.27). The schematism that guides this codification is Aristotle's array of the moral and intellectual virtues, seconded by the Aristotelian assumption that civil society is the necessary means to the humanization of human life.

Maimonides's synthetic understanding of the telic structure and deontic aims of the law is vividly in view when he dissolves the seeming antinomy between the eudaimonist thesis that the virtuous enjoy doing what is right (and feel no urge to evil) and the more deontological doctrine that seeks to recognize the value of moral struggle and effort by promising that rewards are proportioned to the difficulty of the choices obedience demands. Maimonides's well-known response divides the issue: The ritual commands that go beyond the obvious requirements of a perfected human nature are what the Rabbis had in mind when they spoke of the special moral worth of acting out of duty. But the acquisition of a virtuous nature remains the minimal moral expectation of the law.[42] If we include the intellectual with the moral virtues, we find that for Maimonides ritual acts too serve in the perfection of humanity (*Guide* 3.32). And we can see that the schematization is not simply read into Scripture. For the Torah repeatedly states the aims of its legislation in terms of the kind of life that Israelites are to lead (Deuteronomy 21, 22:22, 23:17) and the kind of people it expects those who observe its laws to become, "a nation of priests and a holy people" (Exodus 19:6).

The watchword of the synthesis that does not exclude human fulfillment from deontology and does not confine teleology to the subjective or minimal goals of pleasure, use, survival, or domination is the identity of happiness with the life of virtue (hence, Deuteronomy 33:29). The virtues play a constitutive role in the good life, and obligation is oriented by human dignity and worth. So obligations naturally fuse with their rewards. Thus, in the idea of a mitzvah as biblically articulated and rabbinically elaborated, we find fulfillment in doing God's will. What God commands is not some arbitrary ordeal[43] but a path of life well suited to our human capabilities and aimed toward our perfection and fulfillment as human beings, socially, morally, and intellectually—in keeping with the triad of aims that Maimonides elicits from the Torah and identifies (*Guide* 2.40) as the marks of a law whose authority is not merely human but divine.

Let me say a word about that authority. A sympathetic Catholic philosopher, after reading *On Justice*, remarked that the book "never deviates from a naturalistic interpretation of the Hebrew scriptures," which it presents "as an important, although literary source of insight into human nature and its fulfillment."[44] To this I must plead guilty. How else, I wonder, can we read our sources in a multicultural context, where those who read with us can hardly be expected simply to adopt our traditional perspectives, where our own community is not united in its vision of the status or authority of Scripture, and where even the most wholehearted biblicism would still face the task of interpreting any text that (*per impossibile*) held unquestioned authority?

No one, I believe, can be convincing to others who is not able to convince himself or herself, and self-conviction without self-criticism is worthless. So I have not argued from the premise that the Torah or any document is divinely inspired, but have preferred to seek its guidance and let its wisdom, insofar as we can find it, speak to the issue of its inspiration, through its resonances with the wisdom given us in our own intelligence. In this approach I follow the advice of no less a witness to the law's authority than Moses, who commended God's law to his people in these words: "See now, I have taught you laws and statutes in accordance with what the Lord my God commanded me, for you to observe within the land that you are entering to inherit. Keep them and perform them, for that will be wisdom and insight on your part in the eyes of the nations, who will hear all these laws and say, 'Surely a wise and discerning nation is this great nation.' For what nation is so great as to have the divine so near to it as the Lord our God is whenever we call to Him? And what nation is so great as to have laws and statutes as just as those of this Torah, which I set before thee this day?" (Deuteronomy 4:5–8). As Maimonides says, intelligent people must test the ideas they receive. I can commend no exegesis more highly than his, which seeks the wisdom of the Torah in the transcendence of its aims, rather than arguing from its divine origin, say, to a hidebound ethos alien to its spirit, or projecting onto the life it seeks to guide an inner anxiety about divinity, by way of a dogmatism or positivism as to its authority that is foreign to its announced intentions. For the Torah predicates obedience upon love, not love upon obedience.

A crucial difference between the eudaimonism we can identify as Mosaic and the teleologies of, say, Utilitarianism or Epicureanism is the reductionism I have noted in the more familiar forms of naturalism. Biblical naturalism is grounded in a recognition of the claims to transcendence made implicitly by every being and, self-consciously, by persons. These claims, which come to fruition and explicitness in humanity, are our link to the divine. They ground the dignity of subjects symbolized in the Torah's affirmation of our creation in the image and likeness of God, and they are the very content, in my view, of the idea of an immortal soul—a personhood whose worth is not exhausted by any merely factitious natural or social role or fate.

Within nature and from the finitude of human experience (cf. Job 19:26) we find openings to the infinite, aesthetically, intellectually, and morally. The endeavor to call attention to these openings lies at the heart of my strictures against reductive naturalism and the narrow deontology that is its counterpart. I call the two polarized traditions counterparts. For, just as reductive teleologies seek to generate values out of facticity, so purist deontology verges into positivism, whether from Oedipal anxieties or simply from a vertiginous fear of the absolute intended in every moral choice, conceptual insight, or living act. Just as hedonism, left to its own devices, is morally transparent, having no idea of its own of what constitutes a pleasure, let alone a wholesome or legitimate pleasure, so a purist deontology is morally empty once it has uttered the sheer demand of duty. Thus, the deontology of the Stoics becomes dependent on Roman ideas of fidelity, Confucian deontology is infused with Chinese ideas of filial and political obligation, and Kantian deontology opens itself to Prussian notions of authority and obedience. Openness to the cultural resources of moral data is not in itself a failing. But it is a symptom, the mark of moral hunger. The formalism of sheer deontology can, in all these cases, render the philosophy supine to what it adopts, robbing moral thought of its critical edge and transforming high principle insensibly into rigidity or rigorism. For morals abhors a vacuum.

But if we seek to call attention to the transcendent dimensions of experience and the many ways in which the infinite is intended by the finite, the question remains when and how we are to do so. For we are searching for the foundations of justice in a context where even the value of existence is contested. To argue here from the authority of Scripture would be to preach solely to the converted and presume outrageously upon what needs to be shown even to them. The philosophic principle, par excellence, is that one must not presume what is to be shown. To work from the assumption that the Torah and the Prophets are the word of God, and the Rabbis, faithful and legitimate continuators of the ancient message, would undermine any possibility of showing that there is anything inspired or even instructive in the canon. We cannot discover what we have assumed.

To depart from naturalism is to lean on what needs to be established, revivified, or dismissed. If we want to find a meaning in experience that carries us beyond reductive naturalism, as I think we can, we must begin from experience as we find it, not presume upon the very conclusions that a thoughtful examination of the realia of ethics and nature might suggest and that a thoughtful reading of the ancient texts would confirm, not by the normative authority of a shared past but by appreciation of the sense that our thoughts are not alone but echo the insights that others have reached before us, in a tradition to which we may lay claim, then, not just by birthright, but with intellectual confidence and moral responsibility.

The Torah itself is a good model in this regard. It is never dogmatic or doctrinaire. There is no period at which its audience would have tolerated that. Yet it forcefully communicates a definite set of norms and ideas. It always seems to find stories more effective than theses and symbols more enduring than abstractions. Thus it unites the blessings and the obligations of the good life not in a theory but in a picture: "See how good and pleasant—brothers dwelling together in concord. It is like fine oil on the head running down into the beard . . . like the dew of Hermon that descends on the mountains of Zion. For there the Lord ordained the blessing: life forever" (Psalms 133); again when it pictures each of us under his own vine and fig tree, with none to disturb or cause fear (Micah 4:4; cf. Zechariah 3:10, where the image is made convivial). The vision endures long after the modes of agriculture it presupposes have been forgotten.

The commandments are constitutive in the good life. That view, in my judgment, is the heart of eudaimonism. Clearly[45] the rabbinic and Aristotelian conceptions of the good life are not alike. But, viewed against the background of the deontological-teleological polarity, the biblical project is revealed to be structurally of a piece with the eudaimonism that Aristotle builds on the ontic foundations laid by Plato. That work is continued in Cicero, whose impatience with the exclusivities of Stoic deontology and Epicurean teleology is outspoken in De Finibus—specifically, in his refusal to isolate virtuous actions from their rewards. The theme, implicit in the Torah, becomes explicit when the Rabbis teach that the reward of a mitzvah is another mitzvah (Avot 4:2).

The project of investing the idea of happiness with that of virtue is ultimately Socratic. It is not circular (pace Kant), unless we assume artificially that we know nothing of either happiness or virtue from experience. A Socratic dialectic enhances our ideas of both, by "bootstrapping," or as I prefer to put it, "chimneying" between the two. The Torah achieves the same aim through its vignettes of the good life, but without Plato's reliance on large abstractions, innate ideas, or exile from the physical, and without resort to Socrates's puckish aporetic.

The eudaimonism that Maimonides develops by organizing biblical and rabbinic values in an Aristotelian conceptual scheme does not, of course, equate happiness with pleasure. Pleasures and pains are too contingent and too much the coin of moral exchange to serve reliably as anchors of the moral life. Yet they are not irrelevant. Stoicism can teach suffering humanity that pleasures and pains are not ultimate concerns; but the same Stoic teachings give sorry counsel to legislators seeking to determine the proper limits of self-sacrifice to be laid upon the same suffering humanity. Hedonists would like to judge actions by their outcomes, and outcomes by their pleasures and pains, but I think Aristotle was right to reverse the fields here: We can judge the virtuous and vicious by their pleasures and pains. The virtuous find good actions pleasurable and welcome, and bad actions painful and uncomfortable. The vicious find good actions uncomfortable and unwelcome, and bad actions pleasurable. There is nothing intrinsic in such subjective responses to guide us to the good or away from the bad. Even the most painful actions may be advantageous, worthwhile, or obligatory; there are circumstances in which even death may be our wisest choice—not on hedonistic grounds, but in the interest of honor or other higher principles.

Partly because it relies on the idea of enlightened interests, eudaimonism can (and typically does) enlarge the idea of the self beyond the atomicity typical of the familiarly narrow "rational choice" paradigms of decision making. When it infuses the conception of happiness with the yield of virtue ethics, it judges the moral virtues in a social context, and it does not exclude the social and other-regarding dimensions of a perfected human character. Because the virtues are constitutive in any adequate conception of human fulfillment, eudaimonism captures most of what is worth capturing in deontology. The morally mature or virtuous human being does not conceive of personal identity or personal interest without reference to larger identities and higher interests, in which due weight is given to much that the deontologist rightly respects in the idea of obligation.

As an ethics of tendency, however, eudaimonism does not adequately capture the idea that principled action admits of no exception. Thus it does not afford much basis to the unpleasant but all too necessary idea of sin. Eudaimonists like the idea of refined or perfected humanity, but dislike the idea that actions should be perfect, finding such notions overly rigorist. Legalists highly prize such claims, as the bastion of proceduralism; and liberals (who nowadays often reject deontology in their personal ethics) still insist upon it in the public sphere.[46] For without it there is no guarantarism—no Bill of Rights, nor any real constitutional government. Here, in the prescriptive realm that a eudaimonist like Aristotle barely mentions, when he says that there is no proper mean in theft or adultery,[47] and that Plato badly slights, when he sanctions eugenics, euthanasia, and paternalism, the command ethics of the Torah shines in its explicitness and unwillingness to compromise the matter of principles or procedures.

By avoiding a reductionistic idea of personhood and preserving subjecthood as a matter of principle—whether in the laws against adultery, rape, and incest, or in those against self-mutilation— Mosaic eudaimonism guards the dignity of the subject. And, by grounding ethics in ontology, it leaves room for the relative deserts of other beings, alongside the uncompromisable deserts of persons. Clearly such legislation cannot be equated with any form of hedonism, but it is not joyless or even ascetic. Like eudaimonism, biblical ethics aims for the flourishing, fulfillment, and well being of the individual and the community. These do not exclude pleasure.

Perhaps one of the best things the Torah does for morals is to picture the appropriate modes of pleasure to us. Here modalities matter. We are even told what we should find disgusting. But once the right modalities are found, joy can be boundless. The Torah, after all, founds not just a law but also an ethos and a mythos, an integrated image of the self in its social, natural, and divine milieu. When it sets the commandment that a bridegroom rejoice his bride ahead of military service, it concretely delineates the strength it gives legislatively to the naturalistic-mythic "cleave unto his wife" of Genesis. Pleasure is involved, but the law orders the priorities: He should rejoice *her*, not just anyone, but his bride. The relation, not the pleasure, is paramount. We do not read: "Make love, not war." A certain kind of pleasure is constitutive in the good life, not just for the delight of the individual but for constitution of that individual and of the community whose integration depends on the integration of individuals, inwardly and with one another, as spouses, in families, as neighbors, friends, and fellows.

The Torah's eudaimonia is not an airless intellectualism or isolating mysticism. We will never understand the eudaimonism of Aristotle or of Judaism unless we adopt the inclusive as opposed to the exclusive reading of the summum bonum.[48] Aristotle could not use the virtues to locate eudaimonia if the activities in accordance with the virtues, moral and intellectual, were not constitutive of eudaimonia. True, the virtues are *means* to happiness, but they are such because they are dispositions toward appropriate actions. They are thus constitutive of happiness, understood as the good life, that is, as an optimal ordering of appropriate activities. This means that moral virtues are not left behind by the intellectual reaching out for the fulfillment of the desire for ultimate understanding. Self-cultivation, to use the phrase preferred in the Chinese traditions that are very much in tune with those of Aristotle and the Torah on this point, as we would expect any classic tradition to be, is never merely of the self.

Nor is contemplation, in Aristotle or in Maimonides, isolated from the whole of our intellectual or moral life. The philosopher in Aristotle sees God in nature, through the sciences; and the philosopher can and should guide society as well as himself. Phronesis, an intellectual virtue, is a sine qua non of the moral virtues, and of happiness. And every moral virtue must be guided by reason in discovering the proper mean, implicit in the character of the individual or in the laws and institutions that frame the character and form the ethos that will allow intelligent choices. As Maimonides knows, Moses, the most perfect of men, no more spent his time in sheer contemplation of God than he spent it studying Talmud. He wanted to see God not for the sake of ecstasy, but to be able to govern his people. The perfection of his prophecy, as Maimonides explains, was that the comprehensiveness and purity of his vision allowed him to legislate, not just to find private audience with God. And the vision he was granted was not of God's face, but of God's "back," that is, the tenor of his governance of nature. Moses was said to speak with God face to face, then, not in the sense that he confronted the Godhead without losing conscious individuality, but in the sense that he understood nature and the laws of life and so was able to articulate God's will in terms concretely relevant to human perfectibility. It was only so that he could specify what it means *for us* to realize a likeness to God.[49]

We see a paradigm here, not in the sense that we are called upon to become a Moses or an Abraham and somehow seek to duplicate their work, but in the sense that the ideal held before us is that of an integrated person, in whom the moral and the intellectual serve one another rather than compete, just as the social and the personal fulfill one another rather than compete.[50] Our texts make this plainest, perhaps, when teaching us the complementarity of the deontological and teleological, by their images of the fusion of happiness and obligation. For the purist appeal of the deontological is intellectual; and that of the teleological is practical. But for the Torah, the two are inseparable.

Thus we read: "You shall eat and be sated and bless the Lord thy God for the good land which he hath given you" (Deuteronomy 8:10). No sharp line is drawn between the blessing enjoyed and the gratitude expressed. The commandment drawn rabbinically from the text flows as naturally into practice as joy itself flows from living the fulfillment of the promise. Promise, prophecy, fulfillment, performance, joy—all are fused in the same act, merged at the same table, which the Torah pictures less by describing its cruets and condiments than by establishing the mood shared there. The life of virtue and the acceptance of our obligations are not distinct from happiness. The mitzvot are not simply a means to happiness and certainly not just onerous obligations undertaken for no good reason or for the sake of a reward extrinsic to the life we lead. Rather, these obligations and their fulfillment belong to happiness. Thus the sense of Antigonos of Socho: "Be not like servants who serve their master for the sake of their bonus (*pras*), but be like servants who serve their master not for the sake of receiving a bonus, and let the awe of heaven be upon you" (Avot 1:3). Ernst Renan mistranslated the passage in a way that is happily redolent of the midrashic spirit and method when he rendered its final words, "and let the dew of Heaven be upon you," as though it echoed Psalms 133:3. Every Jew knows that the mitzvot are constitutive of the good life. That is why Jews do not say, "It is my duty," or "It is an obligation," but smilingly, when we have done what we know is right, "Oh, it's a mitzvah." By which we mean, it is a privilege to be able to do the right thing.

NOTES

Early versions of this paper were presented at Harvard and at the Universities of Arizona, Colorado, and Hawaii, as well as at the Academy for Jewish Philosophy meeting in Evanston. The author thanks all the philosophers, colleagues, and friends who discussed its contents with him and extends special thanks once again to Daniel Frank for his editorial skill and philosophical dedication.

    1.   Goodman 1991.

    2.   In a fair spoken review, Warren Zev Harvey (1993) writes, "On the question of justice, one finds different and conflicting views in the Jewish sources. Goodman's book is no less 'authentically Jewish,' even if some books defending rival theories are also authentically Jewish." If one takes the reference to authenticity that Harvey draws from *On Justice* (p. x) in a strictly historicist sense, there is no disputing this claim. But, if authenticity is to evoke commitment, then argument and the coherence of the sources with one another and with the whole of our knowledge and experience must have their say. Philosophically, our concern is not with what is Jewish among the documents in the common human legacy, but with what is credible; so, in the Jewish canon, with what is credible and of enduring worth there. Such questions are not answered from a purely positive historical standpoint. Readers can gauge the outcomes of the philosophical and historicist methods by comparing the discussion of, say, messianism in *On Justice*, chapter 5 with its treatment by Gershom Scholem in his well known essay on the subject. In comparing the two approaches, one finds that the philosophical method is powerless without its historical basis; but outcomes reached by the historical method can also be informed, their standpoint enlarged and their biases counteracted, by findings highlighted by the thematic interests of philosophy.

    3.   Plato, *Republic* 2 (357–360).

    4.   K.D. *(Kuriai Doxai)* 31; cf. Lucretius, *De Rerum Natura* 5 1010–1027.

    5.   K.D. 32. The dictum is a rationale for enslaving tribal peoples.

    6.   K.D. 33.

    7.   K.D. 34.

    8.   K.D. 35. The argument, of course, proves too much. For it also counsels us to do nothing, not even to defend our dignity or property or loved ones, nor our liberty against a tyrant, nor to testify in court against a violent criminal, lest we risk the unremitting threat of reprisal.

    9.   K.D. 36.

  10.   K.D. 37.

  11.   K.D. 38.

12.   *Leviathan*, Pt. 1, sec. x.

13.   See Spinoza, *Tractatus Politicus* 2. 12 (ed. Gebhardt, 3.280); cf. Taylor 1937.

14.   Moses Mendelssohn, *Jerusalem*, trans. Arkush, pp. 36–37.

15.   *De Cive* 1.7.

16.   Hobbes, *Elements of Law* 1.14, 10; *De Cive* 1.10; *Leviathan* 14.

17.   Mark Murphy (in his doctoral dissertation, University of Notre Dame, 1993) has shown Hobbes's continuing debt to Aquinas and other natural law thinkers for such assumptions as the idea that self-interest is a foundation of human obligation. Hobbes's argument is this: Because one's interests are optimized in a civil society and highly at risk in the anarchic state of nature, it follows that one is obligated to obey civil authority. The argument is marred by lack of quantification and particularity (any civil society? this one?). The position is further damaged by Hobbes's assumption that any act of disobedience to civil authority is, wittingly or unwittingly, a choice for anarchy. In using vestiges of natural law theory to shore up his account of political legitimacy and even his conception of self-interest, Hobbes is inconsistent. For the scholastic doctrines assign intrinsic worth to the human project, where Hobbes equates worth with price. Hobbes has powerful motives to resist equating human worth with whatever prideful prelates or boastful barons may claim. But he goes well beyond the rhetorical satisfaction of deflating such pretensions when he categorically rejects intrinsic worth. When he transforms the obligation to protect one's own interests into a law of nature, he proves too much: "I conceive not how any man can bear *animum felleum*, or so much malice towards himself, as to hurt himself voluntarily, much less to kill himself. For naturally and necessarily the intention of every man aimeth at somewhat which is good to himself, and tendeth to his preservation. And therefore, methinks, if he kill himself, it is to be presumed that he is not *compos mentis*, but by some inward torment or apprehension of somewhat worse than death, distracted" (*A Dialogue Between a Philosopher and a Student of the Common Laws of England*, ed. Cropsey, pp. 116–117.) Applying this reasoning to the issue of political obligation yields the conclusion not that rebels are wrong a priori, which is suspect on moral grounds and begs the question Hobbes is seeking to resolve, but that they are all mad or stupid—outcomes suspect on empirical grounds. Clearly Hobbes does not assume that if one had a choice between sanity and madness (as one does, with certain drugs) that choice would be a morally neutral matter. Yet he tries to minimize his reliance on moral notions, because they smack of the dangerous appeal to personal conscience. In short, he is ambivalent. He wants to have his cake and eat it—to use the moral force of the

brickbat that traitors are forsworn, yet not seem simply to wag a finger at them, but to promise them (well deserved, i.e., perfectly expectable) condign punishments and sufferings. The tensions in Hobbes's argument can generate a Socratic kind of paradox that comes quite near the surface in the claim that only a madman would commit suicide. Hobbes leans on the natural law tradition for the force of the claims that madness, suicide, and treachery are evils. But to remain perfectly consistent with his more outspoken conventionalism would undermine his project altogether. For the idea of political obligation is empty without the assignment of intrinsic worth. Beings are the repositories of such worth. I can see no other.

18. See Goodman 1993a, esp. p. 60.

19. See Hardin 1980.

20. See Tannenbaum 1947; Morse 1964.

21. See Goodman and Goodman 1989.

22. By Hobbesian standards, one could argue that predatory gangs survive only to the extent that the state fails to institute a civil society. It would follow that not only is it right and just to punish them, but that any of their depredations that escape punishment are, *eo ipso*, equally legitimate.

23. It is not, as Jude Dougherty (1993) fears, a form of materialism. For the natures in which it finds value are dynamic and open-ended seekers of goals that they themselves help to constitute, but which are never reducible (as matter traditionally is) to the mere facticity of the given. That is, part of what is precious in beings, by my account, is their link to eternity, which, in human subjects, can become, in various ways, self-conscious.

24. Hence Spinoza's distinction between *ambitio* and *humanitas*; see *Ethics* 3, Prop. 29, Schol., and Definitions of the Emotions, 43–44, ed. Gebhardt, 2.162, 202.

25. Maimonides, *Guide* 3.13, cross-referencing *Guide* 1.2.

26. See, e.g., Porphyry, *De Abstinentia*; Ikhwān al-Ṣafā', *The Case of the Animals vs Man*.

27. Hence his reliance on their voluntarism to generate the inference that God has created otiose things on their assumptions; see *Guide* 3.17.3, 25..

28. See Goodman 1981, chapter 1, and chapter 1 in my forthcoming study, *God of Abraham*.

29. See Saadiah on Job 34:17–19, tr., Goodman, pp. 359–361.

30. See Goodman 1993b.

31. Cf. Maimonides's gloss of Job 1:6 in *Guide* 3.22.

32. Operatively, the sniper in the tower must be treated as the exigencies of his pragmatic role demand, as long as he represents an

immediate danger. Once disarmed, he is a full person once again. He may now forfeit many of the civil presumptions that society has accorded him in fleshing out the dignity of personhood, for his actions defeat many of those presumptions. But he does not lose all of them. And never does he lose the basic existential rights of personhood: He may not be tortured to reveal the whereabouts of his accomplices. Even while armed, his deserts as a person are not nugatory. Thus, the moral requirement of phased measures: Deadly force may not be brought against him, even as he fires, if lesser measures would suffice to halt the danger he presents.

33.   For further reflections on the character of ritual, see Goodman 1993c.

34.   See Ikhwān al-Ṣafā', pp. 56–59, 200–202.

35.   Human beings are not self-creating, but they are self-creative. Their own will and wisdom are determinative in their making; see Goodman 1987.

36.   Spinoza, *Ethics* 4, Prop. 18, Scholium, ed. Gebhardt, 2.222–224.

37.   See Leviticus 19:17–19; cf. Goodman 1978, pp. 85–86.

38.   Hume, *An Enquiry Concerning the Principles of Morals*, IV, ed. Niddich, pp. 205–206. Human social arrangements foster the illusion that the two-parent family is no longer necessary. But it is only because many more than two persons assist in child rearing that individuals can contemplate the prospect of raising children "on their own."

39.   Goodman 1991, chapter 3.

40.   Foot 1975; cf. Goodman 1981, pp. 62–68.

41.   Oliver Leaman characterizes as "lukewarm" the paradigm Maimonides chooses for treating Mosaic justice as a virtue rather than simply a rule of fair play. (See Goodman 1991, p. 2 and note, citing Maimonides, *Guide* 3.53, and Leaman's discussion in this volume, p. 60). But I think what is at stake here is much more than the intensity of Maimonides's or the Torah's commitment to the interests of the poor. What is at stake is the issue between legal positivism, which thinks that our obligations are fulfilled when we have behaviorally conformed to certain explicit rules, and virtue ethics, which takes those rules as means to an end, specifically the formation of a certain kind of human character and the foundation of a certain kind of life. Once we know that the rules of a law like the Torah cannot be fulfilled until its aims for humanity are met, we are in a position to seek to modulate the means appropriately to the attainment of those ends. This, I take it, is the whole aim of the rabbinic enterprise; and, as the work of the biblical prophets shows, it is the Torah's conception of our normative aim in history as well; see Goodman 1991, chapter 5.

42.   Maimonides, "Eight Chapters," 6.

43.   See Maimonides, *Guide* 3.26; cf. 3.31

44.   Dougherty 1993.

45.   Here I address questions raised in a thoughtful letter by Hava Tirosh-Rothschild.

46.   Oliver Leaman writes suggestively in his chapter in this volume of the value of distancing oneself entirely from the doings of government; and his words suggest that the point is to be taken generically, rather than simply, say, with reference to the actions of the Roman Imperium, or the Kaiser's Germany, or the empire of the Tsars, for whom Jews were said to pray, "May God bless and keep the Tsar—far from us." But proceduralism has meaning only in the framework of a state, and the liberties that liberals rightly cherish are and can be preserved only by the impersonal institutions of a law. Hence their rise with (and in response to) the centralized, sovereign nation state. The point is seen vividly, long before the rise of such a state, when the Torah commands prospective judges to "recognize no face in judgment" (Deuteronomy 1:17).

47.   Aristotle, *Nicomachean Ethics* 2.6 (1107a9–14).

48.   For the issue, see Hardie 1968.

49.   See Maimonides, *Guide* 1.1, 2, 53, 54, 63; 2.37, 45; cf. *God of Abraham*, chapter 5.

50.   The philosophical work of Halevi is particularly insistent on the need for reintegrating the practical dimensions of life with the spiritual and intellectual, in view of Halevi's clear understanding that neither has meaning without the other; see Goodman forthcoming.

REFERENCES

Dougherty, J. 1993. Review of *On Justice. The Review of Metaphysics* 46: 614–615.

Foot, P. 1975. "Morality as a System of Hypothetical Imperatives." *Analysis* 35: 305–316.

Goodman, L. E. 1978. "Maimonides' Philosophy of Law." *Jewish Law Annual* 1: 72–107.

———. 1981. *Monotheism*. Totowa, N.J.: Allenheld and Osmun.

———. 1987. "Determinism and Freedom in Spinoza, Maimonides, and Aristotle: A Retrospective Study." In *Responsibility, Character, and the Emotions: New Essays in Moral Psychology*, ed. Ferdinand Schoeman, pp. 107–164. New York: Cambridge University Press.

———. 1991. *On Justice: An Essay in Jewish Philosophy*. New Haven, Conn.: Yale University Press.

————. 1993a. "Mythic Discourse." In *Myths and Fictions*, ed. Shlomo Biderman and Ben-Ami Scharfstein, pp. 51–112. Leiden: Brill.

————. 1993b. "Abortion and the Emergence of Human Life: Maimonides and the Judaic View." In *Bits of Honey: Essays for Samson H. Levey*, ed. Stanley Chyet and David Ellenson, pp. 163–190. Atlanta: Scholars Press.

————. 1993c. "Rational Law/Ritual Law." In *A People Apart: Chosenness and Ritual in Jewish Philosophical Thought*, ed. Daniel Frank, pp. 109–200. Albany: SUNY Press.

————. Forthcoming. "Judah Halevi." In *The Routledge History of Jewish Philosophy*, ed. Daniel Frank and Oliver Leaman. London: Routledge.

Goodman, M. J. and L. E. Goodman. 1989. "'Particularly Amongst the Sunburnt Nations . . .'—The Persistence of Sexual Stereotypes of Race in Bio-Science." *International Journal of Group Tensions* 19: 221–243, 365–384.

Hardie, W. F. R. 1968. *Aristotle's Ethical Theory*. Oxford: Clarendon Press.

Hardin, G. 1980. *Promethian Ethics*. Seattle: University of Washington Press.

Harvey, W. Z. 1993. Review of *On Justice. Jewish Political Studies Review* 5:143–144.

Hobbes, T. 1681. *A Dialogue Between a Philosopher and a Student of the Common Laws of England*, ed. J. Cropsey. Chicago: University of Chicago Press, 1971.

Hume, D. 1777. *An Enquiry Concerning the Principles of Morals*, ed. P. H. Nidditch. Oxford: Oxford University Press, 1982.

Ikhwān al-Ṣafā'. ca. 970. *The Case of the Animals vs Man Before the King of the Jinn*, trans. L. E. Goodman. Boston: Twayne, 1978; reissued, Los Angeles: Gee Tee Bee, 1987.

Mendelssohn, M. 1783. *Jerusalem*, trans. Alan Arkush. Hanover, N.H.: University Press of New England, 1983.

Morse, R. M. 1964. "The Heritage of Latin America." In *The Founding of New Societies*, ed. Louis Hartz, pp. 123–177. New York: Harcourt Brace.

Porphyry. ca. 260. *De Abstinentia*, trans. Thomas Taylor as *On Abstinence from Animal Food*. London: Centaur, 1965.

Saadiah Gaon al-Fayyūmī. ca. 940. *The Book of Theodicy: Translation and Commentary on the Book of Job*, trans. L. E. Goodman. New Haven, Conn.: Yale University Press, 1988.

Seeskin, K. 1978. "Is Existence a Perfection?—A Case Study in the Philosophy of Leibniz." *Idealistic Studies* 8: 124–135.

Spinoza, B. 1677. *Tractatus Politicus*, ed. C. Gebhardt. Heidelberg: Winter, 1925.

Tannenbaum, F. 1947. *Slave and Citizen: The Negro in the Americas.* New York: Knopf.

Taylor, A. E. 1937. "Some Incoherencies in Spinozism (II)." *Mind* 46: 281–301.

Is a Jewish Practical Philosophy Possible?

Oliver Leaman

There have been many attempts to link Judaism and philosophy. Some of these attempts are obviously awry, as when Philo suggests that the Greek philosophers were taught by the Jewish prophets! What Philo meant, though, is not obviously wrong. He meant that the teachings of Judaism do not go against the teachings of philosophy or even that an understanding of the latter can be improved by a grasp of the former. Of course, religion and philosophy have different audiences, and it would be inappropriate to expect everyone to approach the truth via philosophy. Yet there is no basic incompatibility between religion and philosophy. Why should there be? Both religion and philosophy are true, and so they cannot be incompatible. We can deepen our understanding of our religion by examining it from a philosophical perspective. We can see how particular religious customs and practices fit into a universal pattern of morally appropriate behavior. We can see how the sorts of religious statements that exist in authoritative texts have philosophical correlates. We can even use philosophical methodology to throw light on religious texts we otherwise find difficult to interpret. Such an approach will naturally find enemies among those religious believers who insist that it is possible to find a clear and unambiguous meaning for all religious texts. For the purpose of this discussion, it will be necessary to assume that there is a role for philosophy in the explication of religious writings, although by the end of the discussion it may seem that the nature of that role is different from that which it is normally taken to be.

Practical philosophy encompasses political, legal, and moral philosophy and is clearly always going to be an important instrument of religious thought for those who think that philosophy is a useful tool in understanding religion. Religion for many people is a profoundly practical set of doctrines. Such doctrines tell believers how to live, how to conduct their lives in relation to the lives of others and to God. In medieval Jewish philosophy there is a well-developed theory according to which philosophy represents the rational kernel of religion. This theory ultimately comes from Alfarabi, who presented a complex account of the relationship between different ways of arguing. He argued that philosophy was essentially a demonstrative discipline, whereby one works from necessarily true and self-evident premises and derives equally powerful conclusions via a valid decision procedure. Not everyone is up to the demanding intellectual standards of such an approach, though, and so people have to be provided with less exacting methods of attaining the truth. Religion has an important role to play here, because religion will present the truth to the whole of the community in a form that it can accept and understand, but without demanding too much of its members. What lies behind religion, though, is demonstration. Philosophers can appreciate this, but the majority of believers cannot. There is a need for prophets, because prophets are superb politicians. They convey the truth in language that the whole of the community can grasp. If philosophers tried to prophesy using philosophical language, they would fail to persuade anyone but their own strictly limited circle and would probably succeed only in attracting the ire of the community as a whole against them. Insofar as that community understood them, it might find its faith threatened and be dissuaded from religious observance. Clearly, then, the demarcation of activities as between philosophers and religious leaders is an important one. That is not to suggest, of course, that they could not on occasion be the same people. Often they were. What is important is that they choose different languages when addressing different audiences.

What are these different sorts of language? As we have seen, demonstration is the appropriate methodology for the philosopher. For the religious leader a whole gamut of techniques is available. There is dialectical, rhetorical, sophistical, poetic, and no doubt other forms of expression. These are designed to move people to action, to accept certain beliefs, and to live in particular ways. These linguistic forms are not illogical nor even alogical. They all have a logical form and in the Middle Ages were regarded as part of the Aristotelian organon of logical techniques, but they do differ in their logical force. Dialectical reasoning is perfectly valid, but it uses as premises statements whose truth and validity depend upon adherence to some range of doctrines, perhaps religious ones, and so cannot share in the universality of demonstrative premises. Poetic reasoning is clearly of a far weaker logical power, depending as it does upon such a heavily subjective level of interpretation, but it is nonetheless a valid method of getting a point over to the community. If one examines the body of religious texts employed by a particular faith, and certainly by Islam and Judaism, one finds the sort of variety of forms of expression that Alfarabi recommends.

What follows from this approach? It follows that we can take a religious text and investigate that component of it which is accessible to philosophical treatment. The way in which we do this will obviously depend upon our philosophical perspective. When we look at the history of Jewish philosophy, we notice that in different periods Jewish religious writings were interpreted very differently. For Hermann Cohen the Torah embodies a Kantian view, which is not at all the approach of Martin Buber or Maimonides. When examining the philosophical meaning of the text we naturally apply our own philosophical perspective. This seems to be a fairly unproblematic procedure. There will be differences, of course, in the skill with which this is done and some accounts will be more plausible than others, and some philosophers will try to make religion fit into a theoretical straightjacket that just will not do. These differences aside, it does seem to be an eminently respectable project to examine religious texts from a philosophical perspective. The question is, though, how is it to be done? How do we take a religious text and analyze it philosophically? What restricts the identification of religious texts with philosophical positions of a particular kind?

This might not appear to be much of a problem. Surely one just looks at a text and then considers it from a philosophical perspective. But the situation is not quite so simple. Let us take as an example, Lenn Goodman's recent *On Justice*, which is subtitled *An Essay in Jewish Philosophy*.[1] When I read this book I felt that it represented Jewish philosophy in its most impressive contemporary form. It is a very interesting analysis of a particular approach to justice, and this approach is shown to accord with aspects of Judaism. How does Goodman establish this? First of all, he describes a theory of justice, which is firmly linked to those philosophers and ethical theories dealing with the topic. Among the philosophers considered are some Jewish philosophers, but there is by no means exclusive use of these, and they often do not seem to be basing their arguments upon religion in any case. The references to Judaism are diverse, sometimes biblical, but often rabbinic and midrashic. Goodman agrees with Alasdair MacIntyre that philosophical argument needs a context, and a religious context provides a tradition in which the argument can be interpolated. This is certainly true of practical philosophy, whose very name suggests that it should be easy to find a tradition within which examples can be found to operate. One then considers the general arguments of moral philosophy within the context of a particular tradition, in this case Judaism, and by "tradition" is meant a whole variety of textual and historical activities. In this way the theory can really be related to the praxis, and once we see the theory in action we are in a better position to understand, and indeed evaluate it. This is how a great deal of Jewish practical philosophy is done, albeit not always as well as by Goodman.

I wonder whether we should feel confident that this can be done. It is worth taking some examples from Goodman's book which suggest that if we examine particular instances of Jewish writing we can see that they are in accordance with a certain philosophical position. For instance, at the beginning of the book he quotes a passage from Maimonides that itself deals with a scriptural passage, and it is worth reproducing this text from the *Guide* in Goodman's translation:

> The word *tzedakah* derives from *tzedek*, which means fairness. Fairness is imparting what is due to any possessor of a right and giving to every being according to its deserts. But the books of the prophets do not call it *tzedakah* in the ultimate sense merely to fulfill your obligations toward others. For if you pay a worker his wages or repay a debt, that is not called *tzedakah*. Duties you assume toward others that distinguish and enhance your character, like mending the hurt of all who are injured—these are what are called out as the virtue of justice. That is why it says (Deut. 24:13) of returning a pawned item to the poor: "This will

be *tzedakah* for you." For when you live a life of moral excellence, you are doing justice to your own rational soul, giving it its due. (*Guide* 3.53; *On Justice*, p. 2).

Goodman takes this passage to say something very important about the Mosaic law. He understands by it that Maimonides is taking up a suggestion of Aristotle according to which we should distinguish between the moral virtue of justice and the mere doing of justice, just carrying out one's formal obligations. Certainly Maimonides seems to be making this point. He is arguing that merely carrying out one's formal obligations does not satisfy all the parties to the transaction, because it may not satisfy the agent himself. We might talk about a weak and a strong notion of justice. According to the former, we act justly if we carry out our basic obligations to others. According to the latter, we act justly if we carry out our basic obligations and go a bit further, for in this way we tend to improve ourselves in more ways than just by developing our disposition to carry out those obligations. We set in train the process of becoming a different sort of person, a better person than the person who administers merely the weak notion of justice.

Why is this an important passage for Goodman? It is important because it appears to counter the view that justice is a matter of convention, and his book is totally opposed to that view. But if we look carefully at the biblical passage it will emerge as far more ambiguous in this respect than one might at first think. The passage discusses the lending of clothes, and it suggests that one will return the clothes to a poor person "when the sun goes down, that he may sleep in his garment, and bless you" (Deut. 24:13). The implication is that the lender gets it back the next day. Now, this is a strange passage to select as the paradigm of *tzedakah*. One is hardly putting oneself out a great deal by returning a possession temporarily to its owner. Indeed, because as a result he will bless you, it might be thought that this is a useful strategy to preserve amicable relationships between rich and poor in the community. If that is a feasible interpretation, then justice could just be a matter of convention. The Bible could be telling the community how to organize its affairs in such a way as to minimize conflict and maximize welfare. It must, of course, be doing more than that, because any religion is going to argue that justice is more than conventional, that justice can really be attained only within the framework of that religion itself.

It is interesting that both the scriptural text and Maimonides should select this rather lukewarm response to the poor as an important example of fairness. Is it, perhaps, because we have here an example of behavior that helps the poor while at the same time not upsetting the division between the rich and the poor? That division is the basis of life in most civil societies, and it would be too much to expect ordinary citizens to give up entirely the claims they have on each other. Possibly through limiting those claims voluntarily in certain contexts they might set up in themselves a disposition to act more generously in the future, with less concern for their own financial well being and superiority over others. God could miraculously change human nature immediately, but he prefers to work with nature, by setting up laws and customs that will gradually allow us to transform ourselves into better people.[2] This gives us the opportunity to attain merit through our own independent transformation, albeit with the assistance of religious law. The scriptural passage could insist that all pledges made to the poor should be redeemed gratis, but it does not. If there were such a policy, no one would make such pledges, and the poor would be disadvantaged in that they could not raise money through loaning their possessions to the wealthy. Both Maimonides and the passage suggest that justice is attainable through going a little further than one need to, and in itself this does nothing to show that justice is more than convention. It does suggest that we may need to broaden the notion of what is conventional, but not very much, and we should hope that both Maimonides and the Bible would come out in favor of a more rather than less sophisticated notion of justice. This is exactly what we get. It would be easy to recommend the permanent return of pledges to the poor or the equalization of incomes and possessions. Because such a policy would completely overturn the conventional relationships between people, it would not be carried out, and so there is no such recommendation.

The important thing about the scriptural passage is not that we can all agree what it means. On the contrary, it is because we can disagree about its meaning that it is important. We assume that what is being described in the passage is more than a technical comment about the rules surrounding the loaning of money against the security of clothes. We assume that this discussion is picked out as representative of fairness because it is of wider significance. But precisely what is this wider significance is unclear. Perhaps it could be taken to say something in general about the relationships between the rich and the poor. Perhaps the rich should help the poor by giving up some of their rights to hold the property of the poor, when this does not seriously inconvenience the rich. Perhaps the rich should transfer some of their property to the poor and so help them escape from complete abjection. Perhaps the idea of allowing someone to sink into such dire straits is itself obscene, and the passage is calling for a refusal to allow this to happen. Then there is another complication. The passage earlier on refers to the poor as being "neighbors." This brings into question who precisely counts as a neighbor. Is it anyone within the community, and is community to be understood in terms of proximity or ethnicity? Perhaps everyone who has commercial dealings with someone else is the latter's neighbor. What I am suggesting here is that it is difficult to take a passage from the Bible and use it to bolster a philosophical theory. That passage can have a whole range of meanings, and selecting just one, the one most appropriate to that theory, seriously misrepresents the nature of the scriptural activity.

Let us take another example, this time from the Talmud. There is a well-known story of a conversation between a Roman officer and Rabbi Eleazar, the son of Rabbi Simeon. The officer was instructed to arrest the thieves in his area, and he wanted to know how to differentiate between the guilty and the innocent. Rabbi Eleazar suggested that he go to the local tavern in the morning and talk to those customers who looked sleepy and had a cup of wine in their hands. He should ask them what their work is. If the person is a scholar, then he has risen early to study. If he is a day worker, then he has risen early for his work. If, on the other hand, he is a night worker, then he might have been busy all night working with metal. If he falls into none of these categories, then he must be a thief and can be arrested.[3] Unfortunately for Eleazar, the Roman officer was so impressed by his advice that he gave him the job of arresting the thieves himself. This was not well received by his coreligionists, as one might expect. Rabbi Joshua ben Karchah rebuked him: "Vinegar, son of wine! How long will you deliver up the people of our God for slaughter?" To this Eleazar replied, "I weed the thorns from the vineyard." Joshua responded, "Let the owner of the vineyard come and weed out the thorns himself!"

What does this passage mean? According to Goodman, Joshua has the best of the encounter. Even thieves are the children of God, and their lives should only be forfeit for the most serious of reasons and on the basis of secure evidence. He did not expect God to intervene directly in the world to pick out and punish such guilty individuals, but he did think that their punishment should be left to God's more indirect form of carrying out justice. Goodman sees this as illustrating his argument that we can "*define justice by the demands of mercy*" (p. 126, his emphasis). We should acknowledge that nature's justice is God's, and insofar as we are able, we should forgive and seek not to punish. As Goodman points out, Eleazar's method of discovering the guilty is inevitably going to involve arresting some of the innocent too. Now, I am sure that Goodman's interpretation of this passage is feasible. But other interpretations are feasible as well. For example, it might be taken as objectionable for Eleazar to collaborate with an occupying power against his coreligionists. Eleazar should not be advising the Roman officer in this matter at all. He should maintain his distance from the Romans, as perhaps his father would have. Joshua hints as much in his insulting address. So the point of the passage may be very little if anything about what attitude we should have toward the guilty. It might be about whether we should work with an occupying power against our community, even where this means against the guilty within the community. In any case, of what are the latter guilty? It could be of opposition to Roman rule, and they might not have been guilty of theft in an acceptable sense at all. Surely there is something very questionable in Eleazar helping the Romans carry out their form of justice against members of *his* community.

But the passage can be taken in an even broader sense to examine the notion that we ought to participate in the decisions of the state. Only God can know for certain who is guilty and who is innocent. If we are put in the position of having to judge people, we should do all in our power to avoid condemning the innocent. We should not play a part in the administration of the unjust state, whatever inducements are offered to us to act on behalf of such a state. We should not assist nor offer to assist and advise the civil authority. Even if such a refusal puts us in a position of danger or disadvantage, we should not involve ourselves in the position of helping the civil authority, where that authority is imposed upon the community. An individual can often escape from the area altogether, if placed in an invidious position by the ruling power. But there are still other readings of the passage. It is not clear that Eleazar is supposed to come out worst in the exchange. After all, he argues that thieves deserve to be punished under any regime, and this is all that he is helping bring about. Whoever controls the state, theft is wrong and punishable. Perhaps it is better for the catcher of thieves to be someone like himself who has concern for the community as compared with a Roman who would not. Although collaboration does not have a very positive image, there is something to be said for it if the alternative is far worse. The Roman officer might pick up a lot of innocent people in his determination to catch some guilty ones. He would not care about the fates of the innocents because his only concern is to punish the guilty. Eleazar, by contrast, would try to minimize the harm to the innocent. Even Joshua's suggestion that the owner of the vineyard should be left to do the weeding can be taken in a number of ways. Who is the owner? The immediate owner is Rome, and he may be taken to argue that it is the Romans who should carry out the arrests. The real owner, though, is God and perhaps justice should be left to him. Yet the de facto owner would treat the Jewish community more harshly than would Eleazar, and the de jure owner would not be seen to do anything at all.

This brings us to yet another implication of the passage. Perhaps the intention is to point out that there are enormous problems whenever the conscientious individual enters into relationships of control over others. Once we abandon our normal way of looking at the world and start to assume power and authority over our neighbors we become different people. Like Eleazar, we fool ourselves that what we do we have to do, because we are linking deserts with punishments. We get into the way of thinking that unless we act in such a way, others will act instead of us and more harshly. We come to think that there is nothing wrong with our actions, that they fit into a broadly acceptable ethical framework. Like Joshua, we condemn those who participate in the activities of the state without offering a clear alternative. We close our minds to the potentially severe consequences to the community of a failure to work with the state. We pretend to ignore the de facto authority by appealing to the de jure authority, yet we know that the latter will not directly intervene to preserve the rights of the individual. Like many of the most interesting talmudic passages, what we have here is a genuine dialogue, a genuine example of what Maimonides called *dialectical thinking*, where a number of ideas come into contact with each other without the necessity to resolve the discussion by drawing a particular conclusion. The point of the passage is to make us think about the issues it raises, but it tells us almost nothing directly. It is certainly possible to find an interpretation of the passage that will fit a particular philosophical thesis about justice, but that is the problem. It is possible to find an interpretation of the passage that will fit virtually any philosophical thesis about justice. We cannot look to the passage as evidence that a particular philosophical theory fits in with Judaism, because on the basis of that passage almost any such theory can be made to fit.

Does this suggest that the meaning of scriptural and talmudic passages can be anything at all? Certainly not. But all one has to do is cast one's eyes over the books in a Jewish library to realize that there has often been disagreement over the precise nature of the meanings involved. There are undoubtedly philosophical ideas, implicit and explicit, in Jewish religious texts, and as we know there has for a long time been a controversy over the relationship between Judaism and philosophy, often characterized as the relationship between Jerusalem and Athens. This controversy has concentrated upon the relationships between the meaning of the religious texts and those of philosophical doctrines. It tends to concentrate upon particular key doctrines, such as the Aristotelian argument for the eternity of the universe with the consequent difficulty of accounting for creation ex nihilo. The sort of relationship I am talking about here is different from these kinds of examples, because the issue is not one of the apparent incompatibility of religious and philosophical texts. On the contrary, the problem seems to be that there is too much compatibility, at least insofar as practical philosophy is concerned.

Why is there so much compatibility? I am tempted to say, following Goodman's argument in *On Justice*, that this is an inevitable aspect of our finitude. Because we are finite, we cannot expect to understand finally those difficult questions that relate to the nature of our existence and our role in God's world. The book of Job is an outstanding illustration of this difficulty. The book starts off with Job bemoaning the injustice of his fate and by implication seeking an explanation for the existence of innocent suffering. Job is a virtuous individual, and he does not deserve the terrible things that happen to him. He wonders why an omniscient, omnipotent, and benevolent God allows these things to happen to him, or even worse, makes them happen. He challenges God for an answer. His friends tend to refuse to rise to the bait, and they suggest that he might not have been as innocent as he thinks. God never answers Job directly. He does respond, though, by showing Job how powerless he is by contrast with the deity. This immediately impels Job to accept his suffering, and by the end of the book he is rewarded by the return, and even improvement, of his possessions. God does not rebuke Job for questioning divine justice. On the contrary, God rebukes Job's friends for having stoutly upheld the existence of that justice!

Many commentators have wondered why Job is satisfied with the divine response. It seems to be little more than the worship of power that eventually brings Job to acceptance of his sufferings. If I have a trustworthy and honest servant who works well for me, and if I subsequently make his life miserable, it is hardly an appropriate response to his questioning my behavior for me to point to the difference in our stations. This is precisely what seems to satisfy Job, and we wonder why. But if we look at the context more carefully we can see that Job is not merely impressed with the power of God. He is more impressed with the difference between the point of view of the deity and its comparison with his own point of view. We have a very limited view of reality, because we are finite and limited creatures. God, by contrast, does not share our imperfections, and he can observe the rationale behind everything. He can know that rationale because he established it in the first place. The implication is that, were the world to be a place in which the virtuous were rewarded and the evil punished in an obvious manner, then it would be banal. The moral organization of the world would be open for everyone to inspect. God's role would be that of a technician keeping the mechanism in working order. Yet Job discovers that the essence of God's participation in the world is based upon mystery, and were it to be otherwise, it would constitute an entirely different notion of religion.

The way in which the book of Job ends could have taken a different form. Job could have insisted upon an answer to his original question, which was why God allowed the innocent to suffer. Job comes to see that he should replace that question with a different one: What is the nature of our relationship with God? God does not really answer this question either, but the important thing is that Job recognized that this is the really important question. It might be said that through his experiences Job grew into replacing the original problem with the new one. He became a different sort of person. The rewards he eventually receives are a material symbol of the spiritual growth he has accomplished. His friends do not change at all through their observation and complacent remarks on his experiences, and so they are chided by God for their conservatism. Job is flexible enough not to stick to repeating the same question all the time. He comes to see that the original question is a quite minor aspect of a much broader question, and he is reconciled to God once he appreciates this. He changes, he develops, he does not allow his experience to submerge him in permanent depression.

I think this tells us something very important about religious language. Such language has to be flexible enough to allow us to grow and develop. Maimonides makes this sort of point when he distinguished between the purpose of religious as compared with civil law. The latter informs us how we are to live with others, in the community and in the state, but the former helps us to perfect ourselves, to go beyond our everyday lives and expectations. For this to be possible it is not enough just to obey a set of rules and prescriptions. We have to become different people in line with those rules, and those rules are there to enable us to bring about such a transformation. We have to work out ourselves how we are to do this. That is not to say, of course, that we have to work out what we are to do entirely in isolation. We can receive a lot of help from the community itself and from the writings of religion, but the important move is one that we ourselves make when we internalize the rules and practices of faith. The process of working out for ourselves how we are to behave is at least as important as the product of such an effort. Job is praised by God for having ended up making the effort to work through his problems; Job's friends are rebuked by God for having stuck to a formula throughout that prevented them from being affected by his experience at all. Religious language has to be open enough for us to enter into it and decide how to use it. If it is immediately obvious what it means, then all that we can do is follow the formula. This might make for an easier journey, but certainly for a less interesting and challenging one.

What are the implications of this discussion for our understanding of Jewish practical philosophy? The main point I hope I have made is that we have to be very careful how we use our examples. We often use examples from the Bible or some other Jewish source to provide evidence of the "Jewishness" of a particular view that comes from outside the tradition. That is not to suggest in every case that the claim is that the philosophical position reflects the religious view precisely, but the implication normally is that the truth represented philosophically is presented in a religious form by the Jewish source. The objection here is that it is all too easy to select religious examples that seem to fit a whole variety of different philosophical positions. This is even more of a problem when it comes to practical as compared with theoretical philosophy. The former is by its very nature related to practical decision making, to the changing needs and circumstances of the individual and the community. Flexibility is of overwhelming significance here, and we find that flexibility in the relevant religious texts. When Maimonides discusses the life of Adam in the Garden of Eden he suggests that Adam had no need of moral concepts. He could regulate his life using reason alone, using theoretical concepts. It was only when he had to attend to his physical and social needs that practical concepts became necessary. Before the Fall, Adam was unchanging. He did not need to change, because he was able to contemplate the most perfect forms of knowledge in the universe, within the limits applicable to a non-divine being. Once he became prey to the vagaries of the natural and social world, he required concepts that would help him deal with the constantly changing conditions of that world, and those concepts could not themselves be fixed and determinate as they were before the Fall. To be appropriate to the world of generation and corruption, those concepts themselves have to develop and change as we do. The relationship that believers as a whole have with a tradition is not fixed forever; rather, it is a continuing dialogue, and as in any genuine conversation, one is never quite sure where and how it is going to end.

When we look at a religious tradition perhaps the first thing we notice is the diversity of forms of expression. There are stories, poems, theology, metaphysics, jurisprudence, folktales, and so on. These forms of expression all have their own rules of construction, and they play different roles in making up the tradition. We tend to think that if we wish to show that particular philosophical views are representative of a tradition, then what we need to do is demonstrate some degree of agreement between the forms of the tradition and those views. I have argued here that it is too easy to do this for it to be worth doing. A tradition is a form of life, and a form of life consists of texts and actions. These are all very varied, and have their own specific rules and conventions. To relate a tradition to a philosophical theory in more than a casual manner is viable only if we have a theory that possesses rules capable of transforming the language of the tradition into philosophical language. Until we have such a theory, we should be very careful about the ways in which we link together religious with philosophical statements. We should be very cautious about what we accept as a Jewish practical philosophy.

NOTES

1. *On Justice: An Essay in Jewish Philosophy.* New Haven, Conn.: Yale University Press, 1991.

2. This point is discussed more fully in chapter 9, "Morality, Law, and Explanation," in O. Leaman, *Moses Maimonides* (London: Routledge, 1990), pp. 129–161. In his *On Justice*, Goodman presents a highly Maimonidean account of how God intervenes in the world.

3. The talmudic passage at hand can be found in *Baba Metzia* 83b. For an extraordinarily interesting discussion of this passage, see E. Levinas, *Jeunesse et Révolution: Données et Débats* (Paris: P.U.F., 1972), pp. 59–80.

Reason in Action:
The "Practicality" of
Maimonides's Guide

Daniel H. Frank

This chapter on Maimonides got its start in Aristotle. I have lectured for many years on Aristotle and when I mention his classification of the sciences, I report that he divided the sciences into three types: theoretical, practical, and productive.[1] And in giving examples I point out that physics is a theoretical science for Aristotle, ethics is a practical science, and so forth. Fine. But what is the status of the *Physics*, the treatise, not the subject matter of it, and how should it be studied? Again, what is the status of the *Ethics*, the treatises not the subject matter, and how should they be studied? Conceptually subject matter and treatise are (apparently) distinct, demarcating a distinction between the objects of study (*ta phainomena*) and the formal presentation of them (*he episteme*). And because of this, there seems to be a "theoretical" (second order) prejudice to *any* sort of philosophical or scientific inquiry, theoretical or *practical*. But this problem is ours, not Aristotle's; for Aristotle, an isomorphic relation obtains between treatise and subject matter. None of the treatises is a metatheoretical inquiry, we might say. The *Physics* like physics is theoretical, to be studied for its own sake. The *Nicomachean* (or *Eudemian*) *Ethics* like its subject matter is practical, to be studied for the sake of action and becoming good.[2] This latter is the more interesting case, for, although we agree that ethics is practical, the treatises themselves by their very nature as works "about" ethics might appear "theoretical." Again, this is *our* problem, not Aristotle's, but my chapter stems from this (faulty) intuition. Indeed, I shall suggest that this theoretical prejudice leads us to overlook the *practical* nature of Maimonides's *Guide*.

THE "PRACTICALITY" OF ARISTOTLE'S *ETHICS*

Aristotle's classification of the sciences, and indeed of his own scientific work, is threefold: theoretical, practical, and productive. The sciences are so defined in terms of their respective goals: the theoretical sciences, such as mathematics and the various natural sciences, have knowledge for its own sake ("theory" as we might say) as their goals; the practical sciences, of which the primary Aristotelian examples are politics and ethics, have good action (or practice) as their goal; and finally, the productive sciences and crafts, such as medicine and poetry, have useful and beautiful products as their goal.[3]

In this chapter we shall need to focus upon the second type of science, practical science. It is crucial to keep in mind the *practical* nature and goal of the practical sciences when *we* are wont to characterize a book "about" a practical subject such as the *Nicomachean Ethics*, whose subject matter is "what is fine and what is just,"[4] as a "theoretical" work, a work in ethical *theory*. For Aristotle, this is a category mistake. For him, the *Nicomachean* (and *Eudemian*) *Ethics* are not theoretical works, concerned with knowledge for its own sake, but practical, concerned with praxis, action determinative of character and human well being. We have an impoverished sense of *practice* in not appreciating the practical nature of Aristotle's enterprise. When we read and discuss the *Nicomachean Ethics* we seem to be engaging in an abstract, second order enterprise. But thinking that this is what Aristotle intended is off the mark. Again, Aristotle is explicit: "The purpose of our examination [the *Nicomachean Ethics* itself] is not to know what virtue is, but to become good, else otherwise the inquiry would be of no benefit to us" (1103b26–9; trans. Irwin). Our discussion of Aristotle's *Ethics* is invariably a discussion of what *he* had to say; we approach the texts as exegetes, as scholars. But in doing so, we are wholly unlike the author and the audience for whom the lectures were presented. That is fine I suppose, so long as we are aware of how alien, indeed un-Aristotelian, our reaction to the text is *as scholars*. To do "ethics with Aristotle," as Broadie has so well shown, is to position ourselves relative to the *Ethics* as would-be practitioners of the good, as a receptive audience desirous to learn about the human good *with a view to achieving and living it.*[5] The question then for us is: How did Aristotle imagine that the *Ethics*, a set of lectures "about" the human good, would make the auditor good, or at least advance one toward the goal? Again, what accounts for the "practicality" of Aristotle's treatises in the practical sciences?

Let us begin discussion of this by asking: Who is Aristotle's audience? For whom was Aristotle writing the *Ethics*? He is clear that the appropriate auditor of the lecture course that is the *Nicomachean Ethics* is the mature human being who has "experience of the actions in life" (1095a3), follows reason not the passions, and finally "has been brought up in fine habits" (1095b4; cf. 1179b25). Only such individuals will benefit from attending Aristotle's lectures; only they will derive such (practical) knowledge as the *Ethics* are intended to provide. But now, of course, one asks: Why do the experienced, rational, and well brought-up (the "virtuous" in *our* sense) *need* to attend and listen to Aristotle's lectures? What knowledge do they *lack*, such that attendance at Aristotle's lectures is prima facie beneficial?

This question takes us to the heart of Aristotle's project in the *Ethics*. It is a project that transports or attempts to transport the mature, well-brought-up, well-behaved, and well-disposed student to virtue. If you prefer, the *Ethics* are an effort to move morality beyond a merely behavioristic framework. There is more to (Aristotelian) virtue and being virtuous than merely behaving in a certain way. The *Ethics* wish to aid in the development of a virtuous character, a state of the soul that, to be sure, entails, but is not exhausted by, the performance of specifiable actions. But now again, what precisely does the student lack, and how precisely are the *Ethics* supposed to fill the lack?

For Aristotle, what the students already bring to the lectures, their good habits and maturity, provides the starting point (*to hoti*) for the inquiry into the nature of the good, "the condition for intelligent study of the subject," as Burnyeat puts it.[6] What the students lack is *to dihoti*, the grounds or explanation for their (so far unreflected upon) habitual actions. As Burnyeat puts it: "[Aristotle] is addressing someone who already wants and enjoys virtuous

action and needs to see this aspect of his life in a deeper perspective"; and again, "[Aristotle] is giving a course in practical thinking
to enable someone who already wants to be virtuous to understand
better what he should do and why."[7] Indeed, the *Ethics* hope to
provide *to dihoti*, the reasoned account for why what the student
is doing and is predisposed to do is the right thing to do. To be
sure, such rational justification for the status quo, what one is
already doing, is deeply conservative—but this much must be said
on Aristotle's behalf: At least his students will be able to give
reasons, satisfying to themselves, for why they choose to be as they
are. The students will become reflective, in the sense that, as Lear
puts it: "The lectures are intended to help them to develop a self-
conscious and coherent ethical outlook: to reinforce reflectively the
lives they are already inclined to lead. Of course, the transition
from unreflectively living a virtuous life to understanding the
virtues and the life one is living is itself of practical value. For this
self-understanding helps to constitute the good life. . . . It is a
reflective endorsement [of it]. . . . So one's understanding of the
ethical life reinforces one's motivation to live it."[8]

In sum, Aristotle's lectures attempt to move the unreflective,
but well-behaved and well-motivated student to the point where he
begins to see his life and aspirations in a wider perspective; and
such "seeing" and "understanding" need to be construed as eminently *practical*, as themselves constituting a measure of the very
life he aspires to live. Such understanding as the lectures bring
about has a decisive impact on the student's motivational structure. In this sense, then, we may understand the "practicality" of
Aristotle's *Ethics*. The treatises are not an attempt to convert the
skeptic who asks: Why be moral? There are no Thrasymachuses in
Aristotle's audience.[9] Maybe there should have been, but that is
another story. He is not writing to convert anyone. His audience
is already primed. And what his auditors lack, the *Ethics* provide.

THE "PRACTICALITY" OF MAIMONIDES'S *GUIDE*

As I turn now to the major portion of the chapter, let me lay out,
unadorned, my thesis. It is this: Maimonides's *Guide* is a work of
practical philosophy in precisely Aristotle's sense. Appearances
notwithstanding, aided and abetted by a Farabian classification of
the sciences,[10] the *Guide* is a work that, like Aristotle's *Ethics*,

serves a practical end, praxis, activity that brings about the human good. Now we must be careful here. The practicality of the *Guide* does *not* mean, any more than for Aristotle, that theoretical activity is precluded as a part of the human good. The theory/practice dichotomy does not fall out in this way. The practicality of the *Guide* does *not* entail, a la Pines, that "the practical way of life, the *bios praktikos*, is superior to the theoretical."[11] My claim that the *Guide* is a practical work, a work in practical philosophy leading to a practical goal, does *not* mean that the life of *moral* virtue is perforce the goal. All that is required for a work to be practical is for it to be concerned with bringing about the human good, *whatever* that may be. To the extent that theory (*theoria*) is part of the human good, it is necessarily part of the subject matter of practical philosophy. Book 10, chapters 7–8 of Aristotle's *Nicomachean Ethics* should make this clear; similarly, I shall contend that all those "theoretical" bits of the *Guide* (in philosophy of language, physics, cosmology, etc.) and the praise of the life of speculation need to be understood as part of the *practical* nature of the *Guide*, not as autonomous theoretical treatises. In sum, neither the *Guide* nor, as is clear, Aristotle's ethical treatises is a theoretical work, concerned with knowledge for its own sake. Nevertheless, both require or lead to theory as the means to achieve the (practical) end, the human good.

The argument may be joined by recalling briefly the old debate between Leo Strauss and Julius Guttmann concerning the nature of the *Guide*: whether the *Guide* is or is not a philosophical book.[12] What this means is whether the *Guide* is best understood as subserving a (nonphilosophical) political goal (Strauss's view) or a (nonpolitical) theoretical, philosophical goal (Guttmann's view). The debate set the contest as one between understanding the *Guide* as political and *therefore* unphilosophical or as philosophical and *therefore* apolitical. But, as our discussion of Aristotle shows, and as I hope our discussion of Maimonides will show, this contrast is a false dichotomy. A rich enough sense of praxis, of practical/ political philosophy, allows us the possibility of understanding the *Guide* as *both* practical and philosophical, as a practical work subserving a practical goal, the good life, which *thereby* is free to be as "theoretical" and philosophical as it wishes. So long as philosophical discussions of cosmology, providence, human freedom, and so forth are contextualized to a practical end, happiness, the "philosophical" work is a work in practical philosophy.[13] So both Strauss's and Guttmann's views are in need of revision: both are insufficiently attentive to the way in which the *Guide* can be a work in practical philosophy.

In a recent article, Joel Kraemer moves us nearer to a fair estimation of the nature, the genre if you will, of the *Guide*. Instead of asking whether the *Guide* is a philosophical or a political work—in large part a non-Maimonidean distinction given that in the *Millot ha-Higgayon* (*Treatise on Logic*), chapter 14, Maimonides makes the latter a species of the former—Kraemer asks, "in Maimonides' terms . . . whether the *Guide* should be classified as a demonstrative, dialectical, or rhetorical work."[14] And his answer, undoubtedly correct, is that the *Guide* needs to understood as a dialectical work.

What precisely does it mean to say that the *Guide* is a dialectical work? Minimally, it means that it starts from *endoxa* (*mashhurat*), beliefs of the many or the wise, and attempts to tease out the truth of them.[15] Indeed, the *Guide* does begin with the beliefs of a smart young man and attempts to provide argument for sustaining them. Quite generally, Joseph, the addressee of the *Guide*, believes that both the law and philosophy are valid. But, alas, they seem to be at odds with one another; so a perplexity arises. It is Maimonides's goal as a dialectician to explode the aporia, Joseph's perplexity, by showing that, properly construed, the belief of Joseph, that both the law and philosophy are valid, is a sound belief. To show this entails a considerable amount of "theoretical" speculation, even demonstrative argumentation, in semantic theory, physics, metaphysics, prophetology, and so on; but again, and this is crucial, such speculation is not done for its own sake, but rather for the sake of assuaging Joseph's perplexity with a view, to be seen later in detail, to placing Joseph's accustomed way of life on a new footing. Viewed this way, the purpose of the *Guide* is dialectical *and* practical.[16] It may reveal, undoubtedly does reveal, many of Maimonides's positions on a variety of theoretical issues, but this is not the goal and purpose of the work. We go astray if we think of the *Guide* as a patchwork of independent treatises on metaphysics, physics, cosmology, and such.

With reference again to chapter 14 of *Millot ha-Higgayon*, the *Guide* may be understood as a work in political governance (*al-tadbir al-madani*). But this must not be construed in too narrow a fashion. A work in political governance is not simply a political work.[17] The latter is a work not concerned with speculative matters or perfected happiness (*sa'adah*), so much as it is concerned with (merely) regulating the political order. In Maimonidean terms, a political work is one concerned simply with the nomoi of legislators, no more. But a work in political governance is concerned not only with social and political arrangements, but also with the inculcation of correct beliefs on speculative matters. This is what Torah attempts to do by means of its prophetic legislation.[18]

We might note in passing that, no more than the *Guide* itself, Aristotle's *Ethics* and *Politics* are not to be understood as (merely) political works. Though hardly governed by revelation, Aristotle's works in practical philosophy have as their manifest goal eudaimonia, human happiness. The governing question is the end at which all our actions aim.[19] The end, studied by politics, is the human good, and it is the express purpose of the *Ethics* to reveal the nature of the human good and how to achieve it.[20] And the *Politics* is clear that the polis and political life are concerned in the final analysis not with life, biological life, but rather with the *good* life.[21] Even if this final goal entails social regulations and political institutions, these latter are (merely) enabling conditions for achievement of eudaimonia.

So far then, the *Guide* may be understood as a work in political governance that proceeds dialectically to make its points. Note that this entails understanding the *Guide* as a sort-of second Torah and Maimonides as a sort-of prophet. The *Guide* is a work that gives to Joseph, in ways appropriate to him, a means whereby he can achieve such measure of truth and happiness as he can.

MAIMONIDES'S AUDIENCE

As we continue to explicate the practical nature of the *Guide*, the sense in which it is a work in practical philosophy, it is imperative that we be clear about the audience for which it is intended. I have written on this previously[22] and will not repeat myself here except to recall the obvious, that Joseph, the addressee of the *Guide*, is one "for whom the validity of our Law has become established in his soul and has become actual in his belief—such a man being perfect in his religion and character, and having studied the sciences of the philosophers and come to know what they signify" (Intro.; trans. Pines). Such a one, perfect in virtue and intelligent, is perplexed, and the *Guide* attempts to alleviate his perplexity relative to the apparent unphilosophical nature of Scripture.

Now my suggestion is that Joseph bears comparison with the typical auditor of Aristotle's *Ethics*. We recall that the auditor of the *Ethics* is a fairly mature adult with experience in life, whose life is not directed by passion. This is an individual brought up in good habits and inclined to do the right thing on the basis of customary opinions (*endoxa*). He lacks the foundations for his habitual activity, however, and therefore acts, as it were, with no *deep* reflective understanding. It is this that the *Ethics* hope to provide, *to dihoti* for his habitual behavior. As Reeve puts it,

> The audience to whom the *Ethics* is addressed consists of people who, having habituated virtue, also have reliable *endoxa* about *eudaimonia*. But their *endoxa* conflict with others and so give rise to *aporiai*. The *Ethics* aims to solve those *aporiai* by means of dialectic, bringing to light the truth that the *endoxa* contain, and thereby converting a vague conflict-ridden grasp of *eudaimonia* into clear-sighted *nous* of what it is. The *Ethics* thus provides to those with habituated virtue precisely what they need in order to be fully virtuous and to possess *phronēsis*. It gives them a clear target to aim at and so makes them 'more likely to hit the right mark'. (1094a24)[23]

How different are these individuals from Joseph? Joseph is mature and, though impetuous to the point that he is led into perplexity, is sufficiently in control of his passions that Maimonides can write the *Guide* for his hoped-for benefit.[24] Further, and more important, Joseph's life is fully framed by halakhic norms—"[the] Law has become established in his soul and has become actual in his belief." Like Aristotle's audience, Joseph does the right thing, but does not understand the *grounds* for his characteristic activity. And it is precisely this, to provide Joseph with foundations for his beliefs and action, that Maimonides hopes to supply. This is "the science of the Law in its true sense," and it is the manifest purpose of the *Guide*. We shall soon discuss the nature of this science, but for the moment let us note its *practical* import. The *Guide*, like the *Ethics*, attempts to provide an intellectual framework for Joseph's life, the life he is *already* leading. As Lear said of Aristotle, we can equally well say of Maimonides: "The lectures [read: *Guide*] are intended to help them [read: Joseph] develop a self-conscious and coherent ethical outlook: to reinforce reflectively the lives they are already inclined to lead. Of course, the transition from unreflectively living a virtuous [read: halakhic] life to understanding the virtues [read: the law] and the life one is living is itself of practical value. For this self-understanding helps to constitute the good life."[25] Now I readily grant that Joseph, unlike Aristotle's auditors, has done some "theoretical" work; indeed, it is for precisely this reason that he has fallen into perplexity, needing the *Guide* to help him out. Yet we should not overlook the common need of *both* Joseph and Aristotle's auditors of *archai*, first principles, by means of which they can begin to see their respective lives in a broader, more philosophical, context, and *thereby* begin to live their lives in a different way and achieve the human good.

THE TRUE SCIENCE OF THE LAW

I now come to the heart of the chapter, my central claim concerning the practicality of the *Guide*. Joseph is floundering in perplexity, torn between his tradition and his new-found wisdom. It is to the resolution of this perplexity that Maimonides presents "the science of the Law in its true sense." What is this science? On the most general level, the science of the law is the *Guide* itself—all of it, the explication of disputed terms and discussion concerning, inter alia, the finitude of human knowledge, the (correlative) incapacity to describe God directly, the nature of the spatio-temporal realm, and so forth. The whole *Guide*, metaphysics, epistemology, cosmology, moral and political philosophy, is offered to overcome Joseph's initial perplexity. It shows him that, properly understood, tradition and "alien" wisdom are commensurable. But put this way, the enterprise seems artificial, indeed overly "theoretical." It sets the problem up as one of intellectual aporiai followed by theoretical resolution. Joseph's problem, even if due to his intellect, has a most practical corollary. Joseph's perplexity entails a correlative worry about how (and how best) to live. Maimonides puts it this way about Joseph and his condition:

> The human intellect having drawn him [Joseph] on and led him to dwell within its province, he must have felt distressed by the externals of the Law. . . . Hence he would remain in a state of

perplexity and confusion as to whether he should follow his intellect, renounce what he knew concerning the terms in question,
and consequently consider that he has renounced the foundations
of the Law. Or [whether] he should hold fast to his understanding of these terms and not let himself be drawn on together with
his intellect, rather turning his back on it and moving away from
it, while at the same time perceiving that he had brought loss to
himself and harm to his religion. He would be left with those
imaginary beliefs to which he owes his fear and difficulty and
would not cease to suffer from heartache and great perplexity.[26]

Simply put, this is the dilemma of someone who heretofore has
done the right thing and lived an upright life and wants to continue in this way, but now craves philosophical edification *for
purposes of motivating and sustaining his way of life*. A "theoretical" answer, an answer that does not carry with it a motivational-
normative component, will be beside the point. We need to understand the *Guide* in this light.

The *Guide* does not disappoint. I have already indicated my
agreement with Kraemer that the *Guide* is a work in political
governance. It is a work that, like the *Ethics*, has as its goal the
inculcation of true opinions *for the sake of happiness*, the goal of
our mortal life. And such opinions, such philosophy as the *Guide*
teaches is constitutive of the happy life for one such as Joseph.

So the *Guide* attempts in its own way to take one who desires
to lead the good life, but is perplexed as to what that entails, to
the point where the desire is fulfilled and the student can see
clearly how the life he is currently living is philosophically defensible while being traditionally kosher. And, again, note the practical
nature of this project. It is pitched to someone who desperately
wants to establish his life upon a firm foundation.

What I have just said is at too high a level of generality to be
of real interest. So let me fine tune the claim. Joseph's life is a life
circumscribed by his halakhic tradition. This is the life he wants to
sustain, but not at the expense of philosophical intelligibility. The
task for Maimonides is clear—to provide in fine detail a defense of
the halakhic tradition, the law, that will satisfy Joseph. This
Maimonides does and does brilliantly.

Much recent work, good work, has been done on Maimonides's
discussion in Part 3 of the *Guide*, chapters 25–49, on *ta'amei ha-
mitzvot*, the purposes or reasons for the commandments.[27] In this

section Maimonides is concerned with providing, for one who can and must follow his discussion, a grounding for the commandments. I suggest that we understand this entire discussion as Maimonides's way of providing *to dihoti*, the grounds or reasons, for *to hoti*, the way of life that Joseph, indeed all in the halakhic tradition, leads. Thus construed, these chapters reprise in small compass the *Guide* as a whole, providing an intellectual framework by which the well-intentioned, but perplexed, addressee can begin to understand how his or her life is defensible, is appropriately conceived in teleological categories. Again, note that this project is practical, for it is offered by Maimonides to Joseph not for the sake of theoretical understanding, knowledge for its own sake, but rather for the sake of becoming truly virtuous. The goal of the commandments, as indeed the goal of the *Guide* as a whole, is to sustain and motivate correct behavior *on the basis of intellectual insight and true opinions*. The aim of the law, as Maimonides says in 3.27, is the welfare of the soul (*tiqqun ha-nefesh*) and the welfare of the body (*tiqqun ha-guf*). And the former is achievable only after the latter. Joseph doubtless possesses the latter as a good member of the community. But he lacks the former, or better, has but a glimpse of true happiness. As a result, he has begun to wonder about the grounds of his obedience. And such grounds Maimonides attempts to provide in his discussion here and in the *Guide* as a whole. In so providing *ta'amei ha-mitzvot* he sustains and motivates Joseph's obedience, and indeed he does so by putting it on a firm foundation.

The whole story is beautifully illustrated by the parable of the palace in 3.51. Detailed discussion of the parable is not now necessary,[28] but what is relevant is precisely *where* Joseph and those like him are located relative to the king (God) in his palace. It seems clear that Joseph is among "those . . . who have come up to the habitation [the king's palace] and walk around it . . . [i.e.,] the jurists who believe true opinions on the basis of traditional authority . . . but do not engage in speculation concerning the fundamental principles of religion and make no inquiry whatever regarding the rectification of belief." Joseph follows the letter of the law without speculating, or, if you prefer, he has a nascent sense, a whiff of speculation, that leads him into confusion. In any event, he has made no systematic study of the law, the very foundation of his life. In this way, again, Joseph is really no different from Aristotle's auditors, who do the right thing on the basis of authority and custom, but have never sought a foundation for their behavior, a broader context for it.

Given Joseph's current situatedness relative to the king (God) in his palace, there is the need of a guide to bring him closer. Indeed, Maimonides commences the chapter by saying that the chapter is only a kind of conclusion to the preceding chapters (25–49) on *ta'amei ha-mitzvot*,[29] adding nothing to them, (merely) explaining the mode of worship practiced by the philosopher ("one who has apprehended true realities") and guiding him toward such worship. The chapter thus picks up the thread of the foregoing discussion and by means of illustration guides Joseph closer to true worship, the human good, or at least indicates to him what true worship entails. Maimonides, like Aristotle, envisions himself as a guide toward true happiness, motivating and directing those in need by means of philosophical argumentation. Both chasten as they edify. Both motivate as they clarify.

And in the end they both motivate their respective students to a seemingly supra-political goal. Aristotle sings a paean to the contemplative life in book 10 of the *Nicomachean Ethics*.[30] Maimonides likewise defends a notion of true worship that is exercised in quite solitary surroundings.[31] But whereas I think this supra-political reading true of Aristotle, that his overarching lesson is to force students to reflect how political life can, indeed ought to, engender its own transcendence,[32] I believe Maimonides's position is rather more complex. The final good that Maimonides urges, the true worship of the creator, is an imitatio Dei, mediated by Farabian political philosophy.[33] For Maimonides, true philosophy, prophecy, entails political activity practiced as an imitatio Dei. Moses is Maimonides's paradigm, and enlightened political activity is the truest manifestation of amor Dei. In the final analysis, the human good differs for Aristotle and for Maimonides. But lest we lose sight of the thread that connects them, it is this: Both the *Ethics* and the *Guide*, each in its own way, are practical guides that transport the would-be leaders of their respective communities to reflect upon the foundations and grounds of their commitments with a view to achieving thereby such happiness as they are capable of.

Perhaps the greatest secret of the *Guide* is this: It is a work in practical philosophy.[34] As I asserted in the beginning, we read the *Guide* as a patchwork of "theoretical" concerns, as providing

Maimonides's considered views on semantic theory, physics, metaphysics, and so on. Maimonides is not writing for himself, however, but for Joseph. And given this dialectical and practical moment, one finds embedded in each discussion (or all of them collectively) normative claims, motivating mechanisms that trigger a response in Joseph. A chapter much longer than this one would tease out the normative ties in each of Maimonides's "theoretical" discussions. In seeing again and again the intelligibility and philosophical foundations of his accustomed mode of life, Joseph is *in principle* released from the bondage of his perplexity and thereby, in time and after much hard intellectual work, positioned to take his place as a leader in his community, living a life in imitation of his creator. And if we scholars think such a life not theoretical enough or, alternatively, too practical for our liking, that is *our* problem, not Maimonides's.

NOTES

1. *Topics* 145a15–16; *Metaphysics* 1025b25, 1064a16–19; *Nicomachean Ethics* 1139a26–28.
2. *Nicomachean Ethics* 1095a5–6, 1103b26–29, 1179a35–b4; *Eudemian Ethics* 1216b20–25.
3. *Metaphysics* 993b19–21; *Nicomachean Ethics* 1139a27–31.
4. *Nicomachean Ethics* 1094b14–15.
5. Broadie 1991, pp. 5–6.
6. Burnyeat 1980, p. 81.
7. Ibid., p. 81; Broadie 1991, p. 23.
8. Lear 1988, pp. 159–160.
9. Burnyeat 1980, p. 81; Sherman 1989, p. 196.
10. Kraemer 1991, pp. 80–98; see also Galston 1990, pp. 68–76.
11. Pines 1979, p. 100.
12. Or, alternatively, a book of Jewish kalam, a defense (ultimately for political purposes) of the law. For Strauss's view on the nature of the *Guide*, see Strauss 1952, pp. 40–46; 1963, p. xiv. For Guttmann's view, see Guttmann 1973, pp. 503–504; 1976. For some recent critiques of Strauss's position, see Buijs 1978 and W. Z. Harvey 1991.
13. Cf. Farabi, *Jadal* 69: 10–18; and Galston 1990, p. 69.
14. Kraemer 1991, pp. 101–104. But note that for Kraemer, "it would not be accurate to depict the *Guide* as a book about practical philosophy, that is, political science, although, again, some facets of political science are touched upon" (101–102; cf. Strauss 1952, pp. 43–44). I disagree. My chapter is an attempt to understand the *Guide* as a work

in (Aristotelian) practical philosophy, though not simply because "some facets of political science are touched upon"; cf. Kellner 1990, pp. 38, 64.

15. *Topics* 100a29–30; *Nicomachean Ethics* 1098b9–12, 1145b1–6; and Kraemer 1989, pp. 85–88; 1991, p. 102.

16. An unpublished paper compares the practical thrust of the *Guide* with a similar motivation in Spinoza's *Treatise on the Emendation of the Intellect* and *Ethics*; for now, see Gregory's remarks in Spinoza 1991, pp. 10–12, and Feldman's in Spinoza 1992, p. 225.

17. The relevant Maimonidean passage is translated by Kraemer (1991, p. 97) and discussed by him on pp. 98–104; for the Farabian background, see *Introductory Treatise on Logic*, p. 232 (Dunlop 1957) and *Enumeration of the Sciences*, p. 24 (Najjar, in Lerner and Mahdi 1963).

18. *Guide* 2.40; and Kraemer 1991, pp. 100–101.

19. *Nicomachean Ethics, ab init.*

20. *Nicomachean Ethics* 1.2.

21. *Politics* 1252b27–30, 1278b21–4, 1280a31–2, b39.

22. Frank 1992, pp. 121–42.

23. Reeve 1992, p. 189.

24. Frank 1992, p. 133.

25. Lear 1988, pp. 159–60; cf. Kellner (1990, p. 64): "Maimonides' book is transformative and not simply expository, subsuming throughout a practical aim."

26. *Guide*, Intro., pp. 5–6 (Pines)

27. See Hyman 1979–80, pp. 323–343; Twersky 1980, pp. 356–514; Stern 1986, pp. 92–130. I have made a small contribution in Frank 1993, pp. 91–94.

28. For some recent discussion, see Kellner 1990, pp. 14–33; S. Harvey 1991, pp. 60–75; Frank 1992, pp. 135–39.

29. Kellner 1990, pp. 13–14.

30. *Nicomachean Ethics* 10. 7–8.

31. *Guide* 3.51: 621 (Pines); and S. Harvey 1991, pp. 66–68.

32. Broadie 1991, pp. 391–392.

33. *Guide* 1.54, 3.54; Berman 1961; 1974; Frank 1985. Though agreeing that the nature of the *Guide* is practical (see note 25), Kellner (1990, pp. 47–53) critiques the foregoing interpretations.

34. Contra Strauss and Kraemer; see note 14.

REFERENCES

Berman, L. 1961. "The Political Interpretation of the Maxim: The Purpose of Philosophy is the Imitation of God." *Studia Islamica* 15: 53–61.

————. 1974. "Maimonides, the Disciple of Alfarabi." *Israel Oriental Studies* 4: 154–178.

Broadie, S. 1991. *Ethics with Aristotle.* New York: Oxford University Press.

Buijs, J. A. 1978. "The Philosophical Character of Maimonides' *Guide*— A Critique of Strauss' Interpretation." *Judaism* 27: 448–57.

Burnyeat, M. 1980. "Aristotle on Learning to Be Good." In *Essays on Aristotle's Ethics*, ed. A. O. Rorty, pp. 69–92. Berkeley: University of California Press.

Dunlop, D. M. 1957. "Al-Farabi's Introductory *Risalah* on Logic." *Islamic Quarterly* 3: 224–235.

Frank, D. H. 1985. "The End of the *Guide*: Maimonides on the Best Life for Man." *Judaism* 34: 485–495.

————. 1992. "The Elimination of Perplexity: Socrates and Maimonides as Guides of the Perplexed." In *Autonomy and Judaism: The Individual and the Community in Jewish Philosophical Thought*, ed. D. H. Frank, pp. 121–142. Albany: SUNY Press.

————. 1993. "*Ad Hoq.*" *S'vara* 3: 91–94.

Galston, M. 1990. *Politics and Excellence: The Political Philosophy of Alfarabi.* Princeton, N.J.: Princeton University Press.

Guttmann, J. 1973. *Philosophies of Judaism.* New York: Schocken Books.

————. 1976. "Philosophie der Religion oder Philosophie des Gesetzes?" *Proceedings of the Israel Academy of Sciences and Humanities* 5: 146–173.

Harvey, S. 1991. "Maimonides in the Sultan's Palace." In *Perspectives on Maimonides: Philosophical and Historical Studies*, ed. J. L. Kraemer, pp. 47–75. Oxford: Oxford University Press.

Harvey, W. Z. 1991. "Why Maimonides Was Not a *Mutakallim.*" In *Perspectives on Maimonides: Philosophical and Historical Studies*, ed. J. L. Kraemer, pp. 105–114. Oxford: Oxford University Press.

Hyman, A. 1979–1980. "A Note on Maimonides' Classification of Law." *Proceedings of the American Academy for Jewish Research* 46–47: 323–343.

Kellner, M. 1990. *Maimonides on Human Perfection.* Atlanta: Scholars Press.

Kraemer, J. L. 1989. "Maimonides on Aristotle and Scientific Method." In *Moses Maimonides and His Time*, ed. E. L. Ormsby, pp. 53–88. Washington, D.C.: The Catholic University of America Press.

————. 1991. "Maimonides on the Philosophic Sciences in his *Treatise on the Art of Logic.*" In *Perspectives on Maimonides: Philosophical and Historical Studies*, ed. J. L. Kraemer, pp. 77–104. Oxford: Oxford University Press.

Lear, J. 1988. *Aristotle: the Desire to Understand*. Cambridge: Cambridge University Press.

Lerner, R., and M. Mahdi (eds.). 1963. *Medieval Political Philosophy: A Sourcebook*. Ithaca, N.Y.: Cornell University Press.

Pines, S. 1979. "The Limitations of Human Knowledge According to Al-Farabi, ibn Bajja, and Maimonides." In *Studies in Medieval Jewish History and Literature*, ed. I. Twersky, pp. 82–109. Cambridge, Mass.: Harvard University Press.

Reeve, C. D. C. 1992. *Practices of Reason: Aristotle's Nicomachean Ethics*. Oxford: Clarendon Press.

Sherman, N. 1989. *The Fabric of Character: Aristotle's Theory of Virtue*. Oxford: Clarendon Press.

Spinoza, B. 1991. *Tractatus Theologico-Politicus*, trans. S. Shirley. Leiden: Brill.

———. 1992. *Ethics, Treatise on the Emendation of the Intellect, and Selected Letters*, trans. S. Shirley. Indianapolis: Hackett.

Stern, J. 1986. "The Idea of a *Hoq* in Maimonides' Explanation of the Law." In *Maimonides and Philosophy*, ed. S. Pines and Y. Yovel, pp. 92–130. Dordrecht: Nijhoff.

Strauss, L. 1952. "The Literary Character of the *Guide for the Perplexed.*" In L. Strauss, *Persecution and the Art of Writing*, pp. 38–94. Glencoe, Ill.: The Free Press of Glencoe.

———. 1963. "How to Begin to Study *The Guide of the Perplexed*." In Maimonides, *The Guide of the Perplexed*, vol. 1, trans. S. Pines, pp. xi–lvi. Chicago: University of Chicago Press.

Twersky, I. 1980. *Introduction to the Code of Maimonides*. New Haven, Conn.: Yale University Press.

Jewish Tradition
and National Policy

Elliot N. Dorff

ENCOUNTERS WITH RELIGION IN
THE PUBLIC SPHERE

During March and April 1993 I served on the ethics committee of Hillary Rodham Clinton's task force on health care. The committee was carefully chosen to mirror America. Of the thirty-two members of the committee, there was approximately an equal number of women and men, four African-Americans, one Latina, one Asian-American, five physicians, three health care lawyers, four secular ethicists, two nurses, and four clergy—a priest, two ministers, and a rabbi. Although all of us served on faculties of universities, and although I have a Ph.D. in philosophy with a dissertation in ethical theory, I was keenly aware that my role on the committee was primarily that of rabbi.

This raised an important issue about which I had thought before, but never with immediate practical consequences. Specifically, how should I as an American Jew integrate my American and Jewish identities in helping to shape national policy? More broadly, what ought to be the role which Judaism plays in national affairs? Note that the question is not what role *Jews* should play in government; as American citizens, American Jews, like all other Americans, should be as active or inactive in government affairs as they choose to be, as long as they fulfill the minimal duties of citizenship like paying taxes and abiding by the law. The harder question is the one to which this chapter is addressed: Should Jews consciously invoke their Jewish heritage in the process of serving their government, and if so, how?

Another recent activity of mine raised the same question in another context. The state of California is the first to mandate teaching about religion in the public schools. The publisher Houghton Mifflin produced a series of books for social studies instruction in grades 1 through 8 that included instruction about the role of religion and about the religions of the world as part of its treatment of world culture. Because of time constraints, however, the books were produced without sufficient review by interested parties, and the Los Angeles Unified School District agreed to adopt the series only if Jewish, Christian, and Muslim scholars reviewed it and wrote a teacher's guide to minimize problematic sections within it. These revisions would, the publisher agreed, not only be published in the teacher's guide, but they would also be taught in teacher-training sessions for those using the series and would be included in the revised version of the series when it appears in several years. I was the Jewish consultant for that project, and that placed me directly in the position of presenting Judaism to millions of non-Jewish youngsters (and some Jewish ones too) in the context of public instruction.

PROBING THE WALL OF SEPARATION BETWEEN CHURCH AND STATE

These activities raise questions from both the American and Jewish contexts. On the American side, the First Amendment mandates that the government shall not establish any religion nor interfere in the free exercise thereof. That has commonly been understood to erect a "wall of separation" between government and religion, and a number of national Jewish organizations have been zealous in defending that wall from all onslaughts. They have done this, in part, because they understand the amendment that way, but also because they believe strongly that Jews and Judaism, as a minority people and a minority religion in the United States, can flourish only if the majority religion is not reenforced by government. Many examples in Jewish history make clear that Jews were at best second-class citizens and at worst persecuted, executed, or exiled when there was a state religion. As a result, one can readily understand why, on the one hand, the Rabbis would say, "Pray for the welfare of the government, for without respect for it people would swallow each other alive";[1] while, on the other hand, they would also say, "Love work, hate lordship, and seek no intimacy with the ruling power" and "Be on your guard against the ruling power, for they who exercise it draw no man near to them except for their own interests; appearing as friends when it is to their own advantage, they do not stand by a man in his hour of need."[2] The respect for authority but the simultaneous wariness of it, as embodied in these early rabbinic comments, shaped the attitude of Jews toward government in most times and places throughout the last two thousand years.

The realities of America, though, have never been as pure as the theory of a wall of separation would require, for national policy or law has long recognized Sunday as a day off for government workers and Christmas as a national holiday; government money supports chaplains in the armed services; tax law exempts religious institutions, not just as nonprofit enterprises but specifically as religious centers; and even the Senate and the House of Representatives hear from a member of the clergy at the start of each day's session. Although United Stated Supreme Court decisions in the 1940s, 1950s, and 1960s asserted that a "wall of separation" exists and that, as a result of that wall, public schools could not be used for religious purposes such as religious instruction and prayer, recent decisions have permitted the display of a religious Christmas scene on public property and the use of public schools by religious organizations after school hours. The Supreme Court ruled that Navy regulations governing attire could legitimately prohibit a religious Jew in the Navy from wearing a skullcap (*kippah*), but Congress overruled the Court through special legislation on that issue. Moreover, Sunday closing laws have long been regarded as constitutional. These breaches in the wall of separation are generally justified as permissible either on the grounds that they assure the "free exercise" of religion and do not constitute governmental establishment of a particular religion or as measures the government may properly take in providing for the citizens' welfare.[3]

The scope of the First Amendment in the future will clearly depend on developing Supreme Court decisions and measures adopted by Congress, but given the background just summarized, to what extent, and in what ways, should a conscientious American

Jew serving the government in some capacity invoke the Jewish tradition in thinking about public issues? The question is as much a moral and pragmatic one as a legal one. What kind of relationship between religion and government do we as American Jews think morally and pragmatically *should* exist? How, then, *should* we respond to our religion while in government service, if at all?

On the Jewish side, what would Jewish sources have us do while in government service, if that can be discerned? Various Jewish philosophers and jurists over the centuries have developed philosophies of government and rules for interaction with it, often in response to similar questions in their time and place, but most of those lived in pre-Enlightenment countries where Jews were at best tolerated. Their treatments of this matter thus always seem at least a bit off-point when one seeks to apply them to the American setting.

Jews living under Enlightenment conditions in other countries have faced similar questions, sometimes very publicly and politically, as in the instance of the questions posed to Napoleon's French Sanhedrin,[4] and sometimes in the writings of specific philosophers, such as Hermann Cohen's equation of the German and the Jewish ethos.[5] The American context, though, is different even from those times and places for two reasons, one legal and one sociological. Other countries whose laws reflect Enlightenment principles have extended full citizenship to Jews, but they have also given special legal status to one particular branch of Christianity. It was the United States that first declined to establish a national church by its constitution, and it still is one of very few countries that does so. Moreover, from a sociological point of view, nowhere has the multiplicity of religions and, indeed, the absence of any religion been consciously part of national identity as in the United States.

In this chapter, then, we shall concentrate on the American setting and ask two questions: (1) How shall we understand and express the American commitments we have in deciding the degree to which our Jewishness should enter our government service? (2) How shall we understand Jewish sources in guiding us on how to play a role in government? As we shall see, the answer to both of these questions depends on our view of what should be the relationship between Jews and non-Jews, which, in turn, ultimately depends on our view of revelation.

THE ROLE OF RELIGION IN CONCEIVING
OF PUBLIC ISSUES

One might reasonably ask why one should bother considering the views of a religion like Judaism on an issue like health care at all. After all, appropriate health care, one might argue, is and should be a medical decision, and so the only factors relevant to making individual or social decisions about them are properly medical.

Not so long ago, many physicians might have thought just that way. In America particularly, medicine was seen mechanistically, such that the task of the doctor was to fix the machine called the *body*.[6] In accomplishing that task, so conceived, the only significant issue is what works and what does not.

We have learned a great deal in the past several decades, however, about the intricate context in which medicine takes place. Many factors, beyond the strictly physical, influence the success of a particular therapy—or the possibility of using it in the first place. One important element is the patient's willingness to carry through with what is necessary to make a given therapy work; without the patient's agreement, even the most accurate diagnosis and the most effective therapy are useless. The patient's inclusion in the process of healing, however, invokes all of his or her views about the body, medicine, the patient-physician relationship, the purpose of life, and in critical cases, the nature of death and the hope for life after death. Such decisions also involve the views of physicians, nurses, and other health care personnel on all these matters. Decisions as to proper treatment are *not*, in the end, exclusively a matter of means, but also of goals; they consequently require broad-based judgments rooted in one's moral views and one's overarching philosophy of life.

It is precisely here that religion plays an important role in medical care. The word *religion* is usually understood to come from the Latin work for link or tie—the same word from which we get the word *ligament*. Religions link us to the broader context of things. They spell out the ways in which we are related to our family, our community, our environment, and to God. They articulate a philosophy of life, a view of all the pieces of our experience and the relationships among them.

Religions, though, go beyond this: They teach their specific philosophy and its implications through story, ritual, prayer, custom, and law within the context of a living community. They are therefore much more powerful influences on humanity than philosophies are by themselves. They share with philosophy, however, the ability to portray an approach to life, and it is such a broad view of the larger scheme of things on which our specific moral judgments are ultimately grounded.

That is true for all religions. Religions differ from each other, however, not only in the region of the world in which they originated or are most commonly found and not only in their ritual practices, but also in their concepts and values. What is the human being like, and what should one ideally be? What are the significance and proper roles of the community? How should we conceive of, and relate to, the environment? How should we respond to that which lies beyond our ability to understand or control—or for that matter, to that which we can understand and control? What do we mean by God, if we hold such a notion? What difference does it make if we do or do not? The answers to these questions from the standpoint of Judaism, Christianity, and Buddhism, for example, will reveal some overlap but also some major differences. These factors play a critical role in determining what kinds of health care are judged to be variously prohibited, permissible, desirable, or required.

How, then, can a pluralistic country like the United States make decisions in these areas? In more monolithic countries, one might expect general agreement on most moral issues—although even there such agreement is sometimes more theoretical than actual as, for example, in the case of Italy's recent sanction of abortions under some circumstances, despite heavy Roman Catholic influence there. In a consciously and avowedly pluralistic country like the United States, though, does its plethora of views make it impossible to make coherent social policy? Put even more strongly, if so many varying views exist on moral questions, does it make any sense to ask what we *should* do as a nation with regard to any specific issue at all? Or is it all a matter of "might makes right," politically, if not militarily?

There are fundamentally two different approaches to this issue. Some would claim that we can identify a common, public viewpoint. Then either the various religious traditions within the nation are simply vehicles for transmitting the values of that view, or alternatively, the common, public theory sets the limits within which the various religions can vary in thought and practice. This approach assumes not only that there are absolute values, but that we can know them with considerable certainty; only then does the society have the moral authority (quite aside from its military power) to restrict variations of individuals and groups with such assuredness. Within Judaism, the early Reform Movement, as articulated by the Pittsburgh Platform of 1885, and some right-wing, contemporary Orthodox rabbis are examples of this approach in one of its two forms.

The second model is based on much greater humility about what we can know about the right and the good. It therefore leads people to anticipate and respect much more variation on those questions. It is, in a word, more pluralistic. It does not even expect to find a single, common moral theory to which all or even most citizens subscribe, for people differ too much for that to be possible. Our epistemological position as human beings makes that so. People may have strong moral convictions, even ones for which they would die, but they never have total moral knowledge; only God has that. Agreement, however, may be found among the various individuals and groups within society on specific matters, and so social policies can be formulated, even though a coherent rationale for those policies may well be lacking.

This second view, to which I subscribe, does *not* entail that we human beings are totally bereft of moral knowledge; we have, after all, the benefit of the moral thought and experience of all human beings in the past and present. It is just that we are not omniscient as God is, and so we must be satisfied with knowing that our knowledge of these matters—like, indeed, our knowledge of science—is partial and flawed. It is not that every person or every society just states what it likes and dislikes when it formulates its moral code and ethical views. Moral subjectivism is not the right position, in my estimation; a context-dependent relativism is. That is, there probably is some absolutely valid way of thinking about human life and the values that should inhere in it; we human beings, however, do not know what that is. Our moral systems and religions thus articulate what we do know and our views of how we should conceive and respond to that and to the far more numerous aspects of life where we do not have indisputable knowledge. Pluralism, then, is the only position that makes sense epistemologically—and, for reasons I shall develop later, theologically.

How, then, do we rise above our varying views of life to come to some kind of social policy on concrete issues that face us all? In some societies, of course, the decision is made by decree of a tyrant or tribal leader, and that is the end of the matter. In others, a high degree of ethnic homogeneity enables a nation to use its heritage to make moral decisions with little, if any, regard for alternative views.

The hard contexts for this question, however, are those like Israel and the United States. The methodological problems in those two countries, though, are different, and they serve as models for other nations of the two sorts that they represent. In Israel, avowedly a Jewish state but also a democratic one, Israeli Jews must find a way to apply the Jewish heritage to contemporary concerns in a way that leaves room for the pluralism that inheres in Judaism and in the Jewish community and for the varying views of Muslims, Christians, secularists, and others who are citizens of the Jewish state. Similarly structured states include France, Italy, and Ireland, with Catholicism, of course, being the dominant (and in some ways official) religion rather than Judaism.

In the United States the context is even more complicated. An overwhelmingly Christian country that nevertheless by constitution separates church and state and that includes citizens of virtually every world religion and view, the United States must find a way to engender social discourse and decision making in a thoroughly multicultural format. England, Canada, and some other former colonies of Great Britain face similar problems, although not necessarily with constitutional support.

How can moral decisions be made in such contexts? Frankly, only if people are willing to discuss issues in a multicultural setting where one's own view of things will be challenged and not necessarily adopted; only if people have sufficient flexibility to see and seize areas of agreement; only if people have respect for the varying points of view presented and for those who hold them; and only if people are resolved to live together not only peacefully, but cooperatively, despite their differing views and practices. No society—and certainly not all of the world's people—can succeed in attaining this high level of civility, humanity, and philosophical appropriateness at all times. If the new technology in medicine and engineering has done nothing else, however, it has brought us together as a global village with the need to get to know each other and make decisions together on the many issues that transcend borders and affect every one of us. Under those circumstances, the cocky assuredness that some might have had when living in isolated conclaves of people who think and act like themselves will need to give way to greater openness and respect. This is not moral laxity or indifference; one might—and ideally would—still argue forcefully for one's convictions. One must, however, come to recognize that one's own way of seeing and doing things is not the only possible way that a person of intelligence and moral character could adopt.

The remarkable thing is that in the two major national discussions on health care—that of the President's commission on health care in the early 1980s and that of the national task force on health care of 1993 chaired by Hillary Rodham Clinton—a remarkable degree of civility and even coherence prevailed. Hence, Daniel Wikler noted this about the essays produced during and for the President's commission:

> It is true that each essay provides a different account of equity in access to health care and insists that rival accounts are mistaken. Yet there is one policy recommendation supported by each of these essays: Every person ought to be assured of access to some decent minimum of health care services. This conclusion cannot be said to have been "proved" by this collection of arguments, but the fact that a recommendation of universal access to (at least some) health care follows from such disparate sets of premises suggests that the recommendation is "insensitive" to choice of moral theory. Even if we do not know which moral theory is correct, then, and thus cannot provide a ground-level-up proof that all should have access to a minimum of health care, such a belief has been rendered reasonable and perhaps even compelling. In this sense, this diverse and inconsistent collection of theories of justice in health care delivery supports the consensus reached by members of the President's Commission concerning the moral obligation of our society to ensure access to health care for all its people.[7]

I can report that the ethics committee of Clinton's health care task force produced similar results. The theoretical debates were many and, in some instances, heated. For example, in formulating the underlying moral principles that argued for universal health care guaranteed by the government, all of us agreed that the moral grounds for such a system included principles enshrined in the nation's constitutive documents, specifically, equality, justice, and "providing for the general welfare." The religious among us, though, wanted to include what the Protestants call "our obligations of stewardship"—that is, our duty to take care of God's property, including our bodies. Even though the ethics committee's subcommittee writing the preamble to the legislation specifically said that religious Americans understand our obligation to provide for health care in those terms and that secular Americans hold that value for other reasons, the secularists on the committee argued strenuously and heatedly to drop the religious language altogether. Ultimately, the committee presented two different versions of the preamble to President and Mrs. Clinton, one with the religious language and one without, leaving it to them to decide. With all this controversy, though, the policy advocated by both sides was the same; namely, that we as an American community have the duty to provide health care for at least all American citizens and perhaps even for undocumented aliens.

Sometimes, of course, religious differences made for differences in policy as well. Early in its deliberations the ethics committee decided not even to talk about whether the benchmark health plan would include abortion services, knowing well that that decision would ultimately be made on the basis of the political consideration of what could get through Congress. I, personally, am sorry, though, that we did not have that discussion. The varying stances on abortion taken by the major denominations in America are well known, but the issue raises an important question about American democratic theory; namely, whether freedom of religion should extend to an issue like this where there is significant moral debate among America's religious and secular communities.

I think that it should, but Presidents Reagan and Bush have thought otherwise. Until now, the freedom to have an abortion has been granted, but the government has refused to pay for abortions for those who cannot afford them. A national health care plan, though, makes the question of whether the government should pay for abortions for the indigent and, indeed, for all Americans who want one all the more acute.

Thomas Jefferson understood the matter this way: "The practice of morality [is] necessary for the well-being of society. . . . The interests of society require observation of those moral principles only in which all religions agree."[8] What would this mean, though, when the issue is not only granting people the freedom to do as they think right, but also the monetary support to carry out their convictions? Jefferson and Madison did not deal with that ripple of the question because they did not conceive of the government providing the many services it now does and the even greater scope of health care services that the government would assure under the new proposal.

We, however, must test the limits of the principles on which Madison and Jefferson founded this nation as we construct a new health care system. With abortion as a particularly poignant example, then, what does freedom of religion entail when a particular medical procedure is required by some religions under at least some circumstances, permitted by others, and forbidden by others? At the moment, that question is being left to the politicians.

The broader point, though, should not be lost. Even if a particular religious argument does not win the day in public debate, it should not be denied simply because it comes from a religious source and uses religious language and reasoning. In his new book, *The Culture of Disbelief*, Stephen Carter has made this point eloquently with regard to court cases,[9] and I would like to extend it to public policy discussions as well. Indeed, as a matter of American principle, all of America's religions should see it not only as a right, but as a duty to articulate their views and advance the arguments for those views in the public forum. Only then can America benefit in forming its public policy from the variety of peoples who constitute America. This effectively imposes an *American* duty on Americans to learn more about their own religions' views so that they can participate in an informed, intelligent, and distinctly religious way in the shaping of American public policy.

A PHILOSOPHY OF JUDAISM ON GOVERNMENT SERVICE

How, though, should we understand government service in a free democratic country from a Jewish point of view? As indicated previously, I believe that a contemporary Jewish philosophy of government service must rest on one's view of the relationships that Jews *should* cultivate with non-Jews and that this ultimately depends upon one's view of revelation.[10]

There are, as noted, historical considerations that would prompt Jews to be suspicious of any interaction with non-Jews. Echoing the rabbi's prayer in *Fiddler on the Roof*, these Jews would say, "May God bless and keep the Tsar—far away from us!" Such sentiments are well-founded in countries where Jews qua Jews had to fear for their lives. In a free and democratic country like the United States, however, where Jews have the right to enter into the process of forming national policy, the question goes beyond simple self-defense and becomes this: Can one develop a theology of Judaism that would permit Jews to interact with non-Jews in shaping national policy, not only from the pragmatic motives of protecting Jewish interests, but also from a genuine appreciation of plural avenues of truth and wisdom, while still retaining one's claim to Jewish notions of what is true, right, and good?

Theological Grounds for Pluralism

Some Orthodox rabbis reject pluralism completely, both within the Jewish community and between Jews and non-Jews. So, for example, Rabbi Walter Wurzburger, past editor of the modern Orthodox journal *Tradition* and hardly among the hardliners within the Orthodox world, has said this: "Religious pluralism borders on religious relativism, if not outright nihilism. It rests on the assumption that no religion can be true and that it does not really matter what kind of myth we invoke in order to provide us with a sense of meaning and purpose."[11] Other Orthodox rabbis, including Joseph Soloveitchik, Irving Greenberg, and David Hartman, have suggested ways in which Orthodox Jews can understand other Jews more appreciatively,[12] but none of their models would open the door to dialogue with non-Jews on national issues except on the most pragmatic of bases. Rabbi Simon Greenberg, a Conservative rabbi, however, has pointed out some features of Jewish theology that warrant pluralism not only among Jews, but between Jews and non-Jews, and I will mention some others. My goal is to explore the *theological* grounding for Jewish involvement in national policy formation.

Rabbi Greenberg defines *pluralism* as "the ability to say that 'your ideas are spiritually and ethically as valid—that is, as capable of being justified, supported, and defended—as mine' and yet remain firmly committed to your own ideas and practices."[13] But what bestows legitimacy upon varying views such that a person should be pluralistic in outlook? Political pluralism, as mandated in the American Bill of Rights, can be justified by pragmatic considerations: The state needs to accommodate differing beliefs to promote the peace and welfare of its citizens. What, however, legitimizes a spiritual or ethical pluralism?

Greenberg says that he knows of no philosophic justification for pluralism, for that would entail the legitimation of accepting a position and its contrary or contradictory. There is, however, a religious justification: God *intended* that we all think differently.

Greenberg learns this from, among other sources, the Mishnah, the authoritative collection of rabbinic law from the first and second centuries. Why, the Mishnah asks, did God initiate the human species by creating only one man? One reason, the Mishnah suggests, is to impress upon us the greatness of the Holy One, blessed be he, for when human beings mint coins, they all come out the same, but God made one mold (Adam) and yet no human being looks exactly like another. This physical pluralism is matched by an intellectual pluralism for which, the Rabbis say, God is to be blessed: "When one sees a crowd of people, one is to say, 'Blessed is the Master of mysteries,' for just as their faces are not alike, so are their thoughts not alike."

The Midrash, the written record of rabbinic lore, supports this further. It says that when Moses was about to die, he said to the Lord: "Master of the Universe, You know the opinions of everyone, and that there are no two among Your children who think alike. I beg of You that after I die, when You appoint a leader for them, appoint one who will bear with [accept, *sovel*] each one of them as he thinks [on his own terms, *lefi da'ato*]." We know that Moses said this, the Rabbis claim, because Moses describes God as "God of the *ruchot* (spirits [pl.]) of all flesh" (Numbers 16:22).[14] Thus God *wants* pluralism so that people will constantly be reminded of his grandeur.

In addition to these sources mentioned by Greenberg, other elements of the tradition would also support a pluralistic attitude. God intentionally, according to the Rabbis, reveals only a part of his truth in the Torah, and the rest must come from study and debate.[15] Study, though, can never remove the ultimate limits to human knowledge, for, as the medieval Jewish philosopher, Joseph Albo, said, "If I knew him, I would be he."[16] Moses himself could not see God directly but only through a lens, and the other biblical prophets, although accepted as true prophets by the tradition, saw God only through nine lenses, and cloudy ones at that: "What was the distinction between Moses and the other prophets? The latter looked through nine lenses, whereas Moses looked only through one. They looked through a cloudy lens, but Moses through one that was clear."[17] Ultimately, one must understand that, according to the Rabbis, even those who stood at Sinai understood the revelation given there through their own individual abilities and perspectives.[18] "Every way of man is right in his own eyes, but the Lord weighs the hearts" (Proverbs 21:2); as Rashi explains, this means that God judges each of us by our intentions precisely because a human being cannot be expected to know the truth as God knows it.

God as understood in the Jewish tradition thus wants pluralism not only to demonstrate his grandeur in creating humanity with diversity, but also to force human beings to realize their epistemological creatureliness, the limits of human knowledge in comparison to that of God. One is commanded to study; one is supposed to be committed to learning as much of God, his world, and his will as possible. One must recognize, though, that a passion for truth does not mean that one has full or exclusive possession of it; indeed, such possessions are humanly impossible.

Moreover, one should understand that everyone's quest for religious knowledge is aided by discussion with others, for different views force all concerned to evaluate and refine their own positions. The paradigmatic disputants, the school of Hillel, reverse their position a number of times in the Talmud, in contrast to the school of Shammai, which did so at most once. The Hillelites understood the epistemological and theological value of plural views and the need to learn from others.

Thus an appropriate degree of religious humility would lead one to engage in spirited, spiritual argumentation; one would not assume that one knows the truth and attempt to exclude others by fiat or by social pressure. One can and must take stands, but one should do so while remaining open to being convinced to the contrary. One should also recognize that others may intelligently, morally, and theologically both think and act differently. From the standpoint of piety, pluralism emerges not from relativism, but from a deeply held and humble monotheism.

These sources indicate that pluralism is a divine creation; as such, human beings should try to imitate it, but they have difficulty doing so. To achieve the ability to be pluralistic is, in fact, the ultimate ethical and spiritual challenge, according to Greenberg. Just as "love your neighbor as yourself"—which, for Rabbi Akiba, is the underlying principle of all the commandments[19]—requires a person to go beyond biologically rooted self-love, pluralism requires a person to escape egocentricity. It is not possible for human beings totally to love their neighbors as themselves, and neither is it possible to be totally pluralistic. We are, by nature, too self-centered fully to achieve either goal.

The tradition, however, prescribes methods to bring us closer to these aims. Many of the biblical directives to gain love of neighbor appear in that same chapter 19 of Leviticus in which the commandment itself appears. The Rabbis' instructions as to how to become pluralistic are contained, in part, in a famous talmudic source describing the debates of Hillel and Shammai: one must, like Hillel, be affable and humble and teach opinions opposed to one's own, citing them first.[20]

Applying These Factors to Discussions with Non-Jews

It is difficult to convince some Jews of these theological reasons to tolerate and, indeed, rejoice in plural views *within* the Jewish community. One can readily understand, then, that such Jews—largely within the Orthodox camp—would have even more difficulty applying this outlook to non-Jews. Moreover, most of the preceding sources are clearly intended only for intra-Jewish dialogue. Nevertheless, it seems to me that some of these same considerations can form the foundation for a mutually respectful interaction between Jews, Christians, and secularists.

History.   Historically, Christianity has been subject to change and redefinition at least as much as Judaism, if not more. Even within the same denomination, creeds created centuries ago are continually changing, sometimes through outright amendment and sometimes through new interpretations, emphases, or applications. This constantly evolving nature of both Judaism and Christianity makes some of the faithful uneasy; they long for certainty and stability. At the same time, though, each religion retains its relevance and its dynamism only by opening itself to change.

In any case, whatever the pluses and minuses, the historical fact is that both religions *have* changed and continue to do so. The certainties of today, *even within the boundaries of one's own faith*, are not necessarily the convictions of tomorrow. History does not undermine one's ability to take a strong stand on what one believes, and it certainly does not prevent the contemporary Jewish community from authoritatively determining that Jews for Jesus are decidedly *not* Jews. History does not totally undermine communal definitions and the coherence they bring. The historically evolutionary nature of both faiths should, however, help contemporary Jews and Christians get beyond the feeling that the present articulation of their faith is the only one possible for a decent person to have; on the contrary, history should teach us that people of intelligence, morality, and sensitivity exist in other faiths too.

Philosophy.   This realization is reinforced only when one turns from historical considerations to philosophical ones. All human beings, whatever their background or creed, suffer from the same limitations on human knowledge. Many of us have sacred texts and traditions that reveal God's nature and will as clearly and fully as we think possible. Others, like Hindus and Buddhists, who are not monotheists, nevertheless have documents that, in their view, articulate ultimate truth, goodness, and wisdom. When we recognize that other peoples make the same claim as our own group, however, we must either resort to debates like those of the Middle Ages as to which is correct or we must confront the fact that none of us can know God's nature or will—or ultimate truth, goodness, or wisdom—with absolute certainty.

At the same time, just as the historical considerations do not make it rationally impossible or inadvisable to affirm a specific faith, so the philosophical factors do not. To see this, Van Harvey's distinction between "non-perspectivists," "hard-perspectivists," and "soft-perspectivists" will be helpful. Non-perspectivists claim that we look at the world through epistemologically transparent eyeglasses, and so all of us should ultimately see the world in the same way if we only are sufficiently intelligent and attentive. On the other end of the spectrum, hard-perspectivists claim that one's own specific view of the world is so entrenched in one's thinking and acting that it makes it impossible for one person to understand, let alone learn from, the views of others. In between these approaches to knowledge is soft-perspectivism, which claims that we each have a perspective that influences how we think and act, but that it is not so hard and fast that it blinds us to the views of others or makes it impossible to learn from them.[21]

If we take a non-perspectivist or hard-perspectivist approach to human knowledge, we will likely affirm our own view of things and think that alternative views are simply incorrect. Because non-perspectivists think that we should all see the same truth, they would likely advance a number of arguments in an attempt to convince those who disagree with them. Hard-perspectivists, on the other hand, might give up on such a project fairly early, convinced that those who disagree are simply too blind to see the truth and that no rational argument will help (although force may). As long as we acknowledge ahead of time, though, that no human argument on these matters can be conclusive, and as long as we assert that our particular understanding of God (truth, goodness, wisdom) is the correct one for all people *as far as we can tell*, we may still leave room for a kind of pluralism in which we appreciate the intelligence and sensitivity of others, even if we disagree with their views on specific issues. One need not deny cognitive meaning to religion to take such a position, as A. J. Ayer, R. B. Braithwaite, and others did in the middle of this century;[22] one need only be humble enough to recognize that none of us is omniscient and that we are all trying to articulate truth, goodness, and wisdom.

Alternatively, we may take the "live and let live" approach embodied in soft-perspectivism. That is, we would recognize that part of the reason that the arguments for my faith seem most persuasive to me is because it is, after all, *my* faith and that of my family and my people. This view has the advantage of recognizing not only that none of us is omniscient, but also that none of us is an objective observer, that we all view the world from one or another vantage point, and that our autobiographical backgrounds inevitably do, and perhaps should, play a role in determining the content of our particular viewpoint.

Such soft-perspectivism affords the strongest foundation for mutually respectful relations among Jews, Christians, and secularists, for it acknowledges the critical role our particular viewpoint has in shaping our knowledge and yet our continuing ability to learn from others who come from other traditions and who hold other views. At the same time, it enables us to affirm what we believe as our view of the truth—whether that be understood as God's will or in nontheological terms—and so it does not dissolve into subjectivism. It is rather a form of relativism, where there is an objective truth to be known, but we recognize that we can only know it through the lenses of our own vantage point.

Even if one takes a non-perspectivist or hard-perspectivist approach to human knowledge, though, mutually respectful relations among people of different faiths are possible as long as one openly recognizes the limits on what anyone can know of God. That is, productive interfaith discussions on matters of national concern must come out of a philosophically accurate assessment of our knowledge of God—that is, that we can and do say some things about God, we do act on our convictions, and our beliefs and actions can be justified by reasons that can be shared and appreciated by others; but, at the same time, other, equally rational, moral, and sensitive people might differ with us and might have good reasons for what they say and do. This is the result to be expected in areas where our knowledge is, by the very nature of the knower and the subject to be known, incomplete.

Theology.   How would the theological considerations mentioned previously apply to a Jewish understanding of Christian views of matters that enter into the national policy debate? In some ways, quite straightforwardly. If all the Israelites at Sinai heard God according to their individual abilities and perspectives, those who came after Sinai—Jews, Christians, Muslims, and even those who adhere to Oriental religions—must surely have heard God in different ways as well. This should open us to listen to other people's understanding of God's will even if we assert our own tradition's view in our own lives.

Moreover, if no two Israelites think alike, how much the more so must we expect that people from different backgrounds vary in their thoughts. If the eternal is to be blessed for the former, God certainly should be blessed for the latter as well.

Furthermore, as master of the spirits of all flesh, God could clearly have created us to think alike. The fact that God did not do this underscores the divine intention that we vary in our beliefs. The Rabbis already drew one significant implication from this:

Non-Jews can attain salvation (however understood) outside the bounds of Jewish law.[23]

Finally, it is just as hard—if not harder—to extend one's empathy and sympathy not only to those within one's own group, but also to those with different affiliations, backgrounds, patterns of living, and aims. One needs all of the qualities ascribed to Hillel, and more. To act in this way surely partakes of the divine.

And yet there are some limitations to this line of reasoning as the basis for Jewish participation in discussion with non-Jews on matters of national policy. It may be that God wants us to think independently, but ultimately the biblical prophets assert that Judaism's Torah is God's true teaching, the one that all nations will ultimately learn.

One should note that Micah, a younger contemporary of Isaiah, copies the latter's messianic vision of universal adherence to the God of Israel but then adds a line of his own that effectively changes it: "Though all the peoples walk each in the names of its gods, we will walk in the name of the Lord our God forever and ever."[24] This is a decidedly pluralistic vision of messianic times: Every people shall continue to follow its own god. Even so, Micah added this line *after* quoting Isaiah's vision that "the many peoples shall go and say: 'Come, let us go up to the Mount of the Lord, to the House of the God of Jacob, that He may instruct us in His ways, and that we may walk in His paths.' For instruction shall come forth from Zion, the word of the Lord from Jerusalem" (Isaiah 2:3; Micah 4:2). Thus even for Micah, apparently, other gods and other visions of the good life might exist, but only Israel has the true understanding of God's will.

God, then, may indeed want multiple conceptions of the divine, as Greenberg maintains, but traditional sources assign non-Jewish views a secondary status. God may like variety among his creatures, and he may even hold people responsible only for what they could be expected to know (the seven Noachide laws); but ultimately only Jews know what is true. This is liberal toleration—and it should be appreciated as such—but it certainly is not a validation of others' views. In that sense, it falls short of Greenberg's criterion that "your ideas are spiritually and ethically as valid— that is, as capable of being justified, supported, and defended—as mine." And, indeed, Greenberg himself may not have wanted to extend his thesis beyond disagreements among Jews.

I would take a somewhat broader view. It is only natural that Jewish sources should reflect a tension between nationalism and universalism.[25] God is, according to Jewish belief, the God of all creatures, but, at the same time, God chose the Jews to exemplify ideal standards for human life. This is how *Jews* understand God's will, the reason why Jews commit all their energies and, indeed, their very lives to Jewish belief and practice.

Despite this nationalistic side of the Jewish tradition, however, what ultimately rings through it is the Rabbis' assertion that non-Jews fully meet God's expectations by abiding by the seven Noachide laws and the Rabbis' statement that "The pious and virtuous of all nations participate in eternal bliss."[26] Jewish sources, then, which speak about God wanting plural approaches to the eternal within the Jewish community can apparently be applied, without too much tampering, to intercommunal relations as well. Of course, the same segments of the Jewish community that have difficulty with the former would undoubtedly have difficulty with the latter, but even some pluralists within the Jewish community would need to stretch their understanding and sensitivity to apply Jewish theology in this way. Nevertheless, a firm basis for this kind of theology exists within the Jewish tradition.

BRINGING RELIGION AND NATION CLOSER TOGETHER

Jefferson and Madison had good reason to fear the entanglement of religion in national matters. The European experience had demonstrated beyond all reasonable doubt that this is not good either for religion or for the state. At the same time, we do ourselves, religion, and the nation a disservice if we think that religion should have no role in shaping national policy. No religion should determine national policy as a matter of right, but each religion must enter the fray of public debate if that discussion is to reflect the nation as a whole and if it is to attain the richness that only multiple parties with differing views can give it. In that sense, religion should not be stuck behind a "wall of separation," but should rather be integrally involved in the process.

Jews can cite ample sources within the Jewish tradition to justify shying away from national affairs. Moreover, the Jewish historical experience might suggest the same, for Jews have been badly burned when governments have done anything but let them be.

The American experience, however, presents distinctly new realities, and Jewish tradition can be read to provide for the pluralism that one must adopt to participate openly in American public debate. This does not mean that Jewish views on any given subject will necessarily prevail in the discussion—or, on the contrary, that they will always be outvoted or ignored. Moreover, participation in American public debate does not necessarily entail that Jewish views will change through exposure to other approaches; Jews may change their minds about matters as they hear other opinions, but they just as surely may become ever more convinced of the wisdom of their own position. It does mean, though, that one must respect other people's views not only on humanitarian or pragmatic grounds, but for theological reasons as well. We Jews may believe that Judaism represents the best articulation of God's wishes for us, and we may live by that belief and even be prepared to die for it; but we must simultaneously recognize that no human being is omniscient, that human knowledge on every subject, including God's will, is limited, and that others may have insights from which we can learn.

Combining the American and Jewish sides of this reasoning leads me to bring the American and Jewish sides of my identity closer together. As one who grew up in the 1950s and 1960s, when Jews like me roundly applauded each new brick being added by the Supreme Court to the wall of separation between church and state, this represents somewhat of a change for me. My experience on the health care task force, however, and my experience with the Houghton Mifflin social studies project, together with the philosophical and theological musings recorded earlier, have convinced me that, although Americans should ever be on their guard to prevent undue entanglement of church and state, a healthy relationship between the two, as defined both by American and Jewish sources, demands open religious discussion of matters of national policy in the public arena. Only then can we be true to both the American dream and the Jewish quest for God.

NOTES

In the following notes, M. = Mishnah; T. = Tosefta; B. = Babylonian Talmud; J. = Jerusalem Talmud; M.T. = Maimonides's *Mishneh Torah*; S. A. = Karo's *Shulchan Arukh*.

1.   M. *Avot* 3:2; B. *Avodah Zarah* 4a; B. *Zevachim* 102a. One was even supposed to pray for the welfare for non-Jewish (as well as Jewish) kings: B. *Berakhot* 58a.

2.   M. *Avot* 1:10; 2:3.

3.   For a summary of the development of the relationship between church and state in the United States on issues regarding public schools and the role of Jewish organizations in establishing that relationship, see Skoff 1988. For a somewhat dated, but exhaustive presentation of the materials up to 1977 relevant to this issue in all of its forms, see Miller and Flowers 1977.

The major Supreme Court cases separating church and state include these: *Everson* v. *Board of Education* (1947), according to which "laws which aid one religion, aid all religions, or prefer one religion over another [are invalid]. . . . In the words of Jefferson, . . . [there is erected] 'a wall of separation between Church and State.'" *McCollum* v. *Board of Education* (1948) forbade "released time" for religious instruction within public schools during regular school hours, but *Zorach* v. *Clauson* (1952) upheld the constitutionality of released time off school grounds. *Engel* v. *Vitale* (1962) banned even nondenominational, "non-preferential" prayer in the public schools; and *Abington Township* v. *Schempp* (1963) banned Bible reading in public schools. In *Lemon* v. *Kurzman* (1971) the Supreme Court established a three-prong test for a statue to be constitutional under the Establishment Clause of the First Amendment: (1) it must have a secular legislative purpose; (2) its primary or principal effect must neither advance nor inhibit religion; and (3) it must not foster excessive governmental entanglement with religion. Numerous attempts to overturn these decisions through constitutional amendment have been made, including President Reagan's efforts in 1982, 1983, and 1984.

The other side of this issue is evident in the Equal Access Law, passed by Congress in 1984, which established the right of high school students to use school facilities for meetings after school hours regardless of the intended religious, political, or philosophical content of the topic of the meeting as long as the meeting was voluntary, student initiated, with no school sponsorship, and not during regular school hours. Moreover, *Braunfeld* v. *Brown* (1961) upheld the constitutionality of Sunday closing laws; and *Lynch* v. *Donnelly* (1984) validated the right of a municipality to allow the display of a nativity scene in a public park during December, even though the mayor of Pawtucket, Rhode Island,

specifically intended thereby "to put Christ back into Christmas." In
Wallace v. *Jaffree* (1985) the Supreme Court declared unconstitutional an
Alabama statute mandating a moment of silence at the beginning of the
school day for "meditation or prayer," but several justices indicated that
they would look favorably on a statute that designated such a moment
of silence only for meditation.

4. For a thorough treatment of this episode from the point of view
of Jewish sources, see Graff 1985.

5. Cohen 1971.

6. This is not by any means the only way to conceive of medicine,
and medical practices in other countries reflect very different conceptions
of the body and of the role of medicine; see Payer 1988.

7. Wikler 1983, p. 48.

8. Cited by Raab 1993, pp. 110–111.

9. Carter 1993. On p. 21, he says specifically, "I speak here not
simply of arguments for or against the adoption of any *government*
policy, although that will, of necessity, be part of my subject. My concern, more broadly, is with the question of what religiously devout
people should do when they confront state policies that require them to
act counter to what they believe is the will of God, or to acquiesce in
conduct by others that they believe God forbids." My chapter, in contrast, concentrates on the former issue—i.e., the shaping of government
policy in the first place.

10. I first developed these themes in Dorff 1982 and Dorff 1992.
What follows draws on some of the thought in those essays as it applies
to the specific issue of government service.

11. Wurzburger 1986, p. 11.

12. For a discussion of these various approaches, see Dorff 1992,
pp. 219–229.

13. Greenberg 1986, p. 23. See also p. 27, where he links pluralism
to the absence of violence in transforming another person's opinion.

14. Ibid., pp. 24, 26. The mishnah cited is M. *Sanhedrin* 4:5; the
blessing cited is in B. *Berakhot* 58a; and the midrash cited is in *Midrash
Tanchuma* on Numbers 24:16.

15. J. *Sanhedrin* 22a; *Midrash Tanchuma*, ed. Buber, Devarim, 1a;
Numbers Rabbah 19:6. These sources are reprinted in their original
Hebrew form and translated in Dorff 1977, pp. 87, 99.

16. Albo, Part 2, Chapter 30, in Albo 1946, vol. 2, p. 206.

17. *Leviticus Rabbah* 1:14.

18. *Exodus Rabbah* 29:1; see also 5:1; *Mekhilta*, "Yitro," chapter
9; *Pesiqta d'Rav Kahana*, "Bachodesh Hashlishi," end of chapter 12, on
Exodus 20:2 (Mandelbaum edition, vol. 1, p. 224); *Tanchuma*, "Shemot,"
#22 (Buber edition, p. 7b); "Yitro," #17 (Buber edition, p. 40b).

108   ELLIOT N. DORFF

19. *Sifra* to Leviticus 19:18. Ben Azzai instead cites, "This is the book of the generations of Adam . . . in the likeness of God He made him" (Genesis 5:1)—a principle that extends love beyond Jews ("your neighbor") and ties it directly to God, whose image should be appreciated in every person.

20. B. *Eruvin* 13b.

21. For the terms, *hard-* and *soft-perspectivism*, see Harvey 1966, pp. 205–230; cf. also McClendon and Smith 1975, pp. 6–8. It is interesting to note that even a medieval, hardline antirationalist like Halevi was open to considering the claims of other faiths and recognized that part of his inability to accept them stemmed from the fact that they were not *his* faiths, that he had not had personal experience of them; see his *Kuzari*, book 1, sections 5, 6, 25, 63–65, 80–91 (reprinted in Halevi 1960, pp. 31–32, 35, 37–38, 41–45).

22. The two non-perspectivists mentioned, A. J. Ayer and R. B. Braithwaite, share the view that religion does not make true or false assertions but rather motivates one emotionally; however, the former thinker sees this as a major limitation on religion, whereas the latter thinks that this description is both accurate and laudatory of religion's role in life; cf. Ayer 1936, pp. 114–120; Braithwaite 1955.

23. *Sifra* on Leviticus 19:18.

24. Micah 4:5. Compare Micah 4:1–3 with Isaiah 2:2–4.

25. See Dorff 1982, pp. 482–484; reprint, pp. 45–48.

26. The doctrine of the seven Noachide laws appears in T. *Avodah Zarah* 8:4 and B. *Sanhedrin* 56a–b; it is thoroughly discussed in Novak 1983. The doctrine that righteous non-Jews inherit a place in the world to come appears in the *Sifra* on Leviticus 19:18.

REFERENCES

Albo, J. 1946. *Sefer Ha-Ikkarim*, trans. Isaac Husik. Philadelphia: Jewish Publication Society of America.

Ayer, A. J. 1936. *Language, Truth, and Logic.* London: Dover.

Braithwaite, R. B. 1955. *An Empiricist's View of the Nature of Religious Belief* (The Eddington Memorial Lecture for 1955). Cambridge: Cambridge University Press. Reprinted in *Christian Ethics and Contemporary Philosophy*, ed. Ian T. Ramsey, pp. 53–73. New York: Macmillan, 1966.

Carter, S. L. 1993. *The Culture of Disbelief.* New York: Basic Books.

Cohen, H. 1971. "The German and the Jewish Ethos." In *Reason and Hope*, ed. E. Jospe, pp. 176–184. New York: W. W. Norton.

Dorff, E. N. 1977. *Conservative Judaism: Our Ancestors to Our Descendants.* New York: United Synagogue of America.

————. 1982. "The Covenant: How Jews Understand Themselves and Others." *Anglican Theological Review*, no. 64, 4: 481–501. Reprinted in revised form as "The Covenant as the Key: A Jewish Theology of Jewish-Christian Relations." In *Toward a Theological Encounter: Jewish Understandings of Christianity*, ed. Leon Klenicki, pp. 43–66. New York: Paulist Press, 1991.

————. 1992. "Pluralism." In *Frontiers of Jewish Thought*, ed. Steven T. Katz, pp. 213–234. Washington D.C.: B'nai Brith Books.

Graff, G. 1985. *Separation of Church and State: Dina de-Malkhuta Dina in Jewish Law, 1750–1848*. Birmingham: University of Alabama Press.

Greenberg, S. 1986. "Pluralism and Jewish Education." *Religious Education*, no. 81, 1: 19–28.

Halevi, Jehuda. 1960. *Kuzari*, trans. Isaak Heinemann. In *Three Jewish Philosophers: Philo, Saadya Gaon and Jehuda Halevi*. Philadelphia: Jewish Publication Society of America.

Harvey, V. A. 1966. *The Historian and the Believer*. New York: Macmillan.

McClendon, J. W., Jr., and James M. Smith. 1975. *Understanding Religious Convictions*. Notre Dame, Ind.: University of Notre Dame Press.

Miller, R. T., and Ronald B. Flowers. 1977. *Toward Benevolent Neutrality: Church, State, and the Supreme Court*. Waco, Texas: Baylor University Press.

Novak, D. 1983. *The Image of the Non-Jew in Judaism: An Historical and Constructive Study of the Noahide Laws*. New York: Edwin Mellen Press.

Payer, L. 1988. *Medicine and Culture*. New York: Henry Holt.

Raab, E. 1993. Untitled essay. In *American Jews and the Separationist Faith*, ed. David G. Dalin. Washington, D.C.: Ethics and Public Policy Center.

Skoff, J. 1988. "Religion in the Public Schools." *University Papers* 7.1. Los Angeles: University of Judaism.

Wikler, D. 1983. "Philosophical Perspectives on Access to Health Care: An Introduction." In *Securing Access to Health Care*, vol. 2. Washington, D.C.: U.S. Government Printing Office.

Wurzburger, W. 1986. In *A CAJE Symposium: Division, Pluralism, and Unity Among Jews*. New York: Conference for Alternatives in Jewish Education.

PART 2

Halakha and the Political Order

Underdetermination of Meaning by the Talmudic Text

Aryeh Botwinick

Most students of the Talmud would probably agree that no one overarching methodology is employed in talmudic argument, but that a plurality of methodologies are invoked on different occasions. The Rabbis themselves were intensely conscious of how talmudic arguments were made, as their concern with biblical hermeneutics attests. Different schools are identified with different approaches to the biblical text, for example, the opposition of those who interpret the text on the basis of *klal u'prat u'klal* (a general statement followed by a specification followed, in turn, by another general statement) and those who adopt the principle of *ribui u'miut u'ribui* (an extension followed by a limitation followed, in turn, by another extension).[1] However, one feature of talmudic argument is so pervasive that it escapes detection and explication by the Rabbis in the Talmud and is not sufficiently highlighted by subsequent commentators. What I have in mind is the underdetermination of meaning by text. This is a recurring feature of talmudic argument animating many of the specific insights into and justifications of talmudic argument offered by the Rabbis.

EXEMPLIFICATIONS OF UNDERDETERMINATION

In what follows, I would like to illustrate what the underdetermination of meaning by text signifies by citing and discussing

113

three concentrated texts, in *Gittin* 76a–b, *Nedarim* 87b–88a, and *Nedarim* 91a, and by analyzing the *shaqla v'tarya*, the give and take of argument, of the *sugya* of *breira* in *Yoma* 55a–56b.[2]

Example 1

> *Mishnah:* [If a man says,] this is your *get* [divorce] if I do not return within thirty days, and he was on the point of going from Judea to Galilee, if he got as far as Antipras [Antipatris, on the borders of Judea and Galilee] and then turned back, his condition is broken [*batel tenao*]. [If he says,] here is your *get* on condition that I do not return within thirty days, and he was on the point of going from Galilee to Judea, if he got as far as Kefar 'Uthnai [on the borders of Galilee and Judea] and then turned back, the condition is broken [*batel tenao*]. [If he said,] here is your *get* on condition that I do not return within thirty days, and he was on the point of going into foreign parts, if he got as far as Acco [Acre] and turned back his condition is broken [*batel tenao*].
>
> *Gemara:* Here is your *get* on condition that I do not return within thirty days [and he got as far as Acco]. This would imply that Acco is in foreign parts. But how can this be, seeing that R. Safra has said: When the Rabbis took leave of one another [i.e., those who came from abroad to study were escorted by those of Palestine as far as Acre], they did so in Acco, because it is forbidden for those who live in *Eretz Yisrael* to go out of it?—Abaye replied: He made two conditions with her, thus: If I reach foreign parts, this will be a *get* at once, and if I remain on the road and do not return within thirty days, it will be a *get*. If he got as far as Acco and returned, so that he neither reached foreign parts nor remained on the road thirty days, his condition is broken [*batel tenao*]. (*Gittin* 76a–b)

There is a systematic ambiguity surrounding the phrase *batel tenao*—"his condition is broken"—in the mishnah. It might mean either:

a. He (the husband) came within the purview of the *tenai* (the condition he had set for himself) and did not meet it—and therefore not only is the condition abrogated, but the *get* (the bill of divorce itself) is declared invalid; or

b. He (the husband) never came within the purview of the condition he had set for himself—and therefore *only* the condition is voided—but the *get* itself remains valid. It would be halak-hically permissible to (re)use the *get* (all other halakhic and factual considerations remaining constant).[3]

The natural way to interpret the third clause in the mishnah that forms the subject matter of Abaye's analysis is as parallel to the two clauses that precede it. Just as in the earlier clauses the terms of the *get* were transgressed—the husband had reached Antipras (the beginning of Galilee) but returned before the conclusion of thirty days; the husband had reached Kefar 'Uthnai (the beginning of Judea) but returned before the end of thirty days—so too in the third clause the most plausible reading would appear to be that the terms of the *get* had been violated—the husband had reached Acco (the beginning of *medinat hayam* or *chutz l'aretz*, foreign parts) but returned before the end of thirty days. Therefore, according to this reading, because the conditions stipulated for the *get* had been violated, not only are the conditions considered transgressed but the *gittin* in the respective cases are considered invalidated.

Abaye, however, on the basis of Rav Safra's identification of Acco as part of *Eretz Yisrael*, trades on the ambiguity implicit in the phrase—*his condition is broken*—in our mishnah and reinter-prets the mishnaic clause so that it is compatible with Rav Safra's assertion. His strategy for doing so consists in individuating the linguistic text in the mishnah so that it issues forth in two condi-tions, not one. In any event, the full content of the condition (its spatial as well as temporal limitations) in all three clauses of the mishnah is a matter of context and is not covered by the explicit stipulations contained in the mishnah. The spatial boundaries of the verbal formulation in each case are determined by where the husband was actually going and not by anything that he directly said. According to Abaye, if the spatial boundaries of the condition remain verbally imprecise and the context helps to determine their content, then we have a logical warrant for stipulating two inter-related conditions in the case at hand and not just one: If the hus-band reaches foreign parts, the document he gave his wife would become a *get* at once; if he remains on the road and does not return within thirty days, it also becomes a *get*. Abaye conjoins what Quine has called the *indeterminacy of radical translation*,[4] the attempt to paraphrase one piece or patch of language into another piece or patch of language, even within the same language, with the porousness and elasticity of context that the mishnah itself semiofficially acknowledges by the way that it is formulated, with a full "milking" of the ambiguity residing in the phrase *his condition is broken*. According to Abaye, what the husband does in the thirty days subsequent to his utterance of the (implicit) two-stage conditional *does not come within the purview of the conditions he has set*. The husband has neither gone to "foreign parts" nor does he stay away for more than thirty days. He has not violated the terms of the conditional. Therefore, the force of the mishnaic phrase—*his condition is broken*—is that not having transgressed the terms of the *get* (but merely not having come within their purview) the *get* itself is potentially reusable on a future occasion when his actions do come within the ambit of the conditions set.[5]

Example 2

Mishnah: [If the husband declares,] 'I know that there were vows, but did not know that they could be annulled,' he may annul them [now]. [But if he says:] 'I know that one can annul, but did not know that this was a vow,' R. Meir ruled: He cannot annul it, while the sages maintain: He can annul.

Gemara: But the following contradicts this: ["Or if he smite him with any stone, wherewith a man may die,] seeing him not [. . . then the congregation shall restore him to the city of his refuge" (Numbers 35:23f.)]: This excludes a blind man [who is not exiled to the refuge cities for manslaughter]; that is R. Judah's view. R. Meir said: It is to include a blind person! [According to Rashi, R. Meir's view is that partial knowledge is in itself not regarded as complete knowledge; hence, without a verse one would assume that a blind person is excluded. Consequently, 'seeing him not' cannot exclude the blind, since for that no verse is necessary, but must be translated, 'though not seeing him,' i.e., though unable to see him, and the verse extends the law to the blind. Thus this contradicts the mishnah, for there R. Meir rules that since he possessed the partial knowledge that a husband can annul vows, he is regarded as having possessed the complete knowledge, and therefore cannot annul after the day of hearing. Likewise R. Judah here is opposed to the sages in the mishnah, by whom R. Judah is meant, when they are in opposition to R. Meir.] . . . Raba answered: In each case [the ruling follows] from the context. R. Judah reasons: Concerning a murderer it is written, As when a man goes into a wood with his neighbor, etc. [Deuteronomy 19:5] implying whoever can go into a 'wood,' and a blind person too can enter a wood. Now, should you say that 'seeing him not' teaches the inclusion of the blind, that could be deduced from 'a wood.' Hence 'seeing him not' must exclude the blind. But R. Meir maintains: It is written [Whoever kills his neighbor] without knowing [Deuteronomy 19:4], [which implies] whoever that can know, whereas a blind person cannot know. Now, should you say that 'seeing him not' excludes the blind, that would follow from, 'without knowing.' Consequently, 'seeing him not' must teach the inclusion of the blind. [Thus their dispute does not center on the question whether partial knowledge is as full knowledge or not, and hence has no bearing on our mishnah.] (*Nedarim* 87b–88a)

Example 3

> *Gemara:* The scholars propounded: What if she declares to her husband, 'You have divorced me'? [Is she believed in spite of his denial, or may it be a ruse to gain her freedom?]—R. Hamnuna said: Come and hear: She who declares, 'I am defiled to you': Now even according to the later mishnah, which teaches that she is not believed, it is [only] there that she may lie, in the knowledge that her husband does not know [whether her statement is true]; but with respect to 'you have divorced me,' of [the truth of] which he must know, she is believed, for there is a presumption [that] no woman is brazen in the presence of her husband [i.e., she would not be brazen enough to tell such a lie in his presence, wherefore she is believed]. Raba said to him: On the contrary, even according to the first mishnah, that she is believed, it is [only] there, because she would not expose herself to shame [if she had not actually been ravished]; but here it may happen that she is stronger [in character] than her husband,[6] and so indeed be brazen. (*Nedarim* 91a)

The mishnah and gemara on 87b–88a[7] are a striking exemplification of the elasticity of presuppositions, of how the formulation of a statement does not hook up with just one presupposition or set of presuppositions but rather with multiple sets from which we cannot factor out the element of choice. The dispute between R. Meir and R. Judah in the mishnah on 87b can be explicated in terms of either the large substantive principle of partial knowledge being regarded as full knowledge or the more restricted hermeneutical issue of when a verse in the Torah is susceptible of the *drasha* (interpretive technique; hermeneutical principle) of both *ribui achar ribui* (amplification after amplification)—which signifies attendant limitation—and *miut achar miut* (restriction after restriction)—which signifies augmentation of possibilities—which *drasha* is supposed to prevail. The gemara thus deflates "presupposition" to the status of "implication," showing how the former has no greater stability than the latter.

The gemara on 91a, which serves as implicit commentary on the mishnah on 90b, is illustrative of the uncontrollable, elastic, and unbounded character of implications. A set of contradictory implications can be derived from the mishnah on 90b with regard to the case of a woman who declares to her husband that he had divorced her. One set of implications focuses on the implicit constraints of the husband-wife relationship and the other set focuses on the interplay between character and social setting in governing human behavior. Different combinations of implications give rise to contradictory outcomes, each of which receives its sanction from the literal language of the mishnah. The upshot of these two mini-*sugyot* from the tractate *Nedarim* is that both presuppositions and implications remain in a crucial sense underdetermined by text. What you can read out of a text is what you supply it with, both by way of presupposition and by way of implication.

Example 4

The gemara in *Yoma* begins by citing a mishnaic text (attributed in some versions at least to R. Judah) to the effect that no money chests were provided for obligatory bird offerings to prevent confusion (*mipnei hatarovot*). The mishnaic statement explains why no chests were established for obligatory bird offerings comparable to the chests established for voluntary bird offerings. The gemara then asks what *to prevent confusion* means in this case? R. Joseph answers that it indicates the possible confusion of an obligatory bird offering with a voluntary bird offering. Perhaps the chest containing the one will be taken for the other and the monies set aside for the obligatory sacrifices (*qorbanot chova*) will be sacrificed as voluntary offerings (*qorbanot nedava*) or vice versa and the sacrifices would then be invalidated. The obligatory bird offerings that, for example, a woman brought after childbirth consisted of one sin offering (*chatat*) and one burnt offering (*olah*) and the voluntary bird offerings were all sacrificed as burnt offerings (*olot*)—and the ritual for sacrifice of sin offerings (*chataot*) and burnt offerings (*olot*) was different. Abaye then says to R. Joseph: Let him designate two money chests and inscribe on each of them which is for voluntary offerings and which for obligatory offerings. The gemara then interjects that R. Judah does not subscribe to the principle of writing, that is, writing (labeling) is not a sufficient safeguard against a mistaken exchange of the two sets of monies because on occasion the kohen engrossed in performing the sacrifice will withdraw money without looking. In substantiation of this point the gemara cites the statement by R. Judah in the mishnah in *Yoma* 53b where he says that, with regard to the rituals attendant to the Yom Kippur sacrifices, "there was no more than one stand." The gemara draws the inference from this statement that two stands, one for the blood of the bullock and the other for the blood of the he-goat that needed to be sprinkled in a particular order, are rejected by R. Judah lest the kohen exchange the blood of the one for the blood of the other. Implicit in R. Judah's rejection of the "two stands" is his finding unacceptable their separate labeling, one for the blood of the bullock and the other for the blood of the he-goat. The warranted inference to be drawn from R. Judah's statement in our mishnah in *Yoma* is that he rejects the principle of writing (labeling).

The gemara raises an objection to this construal of R. Judah's position from a mishnah in *Sheqalim*: There were thirteen money chests in the Temple on which were inscribed: "new shekels," "old shekels," "bird offerings," "young birds for the burnt offering," "wood," "frankincense," "gold for the mercy seat," and on six of them: "voluntary offerings." The mishnah then goes on to define the first four categories. *New shekels* refers to those shekels that were not contributed in Adar when a general levy was placed on the Jewish population to provide a fixed sum from which the *qorbanot tzibur*—the communal offerings—would be brought during the subsequent year. Anyone who did not participate in the original collection could place the required amount afterward in the money chest in the Temple marked *new shekels*. *Old shekels* refers to offerings from someone who did not contribute his levy in the previous year and contributes it the following year, and the treasurers use this money to repair the walls of the city and its towers. *Bird offerings* refers to turtledoves; *young birds for the burnt offerings* refers to young pigeons. And these latter two are to be used for burnt offerings. These are the words of R. Judah. He is consistent here with his view noted earlier that all the monies in the chests utilized for bird offerings are to be used exclusively for burnt offerings. Now, however, we see from the language of the mishnah that states "on which were inscribed" (*"vehaya katuv aleihen"*) that what motivates R. Judah's opinion with regard to the monolithic use of bird offering funds cannot possibly be his rejection of the principle of writing (labeling).

This is the first manifestation in our *sugya* of the underdetermination of meaning by text. Initially, the gemara thought to make sense of R. Judah's requirement that bird offering funds be used exclusively for burnt offerings because he did not believe that writing (labeling) was a sufficient safeguard for the kohen to disburse the funds in the mandated way, that is, burnt offering funds for burnt offerings and sin offering funds for sin offerings. Now with the citation of the language of the mishnah in *Sheqalim* a decoupling is effected between the requirement of the monolithic disbursement of bird offering funds for burnt offerings and a rejection of the principle of writing (labeling). We are thus bereft of an appropriate conceptual background to make sense of R. Judah's dictum that bird offering monies are to be put to only one use.

The gemara responds by saying that when R. Dimi came from Israel to Babylonia he reported on the approach taken in the Israeli yeshivot to the effect that R. Judah is concerned about a sin offering whose owner had died after the animal was consecrated. The halakha in such a case is that the money contributed by the owner has to be thrown into the Dead Sea, that is, the money needs to be destroyed, because the death of the owner precludes atonement for his sin through the offering of the sacrifice. The kohen not being apprised of this and taking money indiscriminately from the chest marked sin offerings would thus disqualify all of the monies contained therein and all of the sacrifices brought on their basis. We now have a new gloss on the phrase *mipnei hatarovot*—"to prevent confusion"—cited at the beginning of our *sugya*. *Tarovot* does not mean a mixing up of the funds of sin offerings and burnt offerings because of the kohen's inattentiveness to the labels on the diverse money chests. It refers rather to the mixing together of the sin offering monies of those owners who remained alive at the time of sacrifice with the money of that owner who had already died.

The gemara then goes on to raise the question: Is this a valid anxiety? Have we not learned in a mishnah that if someone sends his sin offering from a faraway place (*mimedinat hayam*), it is sacrificed on the assumption that he is alive? (Barring a factual confirmation to the contrary, the *chazaqa*, the presumption, is that the previous status—the person was alive at the time he sent the sacrifice—continues into the present.) The gemara responds by saying that we are dealing with a case where we know for sure that the owner of a particular sin offering had died and that the kohen through his absorption in the multiple tasks associated with a sacrifice will sacrifice that sin offering along with the rest.

At this juncture the *sugya* introduces the notion of *breira*. The gemara asks why we do not simply separate out the four *zuzim* (the cost of a sin offering) and cast them into the sea, and the rest of the money in the chest would thereby be released for its regular use for sin offerings? This would be in accordance with the principle of *breira*, that a subsequent action (in this case, the throwing of *these* four *zuzim* into the sea) retrospectively determines the character and identity of a previous "action" (the sending of four *zuzim* to the Temple for a sin offering). The gemara responds by saying that R. Judah does not accept the principle of *breira*. In Rashi's gloss, R. Judah does not rely on *breira* to relax a prima facie halakhic prohibition. We know that one of the contributors to a money chest containing money for sin offerings has died, so that until his portion of the money is removed, the rest of the money is "contaminated" and is disbarred from being used for sin offerings.

The gemara then inquires how we know that R. Judah does not adhere to the principle of *breira*. It is perhaps from the following mishnah: If a man purchases wine from Cutheans (before the Rabbis had prohibited their wines due to idol worship) immediately before the Sabbath while it is getting dark—he needs the wine for kiddush on the Sabbath but the lateness of the hour and, according to Rashi, the absence of utensils, prevent him from removing the requisite heave offerings and tithes to render the wine permissible on the Sabbath—there is a difference of opinion between R. Meir, on the one hand, and R. Judah, R. Jose, and R.

Simeon, on the other. According to R. Meir, the purchaser can say
that the two *logs* that he shall give to the kohen as *terumah* (heave
offering) are now *terumah* within the total mixture; the ten *logs*
that he shall give as first tithe (to the levite) are now first tithe
within it; the nine *logs* that he shall drink in Jerusalem as second
tithe are now second tithe within it; and he redeems the second
tithe for money—because that can be done on the spot—and
drinks immediately. R. Meir apparently adheres to the principle of
breira so that what he drinks on the Sabbath is taken to be *chulin*
(nonsanctified), and what he eventually offers as his heave offering
and first tithe is taken to be *huvrar lemafrea*—retrospectively
determined that these particular *logs* would be offered under their
respective categories. R. Judah, R. Jose, and R. Simeon prohibit
him from engaging in this stratagem. We have thus apparently
found proof for the notion that R. Judah does not adhere to the
principle of *breira*.

The gemara's rejoinder to this is to say that perhaps the conceptual background to R. Judah's prohibition has nothing to do
with *breira* but is as formulated in the challenge that the opposing
team of rabbis posed to R. Meir: Do you not acknowledge that if
the bottle (containing the hundred *logs* of wine) burst (before he
actually had a chance to give the heave offering and first tithe to
the appropriate persons), he will have been found to have drunk
untithed wine retrospectively? And he answered them, "when it
bursts"—that is, this is a remote eventuality because he can take
precautions by hiring a guard to watch the wine.

The gemara's retort here severing R. Judah's prohibition of the
stratagem from the principle of *breira* is a classic instantiation of
the notion of the underdetermination of meaning by text. The
gemara is saying in its response that it is possible to impute to R.
Judah the principle of *breira*. Nonetheless, the prohibition would
still make sense because R. Judah takes account of the possibility
of the bottle bursting before he actually has a chance to give the
first tithe and heave offering to the appropriate persons. If that
were to happen, the principle of *breira* would have no realia, no
material object, upon which to devolve. So this circumstantial
factor, rather than the larger principle of *breira*, accounts for R.
Judah's prohibition.

The gemara then says that R. Judah's rejection of the principle
of *breira* is to be derived from a *b'raita*,[8] which Ayo taught. Ayo

stated that R. Judah said that a person is not allowed to stipulate concerning two entities (in this case, two persons) at the same time. Thus a person is not allowed to lay down two separate *eruvei techumin,*[9] one in an eastward direction and the other in a westward direction—with the understanding that two different scholars will be coming to lecture at two different locations on the Sabbath, and relying on the principle of *breira* to fix retroactively which *eruv techumin* was operative *erev shabbat bein h'shm'shot,* the twilight zone on Friday before the Sabbath has halakhically commenced. *Breira* would then enable him to invoke the legal fiction that only one *eruv techumin* had been operative before the Sabbath began. This would not be permitted because R. Judah does not adhere to the principle of *breira*. What is permitted according to R. Judah, says Ayo, is when only one scholar is coming to lecture on the Sabbath and it is not known whether he is coming to an eastward destination or a westward destination, then a person is allowed to place two *eruvei techumin* and say that he wants that *eruv techumin* to be efficacious for him that coincides with the direction in which the scholar actually comes.

The gemara now proceeds to call into question the central distinction which Ayo draws. The gemara asks if R. Judah truly rejects *breira*, then on what basis can a distinction be drawn between two scholars coming to speak or only one scholar coming whose direction is unknown? The principle of *breira* would seem to be operative either way. R. Yochanan answers that the distinction which Ayo draws in the teaching of R. Judah must therefore be predicated on a factual consideration. In the case where the stipulation concerns only one scholar, the scholar had already come *bein hashmashot,* before the Sabbath had halakhically commenced. There is therefore no relevant *lemafrea*—retrospective filling in the content of what went on—to require or justify invoking the category of *breira*. In the case of one scholar coming, the person placing the double *eruv techumin* (in the East and in the West) is effective because of the laws pertaining to how stipulations work—and has nothing to do with *breira*. According to R. Yochanan, if the scholar had already come to his proposed destination before the Sabbath had begun, even though the person stipulating did not know which direction that was while he was stipulating, then there is also no scope for *breira* to be operative. When a "future" fact has already occurred in the present, even though the person who is halakhically affected by it does not yet know it, the principle of *breira* is not applicable. If you transform the conceptual counters of *breira* from states of mind to states of affairs intersubjectively observable within the world, then you subvert and deconstruct the category of *breira*.

We thus see at work in the second instance cited by the gemara to prove that R. Judah does not hold the principle of *breira* a mechanism analogous to that present in the first example discussed above. Just as there the underdetermination of meaning by text leads the gemara to point to a factual set of considerations that lies in the background to R. Judah's prohibition of engaging in the proposed stratagem, so too here a comparable devolution takes place from principle to fact. A factual set of considerations is introduced by R. Yochanan (the scholar had already arrived at the time of *bein hashmashot*) to sever the conceptual link of the case of one scholar coming from the category of *breira*.[10]

From the perspective that I have been advancing in this chapter, *breira* itself can be seen as the halakhic category that on a metaphoric level encodes the idea of the underdetermination of meaning by text. However we choose to interpret—whichever conceptual category(ies) we designate as appropriate for pinning down the meaning and determining the reference of particular texts—*that is huvrar lemafrea*, the conceptual and categorical background to the text at hand. There is no accessible set of original meanings or referents to pierce through in our analysis of particular texts. What is is always determined (only) *lemafrea*, retrospectively. In the end we might say that *breira* on a submerged level is a self-referential category about the halakhic process itself and the roles of innovation and interpretation within that process.

PHILOSOPHICAL AND THEOLOGICAL IMPLICATIONS OF UNDERDETERMINATION

What larger issues and implications flow from the virtually omnipresent talmudic methodological principle of the underdetermination of meaning by text? I discuss seven.

1. One thing to notice about underdetermination is that it goes a long way toward helping to account for how innovation and

application to unanticipated circumstances take place within Jewish law. Decontextualizing previously received biblical and tannaitic and earlier amoraic texts enables one to reconstitute them with a conceptual background that makes them relevant to new circumstances.

2. Underdetermination also introduces an element of complexity into the project of giving a historically faithful rendition of Jewish law. A good part of what the talmudic sages were doing was precisely to subvert an historical approach to the biblical and tannaitic and earlier amoraic texts they were dealing with. They relate very often to those texts as if they are there to be endlessly played with and reconstituted. In the Talmud, there is an ineradicably aggadic element in even the most austerely halakhic discussions. The paradox thus emerges that if one wants to give a historically faithful account of talmudic discussion and legal analysis, one has to be able to integrate within it its resolutely antihistorical character.

3. A jarring theological issue also emerges out of the centrality I assign to the underdetermination of meaning by text in talmudic argument. This thesis after all points in the direction of skepticism, the absence of secure external supports for the interpretations we evolve. Once skepticism is unleashed with regard to the textual sources of Jewish tradition—the articulation of its canon of binding halakhic texts is inconceivable outside of a framework of skeptical reinterpretation—how can it be reliably and validly contained with regard to the behavioral patterns that those texts sanction and require? A serious tension emerges between the end of decontextualizing the Torah text and its later canonical halakhic offshoots and making them relevant in transformed contexts—temporally extending the normative reach of Torah in the broadest sense—*and* the skeptical strategies of underdetermination employed or invoked for the realization of that end. I am not just asking an inescapably existential question about myself—how can I believe and practice?—but a question that goes to the heart of the identity of the Rabbis and founders of Jewish tradition.

4. The underdetermination thesis explicates the priority assigned to speech over writing in talmudic discourse. It is only because

of *eit laasot laShem heifeiru toratekha*[11]—that reduction to writing is rendered permissible—and then, too, apparently with the proviso that the writing as far as possible resemble the highest form of speech; that is, that it be dialectical in character. Writing engenders an illusion of fixity and finality that the articulation of words continually belies. Only speech can be in good faith. Writing is always in bad faith. The fact of persecution and the potential loss of collective memory yield a set of extenuating circumstances permitting recourse to writing.[12] If the writing is dialectical in character, this, too, is a redeeming factor, because dialectical writing with its tentativeness and recursiveness incorporates the continually interrogatory aspects of speech.

5. From the perspective that I am introducing here, the contrast that is typically drawn between talmudic-legalistic and philosophical modes of argument, the former being practically oriented and the latter being theoretically designed, loses its force. The vast canon of talmudic-legalistic argument itself entails a monumental philosophical statement. Articulation constitutes simultaneously erasure, the effacing of possibilities that have just been put into words. What one says can always be decomposed and reconstituted along lines other than those in which one appears officially to be pointing. The formulation of sentences posits their silent others (in the form of presuppositions and implications) that can always be regrouped and rearranged to yield different configurations of meaning and different constellations of referents from what one is officially intending, and thereby making a mockery of the whole notion of the primacy of intention. One can argue that the concept of intention presupposes a specific hierarchical relation between presupposition, statement, and implication that is itself metaphysically up for grabs, systematically undecidable. The putting into words of one's intentions is as vulnerable to an infinite regress of interpretation (each sentence that specifies meaning must be interpreted in turn) as any other sort of statement that one might make. Talmudic argument from this perspective constitutes one of the most imposing rhetorical edifices ever erected in defense of the notion of the floating statement, the endlessness of the process of decontextualization and recontextualization.

6. The mitigated skepticism of the Rabbis evinced in their textual strategies cannot be safely contained within the boundaries they might have wished. Issues of reflexivity, of self-reference in a fairly loose, nontechnical sense, collapse formulations of limited skepticism into statements of extreme skepticism. Consider, for example, the epistemological theory distinguishing between primary and secondary qualities. This theory grounds what appear to be objective properties of an object such as colors, sounds, tastes, and smells in us. It marshals skeptical arguments in support of what it designates as the whole range of secondary qualities as a means of safeguarding a preserve of nonhumanly dependent properties such as extension, mass, charge, and the various field intensities,[13] which are realistically claimed to be situated in the world. Primary qualities describe the world as it is, independent of our constitution, whereas secondary qualities "depend on psychological factors."[14]

The categories of primary and secondary qualities have an external validational use as well as an internal explanatory one. Their internal explanatory use is that summarized in the previous paragraph. Their external validational use has to do with the choice of these two categories to capture a distinction between the given and the made in contrast to more holistic epistemological categories such as those found in traditional idealism, which emphasize the fashioned, constructed character of even the most basic units of what we take to be "out there" in the world.[15] The philosophical content of primary and secondary qualities buttresses these notions as descriptive categories but does not speak to or support their external role as validational categories. The drawing of the distinction between primary and secondary qualities, the carving-up of the epistemological map in such a way that this distinction results and has point, exceeds the warrant of the descriptive content introduced under either half of the distinction and is in this sense reflexively unsustainable. For every stage of philosophical reasoning there is always an external component that links up to the next higher level of philosophical argument and abstraction, and thereby defeats the attempt to derive the *drawing* of particular distinctions from the content introduced under either half of a distinction.[16] Because what I am saying would be true for every level of abstraction in a philosophical argument, there is a sense in which philosophical argument in any domain is not able to yield a full account of itself.

The excess of the made and the constructed over the assimilated and justified in any particular structure of philosophical argument that this analysis underscores raises the specter of extreme skepticism. The theoretical slack disclosed in our whole edifice of argument evokes the possibility that our individual judgments, even though internally supported by our reigning concepts, categories, and distinctions, remain unanchored from a more external, synoptic perspective. Internal sense might rest on external arbitrariness. *Coherence* might be a function of arresting the flow of argument to an internal, descriptive level and curtailing the attempts to ascend to more far-reaching, comprehensive levels. The dual functioning of concepts in a descriptive and validational sense eventuates in an uncontainable skepticism that unhinges the certainty of all of our philosophical judgments. Skepticism, however, is an unsustainable philosophical thesis. To be consistently skeptical requires one to be skeptical of skepticism itself, as well as of all competing and alternative philosophical theses. The presuppositions of the skeptic's argument are in tension with his or her explicit formulations. In formulating his argument, the extreme skeptic is presupposing that it is possible to doubt everything, whereas to render consistent the individual statements that go to compose the argument the skeptic is required to be skeptical of his or her own skepticism and thus to withdraw from the extreme position that he or she originally set out to formulate. Thus, skepticism ends up limiting itself to remain consistent with its own tenets. The need to reconcile presuppositions with explicit statements of argument is also evident in the structure of philosophical argument. Engaging in argument defeats the possibility of argument. We engage in argument to justify rationally our position(s), but given the simultaneously descriptive and validational use of the terms and concepts that we employ, the validational component always presupposes one level beyond the level we are actually on, and thus undermines the prospect of ever rationally justifying anything. Engaging in rational argument is the very instrumentality that ensures that rational argument will never suffice.

Given the pervasiveness and deep-rootedness of the dilemma highlighted in the case of the skeptic, it becomes apparent that what is at stake in the analysis is not just a matter of false dichotomizations and distortions of the appropriate alternatives of diverse arguments; it is rather a revised understanding of what is involved in thinking. The most parsimonious way to proceed is to acknowledge that paradox needs to be converted into platitude, with the gap between presupposition and explicit statement of argument closed by a receptivity to multivalued logics. The argument of the skeptic, as well as our notion of the structure of argument conceived as a whole, needs to be moved in the direction of a generalized agnosticism. This stance posits that our knowledge of objective reality remains incomplete and holds that a multivalued logic, one that maps the suspension of the law of excluded middle,[17] might encode reality more accurately than the traditional Aristotelian logic. Our alternatives are thereby increased beyond A and not-A, and we are able to circumvent the law of contradiction and refer to skepticism in all cases without either affirming or denying its predication upon not-skepticism. The skepticism undercutting structures of argument in all domains of thought would thus also be salvaged by the same strategy.

Analogously, in the case of the textual skepticism of the Rabbis, their rampant decontextualizing is suggestive of the absence of any firm correspondence between our verbal and textual formulations and reality. Overall, they appear to opt for a methodological nominalism that assigns centrality to our naming and categorizing capacities above any putatively given textual or other reality. Even if one were to embrace a less extreme reading of rabbinic methodological nominalism, so that somehow the reality of an external world is preserved while the stability of texts gets badly shattered, the mitigated skepticism that results would also devolve into a form of extreme skepticism. As I have already argued, issues of reflexivity become our probe highlighting the way(s) in which mitigated skeptical positions destabilize into extreme skepticism. The drawing of the distinction between textual skepticism and realism about the external world (as well as drawing the distinction between skepticism and realism more generally) exceeds the warrant of the epistemological content introduced by either half of the relevant distinction. The descriptive content of both sets of concepts is amply covered by what would ordinarily be subsumed under the rubrics "textual skepticism" and "realism." However, the validational content in question points us in the direction of an infinite regress as our argument ascends through higher and higher levels of abstraction and generality without coming to a satisfactory repose. The regress can be sealed off by acknowledging the ultimately humanly supplied character of at least the most primary concepts that we use to talk about our experiences of the world.[18] Nominalism in whatever guise, methodological or otherwise, is thus evocative of extreme skepticism and cannot be construed as a variety of mitigated skepticism.

Consider, for example, how the distinction between descriptive and validational uses of concepts works to unhinge Hilary Putnam's distinction between general names and proper names in his critique of Nelson Goodman's nominalism in *Ways of Worldmaking*.[19] Goodman poses a rhetorical challenge to his realist opponents: "Can you tell me something that we didn't make?" Putnam responds to this by saying that Goodman conflates general names with proper names. Although it is true, for example, that we conferred the name "Sirius" upon a particular star, we did not make the general name "star." That simply corresponds to something already existing in the world that the word "star" in some incomplete way refers to. The problem with Putnam's defense of realism against Goodman's nominalism is that the distinction between general name and proper name is not sustainable. The drawing of the distinction between general name and proper name is not itself derivable from the content introduced by either half of the distinction. The descriptive content of general names and proper names helps to confer internal sense upon these terms, but to get clear why the distinction is drawn along these lines, with the splits taking place at the precise fault lines at which they occur, we need to ascend to higher levels of generality. We need to contrast this way of demarcating between concepts with nominalist ways of distinguishing between concepts that are more likely to assimilate general names to proper names. At this higher level of generality, the issue of reflexivity recurs, with the terms in the operative contrast being able to account for themselves descriptively but not validationally, which requires ascent to a still higher level of generality, and so on indefinitely,[20] with the result that no validational exercise can be effectively completed, thereby calling attention to the ungrounded character of all of our concepts.

One possible way of construing the nominalism vs. realism debate is that it centers around the question of whether the moves from an internal, explanatory level to an external, validational level are inexorable or whether they can be blocked. The nominalist believes that they are inevitable and the realist believes that they can be blocked. For the realist, at some point in the chain of conceptual derivation there is correspondence between a concept and some feature of or element in the world. Because both the nominalist and the realist can adduce systematic patterns of argumentation to support their opposing positions—the realist by invoking the issue of correspondence and the nominalist by highlighting the claims of reflexivity— there appears to be no way that either approach can be rejected on the basis of a move (or moves) internal to the *other* system. In this negative, indirect way logical space is carved out for tendering nominalist rejoinders to realism.

A case in defense of nominalism as an ontological doctrine can be made by capitalizing upon the realist's inevitable concession that only through a verbal medium are we able to pinpoint what the nature of reality is and to have it serve as a direct constraint upon our theoretical formulations. Words can never have that immediate, overwhelming, univocal relationship to things, so as to effectively forestall the nominalist claims. The epistemologically limited claims of the realist presuppose a nominalist ontology. If even the realist concedes that we get to things only through words and the connotations and denotations of words need to be continually delimited and purged of ambiguity, then we truly do not have an external world that is not the function of a prior naming and describing process. The realist's insistence that there is an external world that independently constrains our theorizing cannot serve as a sufficient basis to ground the claims of realism, because of the indispensable role of language in capturing that reality with which our verbal formulations must be correlated. Getting to the world through language concedes to the nominalist all that he or she needs to make the ontological case that what there is depends in a crucial sense upon our denominating it. Even the epistemological realist must concede in certain key respects the truth of nominalism as an ontological claim to delineate appropriately *his or her* own position.

Words, of course, can be adequately translated, para- phrased, and clarified only through the medium of other words, which means that the whole process of naming is irredeemably circular, engendering an infinite regress that can never be noncircularly halted by invoking the objects of experience themselves. Material objects remain even from the realist's perspective Kantian 'things-in-themselves' that, paradoxically, can be more closely approximated only by the endlessly *distancing* mechanisms of language.

Stated more sharply, one can say that the realist is already behaving as nominalism decrees to espouse the realist position. To refer to physical objects, states of affairs, events, and so forth, in the world is already to be selecting out of the lin- guistically multiple categories available to us. Given the inde- pendent constraints exerted by language upon both small-scale and large-scale acts of theorizing, the realist must be behaving nominalistically to put forward the tenets of realism.

From the perspective of this analysis, nominalism also con- fronts an infinite regress. If there is no object to name outside of the distinguishing, qualifying, and differentiating resources of language, then *naming* is not the right name for the process either. An issue of reflexivity is attendant to formulations of nominalism, analogous to dilemmas of reflexivity present in formulations of realism. The realist presupposes the truth of nominalism in the inability to circumvent the centrality of language for identifying and delimiting objects. For the realist, realism cannot be about the location of antecedently existent objects. Analogously, for the nominalist nominalism cannot be about naming, if the location and identification of objects outside of a linguistic ambit gets endlessly deferred. Realism therefore must be construed as harboring key elements of nominalism, and nominalism needs to be understood in a gen- eralized agnostic way so that a connection with a firm and enduring "reality" remains endlessly staved off. Nominalism needs to be formulated in such a way that no permanent commitment follows from it concerning the objects of nominalist designation. In other words, nominalism needs to be construed in a generalized agnostic fashion creating space for multivalued logics to ward off the inconsistency that nominalism both does and does not refer to external objects. It refers to them to counterpose itself to realism, but under no circumstances does it certify to achieving an autonomous hook-up with them.

Issues of reflexivity are not alien to talmudic discourse. A locus classicus where they are manifested is in the dispute between Abaye and Raba in *Temurah* 4b. Abaye says concerning any act that the Torah prohibits that, if it were undertaken, it would be efficacious. If one were to think that it has no effect, how is one punished for a transgression? Raba, by contrast, says that such an act has no legal effect and the reason why it is punishable (with lashes) is because one has gone against a command of the Torah.

Taking my cue partially from R. Yaacov Yisroel Kanevsky (the Steipler Rav),[21] I believe that a plausible way to explicate the dispute between Abaye and Raba is the following: This is a metaphysicalized halakhic dispute that belongs to the same family of *machloqot* as *breira*.[22] Both Abaye and Raba in different ways are responding to the challenge of reflexivity. If the Torah prohibits certain classes of action, its delegitimation remains in some sense inconsistent if the prohibition is predicated upon a person's engagement in the very action. The prohibitions enumerated in the Torah presuppose the continued maintenance of those very possibilities of action that their formulation was designed to discredit and inhibit. The issue of consistency here is more metaphoric than real because we are dealing with a realm of "ought," what should be done, rather than a domain of "is," what is the case, so that logically speaking it would appear to be entirely acceptable for the normative injunction to presuppose a different ontology from the factual states of affairs to which it is addressed. Nevertheless, I believe that it is a metaphoric extension of a reflexive dilemma from an "is" domain to an "ought" realm that vexes both Abaye and Raba and to which they offer their contrasting resolutions.

Abaye resolves the dilemma of reflexivity by propounding an operationalized definition of a biblical prohibition.

According to Abaye, the prohibition just is the punishment, that is, what Jewish political and judicial authorities are prepared and able to do to enforce it. The motive behind this reformulation is the circumvention it affords in enabling us to identify the prohibition with the penalty, thereby releasing us from the reflexive tensions surrounding a nonconsequentialist construal of the prohibition. Raba, on the other hand, opts for a more logically resourceful strategy than Abaye, one reminiscent of the skepticism discussed in this chapter, that seeks to neutralize its paradoxes by invoking a multivalued logic. Raba (implicitly) points to a systematic ambiguity surrounding the biblical prohibition: X (the relevant halakhically designated person or class of persons) should not do it (the relevant halakhically designated action or class of actions). This formula can be variously inflected. It can be read "X should not *do* it" or "X should not do it." Abaye opts for the first, more conventional reading that places its emphasis on the action done, and that, as we have seen, encounters extensions of the dilemmas of reflexivity in individuating the action concerned.

Raba, by contrast, places the emphasis on the subject, "X should not do it." Every prohibition found in the Torah can be variously interpreted as subsisting in either the active or the passive voice: A person should not engage in a prohibited action or a prohibited action should not be done. If the active reading predominates with the emphasis falling on the person as doer rather than upon the action as done, then according to Raba we would be licensed in substituting a counterfactual conditional for the verbal component of the formula as long as we preserve the primacy of the subject. If the Torah had not in fact prohibited the particular action, then we would experience no logical scruples in attributing the action to the doer; so now, too, in our active paraphrase of the sentence, we can acknowledge simultaneously that the prohibited action has no efficacy and the subject is still culpable because of the tacit conjunction of the counterfactual conditional with the subject of the sentence.

7. It seems to me that the theological pedigree for talmudic argument is the tenets of monotheism. The utterance of the word *God*, as Maimonidean negative theology has classically emphasized, initiates a process of endless displacement that finds no

resting place anywhere. All we can ever do in terms of assigning a content and pinpointing a reference for the term *God* is to say ad infinitum that God is not to be construed in this way or that, and so forth, and that he is not to be found in a humanly cognizable sense here or there or elsewhere, and so on. Human utterance from a talmudic perspective mimics the evaporation of the God concept. Its stability, too, is to be identified with an endless process of deconstruction and reconstruction rather than with some positive content. The allegorizing of positive attributes of God gets translated in the Talmud into an implicit acknowledgment of the ultimately ungrounded character of our linguistic formulations. In this negative sense, God for the talmudic speakers and editors becomes the paradigm-case of the humanly sayable.

NOTES

I am grateful to Zev Harvey, Matthew Kramer, and David Riceman for their comments on earlier drafts of this paper.

1.   According to Rabbi Ishmael, *klal u'prat u'klal* forms one of the thirteen hermeneutical principles by which the Torah is expounded, and Rabbi Akiva, his constant controversialist throughout the Talmud, invokes the principles of *ribui u'miut u'ribui*. (Compare the two *sugyot* in the Babylonian Talmud of *Sanhedrin* 45b and *Sukkah* 50b and Rashi's commentaries thereon.) Rashi says in *Sanhedrin* that the principle of *klal u'prat* means that the *prat*, the particular, is *peirush haklal*. It restricts and delimits the generalization to what the particular enumerates. But the tannaim who follow the principle of *ribui u'miut* do not dislodge the generalization from its place. The generalization, however, must take off from the specification that follows and is not as wide in scope as the original formulation of the generalization itself might suggest. The upshot of these divergent hermeneutical approaches is that *klal u'prat* excludes far more than *ribui u'miut*. *Ribui u'miut* excludes what is at antipodes from the specification, allowing all else to be subsumed under the original generalization, whereas *klal u'prat* includes only what is specified after the generalization and excludes all else. The very undecidability of how to codify the rules of logical inference with regard to the text of the Torah is itself a manifestation of the underdetermination of meaning by text.

2.   The term *breira* will be explicated in the course of my exposition of the *sugya*.

3.   Saul Lieberman (1973, pp. 879–880) argues that, according to
the Tosefta's construal of the clauses in our mishnah, if the husband
returns before fulfilling the conditions he had set for the *get*, his very lack
of fulfillment of the terms (even if by way of not coming within their
purview—rather than by directly transgressing them) is sufficient to
invalidate both the *tenai* and the *get*. The Meiri (1967, p. 283) on *Gittin*
codifies the view that, in those circumstances where the husband's actions
at first do not come within the scope of the conditions he had set and on
a subsequent occasion they do, the woman becomes a *safeq megureshet*
(doubtfully divorced)—i.e., we impose upon her the stringencies of both
being single and being divorced. She is prohibited from marrying a kohen
(priest) as if the *get* were valid, and she requires another *get* to be able
to remarry (even her first husband). Apparently, according to the Meiri,
there is an implied condition that needs to be read out of the interstices
of the condition that was uttered, namely, that the substantive condi-
tion(s) needs to be fulfilled upon the first occasion after its utterance and
is not to be deferred. Because this temporal constraint is possibly implied
by the original utterance of the condition, the woman remains *safeq
megureshet*. Lieberman (p. 880, n. 52) cites a commentary called *Shaarei
Torat Eretz Yisrael* (p. 422) that interprets R. Yochanan's gloss on the
fourth clause in our mishnah in *Gittin* in conformity with the way that
I analyze Abaye in the text: *Batel Tenao* means that only the condition
remains unfulfilled (the husband's actions did not fall within its purview),
but that the *get* itself remains valid. Lieberman invokes a number of
forceful objections against the *Shaarei Torat Eretz Yisrael* to the effect
that the invalidation of the *tenai* in the mishnah must be extended to
include the invalidation of the *get*. My analysis in the text can be construed as an argument on the other side: an attempt to show how a
conceptual split can appropriately be effected between the condition and
the *get*. In any event, the point of underdetermination is not to endorse
particular readings of the text, but to account methodologically for the
turbulence of possibilities residing within it.

4.   Quine 1960, chapter 2; also see Quine 1969, chapter 2.

5.   Rashi in his commentary on our *sugya* appears to learn that
even according to Abaye the phrase *batel tenao* encompasses the invalidation of the *get*. Once the condition was not fulfilled in the husband's first
"attempted" implementation of it, even though the nonfulfillment consisted in the husband's not coming within its purview altogether, the *get*
itself automatically becomes invalidated. Apparently, according to Rashi,
the analytical distinction between not coming within the purview of a
condition and transgressing it is blurred on a practical level, because
nonactualization of a condition for whatever reason renders a *get* vulnerable to revocation.

There thus appears to be a *machloqet* (division of opinion) between Rashi and the Meiri cited in note 3. Rashi invalidates the *get* even where the husband's actions subsequent to his stipulation of the *tenai* do not fall within its purview, whereas the Meiri considers the woman under such circumstances to be *safeq megureshet* (doubtfully divorced). Apparently, what motivated the Meiri in imposing upon the woman the stringencies of a divorced state is the analytical distinction developed in the text between transgressing a condition and engaging in action that does not fall within its purview. In the latter case, it is as if the *get* did not come into play at all, so that it remains available for use on future occasions. When it is invoked subsequently, at least part of its efficacy remains in force.

6.   This is the way the Ran construes the *sugya*. Rashi learns it differently.

7.   Even though *Nedarim* is in many respects sui generis in the Babylonian Talmudic canon, the Jerusalem Talmudic influence is primarily manifested in the shortness of the *sugyot* presented and their often rampant disconnection from what precedes and what follows them, rather than in the substantive content of the arguments presented. Here, as in the examples cited in the text, the *sugyot* developed in *Nedarim* often constitute heightened versions of what is found in the remainder of the Babylonian Talmud.

8.   A *b'raita* is a tannaitic text that enjoys a lesser canonical status than a mishnah, those sets of tannaitic statements codified by R. Judah Hanasi.

9.   The word *eruv* signifies mixing-up, conjoining what was previously kept distinct. *Techum* means limit (in this case to walking), which the Rabbis fixed at 2,000 cubits in every direction from the town or location where one has his abode for the Sabbath. To extend these limits, the Rabbis allowed for purposes of performing a mitzvah (such as going to hear a scholar's lecture) the placing of two Sabbath meals at a point that is 2,000 cubits beyond the borders of one's original location, which accords one the mobility of traversing another 2,000 cubits in the direction in which the food has been placed. The second boundary is thus superadded to the first boundary and one has freedom of movement for a combined 4,000 cubits in the direction in which the food was placed.

10.   The *sugya* of *breira* in *Yoma* terminates in an anomalous way, because the point of the whole discussion in the gemara appears to be that R. Judah's position in the tannaitic texts cited is independent of the issue of *breira*. He can maintain the principle of *breira* and still adhere to the positions attributed to him in the tannaitic texts cited. Yet, at the conclusion of the discussion, the gemara draws the inference (at 56b), "and now that we say that according to R. Judah there is no *breira*,"

as if the gemara discounts the whole previous discussion, regarding it as a manifestation of dialectical playfulness having nothing to do with R. Judah's true opinion. This is analogous to the gemara's treatment of the *machloqet* between Abaye and Raba concerning the question of whether acts that the Torah forbids, if undertaken anyway, are efficacious or not, discussed in the conclusion of the chapter. See note 22.

11.   "It is time to work for the Lord; they have made void thy law" (Psalms 119:126). In the last mishnah in *Berakhot* (54a) the Rabbis extrapolate from this verse the general principle that in times of dire exigency the Rabbis are authorized to suspend specific halakhic requirements for the sake of keeping the Halakha itself alive as the organizing set of guidelines for the Jewish people. In times of emergency, the Rabbis as custodians of Jewish tradition are empowered to sacrifice the letter of Halakha for the sake of preserving its spirit and influence. The Rabbis' dichotomization of Torah into *Torah shebikhtav* (written Torah) and *Torah shebaal peh* (oral Torah) is suggestive of the need to keep large segments of the interpretive apparatus of Torah oral, which was transgressed by the Rabbis for the reasons alluded to in the text.

12.   Maimonides also in his Introduction to *The Guide of the Perplexed* concedes that, although his treatise is addressed to topics that the sages have concealed, he was entitled to innovate through an act of writing by the verse in Psalms cited previously, as rabbinically interpreted.

13.   Putnam 1992, p. 82.

14.   Williams 1978, p. 241; quoted in Putnam 1992, pp. 91–92.

15.   These strictures concerning the "fashioned, constructed character" of the world are violated by even the most sophisticated versions of idealism in their legitimating of an "unconstructed" subject, at least at the moment of perception. Relativization has its limits in the necessary positing of a nonrelativized, nonconstructed subject at the moment of perception. Thus serious issues of reflexivity haunt even those versions of idealism most obsessed with the evanescence of the subject. (I am indebted to Matthew Kramer for raising this issue in a letter of June 24, 1993).

16.   The distinction between "the differentiated" and "the undifferentiated" is formulated on such a general and comprehensive level that it would be pointless to invoke the critical canon of reflexivity in relation to it. In this sense the idea of drawing distinctions is a pervasive cultural norm that defines the limit of an extremely widespread cultural and critical vision. The activity of differentiating and the requirement of consistency are what I need to assume to give adequate scope to my critical apparatus centering on issues of reflexivity and "self-reference." The generalized agnosticism that underpins my critical apparatus highlights the posited, provisional character of the notions of "distinctions" and "consistency," and situates them in such a way as to render further

revision and eventual supersession possible. (The issue of "the distinction between the differentiated and the undifferentiated" is raised in Kramer's letter of June 24, 1993.)

17.   The denial of the law of excluded middle is not contradictory. It does not constitute a violation of the law of contradiction.

18.   In this context, I am using the term *world* heuristically—to enable me to make the point I want to make, rather than investing it with substantive content. A more systematic resolution of this inconsistency, teasing out some of the implications of a generalized agnosticism, is presented later in the chapter.

19.   Putnam 1992, pp. 114–115; Goodman 1978, especially chapter 1.

20.   At a higher level of generality the operative contrast might be between philosophical categories that individuate discrete objects in experience and those whose principles of individuation are blobs or agglomerations of sounds, colors, or other units of sensation.

21.   Kanevsky 1990, pp. 52–53. For a further discussion of the metaphysical and political ramifications of issues of reflexivity, see Botwinick 1993.

22.   The dispute between Abaye and Raba seems to be a true philosophical *machloqet*, concerning how to understand the nature of halakhic negation, the prohibition of certain courses of conduct, rather than one that issues forth in concrete differences in practical halakha. After a *sugya* that extends for two pages, R. Aha, the son of Raba, says to R. Ashi: "And now that you have given all these [various] answers, wherein do Abaye and Raba really differ?" (*Temurah* 6a). In case after case cited in the gemara, basing themselves upon rabbinic inferences derived from particular texts of the Torah, Abaye and Raba end up agreeing in one area of halakha after another as to what the practical outcomes should be. R. Aha is therefore questioning what the point of the *machloqet* is.

At first the gemara wants to say that they differ in the case of stipulated usury (*ribit qetzuzah*), whether it is legally recoverable or not. Further scrutiny of this area of halakha discloses, however, that stipulated usury is no different from all the other areas of halakha discussed previously in the *sugya*, where different halakhic positions can be grounded squarely in interpretation of biblical verses confined to the particular area in question and do not impinge upon the larger theoretical issues raised by Abaye and Raba.

The gemara repeats the question on 6b: "But then wherein do Abaye and Raba differ?" The gemara then invokes a different area of halakha, whether *shinui* is *qoneh* or not. Does transformation of the material stolen by a thief into a finished product (wood into vessel; wool into garment) enable one to acquire ownership, so that one has only to return the price of the material to the original owner, *or* does one not acquire ownership of the raw material, and therefore must restore the finished product? Previously, the gemara had subjected the issue of *shinui qoneh* to the same treatment of localization to Torah context that it had applied to all of the other areas of halakha invoked to try to clarify the application of the dispute between Abaye and Raba. The gemara does not introduce any argument to justify the expansion of horizons to encompass philosophical considerations in making sense of the dispute surrounding *shinui qoneh*. Raba is able to achieve a practical result that approximates to Abaye's philosophical position based exclusively upon an inference drawn from the wording contained in the local section of the Torah dealing with the laws of theft: That he shall restore [that which he took by robbery] (Leviticus 5:23)—the thief returns to the owner the value of the materials as they were at the time of the robbery (but not according to their value at present, after being changed and improved). The *sugya* thus ends irresolubly with no alternative worked out for illustrating the practical relevance of the dispute between Abaye and Raba.

REFERENCES

Botwinick, A. 1993. *Postmodernism and Democratic Theory.* Philadelphia: Temple University Press.
Goodman, N. 1978. *Ways of Worldmaking.* Indianapolis: Hackett Publishing Company.
Kanevsky, Y. Y. 1990. *Birkat Peretz.* Bnei-Brak.
Lieberman, S. 1973. *Tosefta Ki-Fshutah,* Part 8: Order Nashim. New York: The Jewish Theological Seminary of America.
Maimonides. 1963. *The Guide of the Perplexed,* 2 vols., trans. S. Pines. Chicago: University of Chicago Press.
Meiri, M. 1967. *Beth Habehira on the Talmudical Treatise Gittin,* ed. Kalman Schlesinger. Jerusalem.
Putnam, H. 1992. *Renewing Philosophy.* Cambridge, Mass.: Harvard University Press.
Quine, W. V. 1960. *Word and Object.* Cambridge, Mass.: M.I.T. Press.
———. 1969. *Ontological Relativity and Other Essays.* New York: Columbia University Press.
Williams, B. 1978. *Descartes: The Project of Pure Enquiry.* Harmondsworth, Middlesex: Penguin Books.

Nachmanides's Conception of Ta'amei Mitzvot and Its Maimonidean Background

Josef Stern

It has been common among scholars and lay readers to interpret Nachmanides primarily as a critic, even an opponent, of Maimonides.[1] For many readers, to paraphrase the *Guide*, the two Moses have no more in common than the name alone. There is, of course, some reality beneath this appearance. Despite the many references to Maimonides in his writings, the reader is usually left with the impression that Nachmanides cites the "Rav" primarily to disagree with him. However, a closer look reveals a more subtle, less polarized, relation between the two, as a number of more recent scholars have argued.[2] Nachmanides's stance toward his predecessor is also at times simply obscure. As we shall see, in some instances their disagreement appears to be largely the result of misunderstanding, and perhaps even deliberate misrepresentation, of Maimonides's actual words by Nachmanides. In other instances, Nachmanides coopts the Maimonidean approach and takes it one step further than Maimonides himself did, even while he presents his interpretation as if it were in opposition to Maimonides's. In some of these cases, Nachmanides's view remains within the broadly philosophical framework in which Maimonides wrote. In other contexts, Nachmanides's dissatisfaction with Maimonides's philosophical solution to the problem at hand prompts his turn to kabbalah or leads him to transform a philosophical concept into a kabbalistic one. But in none of these cases is Nachmanides's stance toward Maimonides simply one of opposition.

In this chapter, I shall examine one instance of this complicated relation between Maimonides and Nachmanides: their respective conceptions of the project of *ta'amei mitzvot*, the explanation of, or reasons for, the commandments of the Mosaic law. Maimonides and Nachmanides were arguably the two greatest medieval exponents of *ta'amei mitzvot*, and their disagreements over reasons for particular commandments are well known. However, despite these many differences in the contents of their reasons, the strong influence of Maimonides's method on Nachmanides's approach can be discerned at the deeper formal level. Nachmanides, as is well known, typically offers multiple reasons for individual commandments, just as he frequently offers multiple interpretations of specific verses and texts. In the latter case, as Elliot Wolfson has recently observed, Nachmanides's model of interpretation is "highly reminiscent" of Maimonides's theory of multi-leveled parabolic interpretation.[3] I shall argue that this resemblance runs very deep and, furthermore, that the Maimonidean conception of the multi-leveled interpretation of parables, which he himself extended to the explanation of commandments, also underlies Nachmanides's approach to *ta'amei mitzvot*.[4] First, I shall present Maimonides's own two-leveled account of external and internal reasons for the commandments, an explanation that emerges from his conception of a parable. Then, I shall show how Nachmanides adapts the same kind of schema for his account. Finally, I draw some implications from this account for Nachmanides's view of the obligatoriness of the commandments.

MAIMONIDES'S PARABOLIC EXPLANATION
OF THE LAW

The largest self-contained bloc of Maimonides's *Guide* explicitly devoted to a single topic is chapters 26–49 of the third part, which lay out a systematic explanation of the reasons for the Mosaic commandments. The general outline of this account is well known; for our purposes I would emphasize three themes. First, in opposition to the Ash'arites who claimed that all the commandments of any divine law are necessarily willed by the deity "without being intended toward any end at all" (*Guide* 3.26: 506 [trans. Pines])

and against the Mu'tazilites (including their Jewish followers, such
as Saadia) who claimed that this is true of only some divine laws,
Maimonides argues that every commandment must serve an excellent end if only because it was legislated by the paradigm rational
agent, the diety, who acts and commands only out of wisdom.
Furthermore, in his legislation of the commandments, Maimonides
argues that the deity acts, not for his own good or utility, but
always for a utility or good for humankind, for human happiness.

Second, Maimonides attempts to show how each commandment is a means toward one of two general aims of "the law as a
whole," both of which are directed at the "welfare" of the general
community. The first of these is what Maimonides calls the *welfare
of the body*, namely, the political and social well-being of the
general community and the moral improvement of its individual
members. The second, for which the first is itself a means, is the
welfare of the soul, by which Maimonides means the acquisition
by the members of the community-at-large of "correct opinions
corresponding to their respective capacity" (*Guide* 3.27: 510).
Maimonides goes on to distinguish these two kinds of communally
oriented "welfare" from two corresponding kinds of individual
"perfection," but he emphasizes that the law is specifically directed
at, and attuned to developing, the former rather than the latter.[5]
That is, the law is specifically addressed to the communal good, be
it intellectual or social-political, rather than individual perfection.

Third, and probably most distinctive, Maimonides makes extensive use of (allegedly) historical-anthropological information
about the pagan environment of ancient Israel to show how the
particulars of many commandments—related to the Temple, sacrifice, purity and impurity, agriculture, and dress—were legislated
to wean the people away from idolatry, either through counter-
practices or through accommodation, and toward worship of one
incorporeal deity. As I have argued elsewhere, this broad class of
commandments, whose reasons cannot be known apart from
historical knowledge of the circumstances of their legislation,
constitutes Maimonides's reconstruction of the class of laws distinguished by the Rabbis as *chuqqim*, commandments whose reasons
are not known (or, as some hold, are unknowable).[6] As qualified
by Maimonides, the reasons for these commandments are not
known *by the multitude*, those who lack such historical knowledge. Furthermore, Maimonides also holds that these *chuqqim* are

laws whose reasons are best left unrevealed to the multitude, because knowledge of those reasons might easily lead to antinomianism. Thus, given his historical, context-dependent explanation for their legislation, the objection will undoubtedly be raised: Why, in different historical circumstances (say, already in Maimonides's twelfth century Andalusia in which idolatry was no longer a live threat), should one nonetheless be obligated to perform these commandments? Lacking a good answer to this question, or at least a persuasive answer for the community-at-large, Maimonides suggests that the Rabbis thought it best not even to suggest that there exist these problematic reasons for the commandments.[7]

The impact of Maimonides's naturalized, Aristotelian conception of ta'amei mitzvot, and especially his interpretation of the chuqqim, was enormous. Among the Jewish philosophers, it provided the impetus for a continuing literature that carried on Maimonides's rationalist program of ta'amei mitzvot, while being at the same time largely critical of his more radical explanations.[8] Among the emerging kabbalists in Spain and Provence, Maimonides's naturalized account, which was ipso facto a devaluation of their older esoteric understanding of the commandments, precipitated both a vigorous polemical literature and a new genre of commentaries on the mystical significance of the commandments.[9] The influence, or effect, of Maimonides's analysis of the chuqqim on Nachmanides in particular deserves a chapter of its own.[10] For our present purposes, I would emphasize that the possible antinomian implications of his naturalized account of the reasons for the commandments and the questions these implications raise about the permissibility of engaging in inquiry into ta'amei mitzvot were not lost on Maimonides himself. At the conclusion of the Book of Commandments, commenting on negative commandment 365 (based on Deut. 17:16–17), Maimonides cites the well-known example of Solomon who, knowing the reason for his prohibition, was thereby led to disregard and ultimately transgress it, thinking that he could achieve its purpose or end without the specific Mosaic commandment as a means. "For this reason"—concerned that the vulgar multitude would surely be led to such 'enlightened antinomianism' if Solomon could not resist its temptation—Maimonides concludes: "the Exalted One has concealed (histir) the reasons [for the commandments]."[11] Of course, this danger did not in the least stop Maimonides from going ahead with his philosophical explanation of the commandments. But the danger was real and, as we shall see, it was not ignored by his contemporaries, including Nachmanides.

Although Maimonides's explanation of the commandments in *Guide* 3.26–49 is his longest, most explicit, and best known discussion of the subject, it is not his only account of *ta'amei mitzvot*. In chapters 51–2 of the third part he presents, in very succinct form, a second general account that is eclipsed, or concealed, by the prominence of the earlier account. According to this second account, the "actions prescribed by the law" (*Guide* 3.52: 630) or "the practices of the worship, such as reading the Torah, prayer, and the performance of the other *commandments*" (*Guide* 3.51: 622), "have only the end of training you to occupy yourself with [God's] commandments . . . rather than with matters pertaining to this world." In contrast to the first account, this explanation of the ends of the commandments is not based on the good or well-being of their agents, be it the welfare of their bodies or the welfare of their souls; both of these kinds of goods fall under what Maimonides categorizes here as "matters pertaining to this world." Rather, the sole end of the commandments on this second account is "training," or discipline, designed to detach the agent from anything pertaining to this world; that is, any needs or desires that would concern one as a creature composed of matter as well as form. This account of the commandments, Maimonides tells us, is not for everyone; it is directed to the individual who has already "attained perfection in the divine science," indeed the "rank of the prophets" (*Guide* 3.51: 620). It is only when this sort of person achieves this kind of detachment from the world, only when one disassociates oneself from the impulses of one's matter or body to the fullest extent possible, only when one empties one's thought of all concern with the material world—it is only then that one can reach the state of an acquired intellect, fully and solely engaged in contemplation of the deity, or divine science, the state of a fully actualized intellect totally absorbed in apprehension of intelligibles.

It is perhaps worth adding that the claim, according to this second account, that the commandments were legislated to "train" people to be "occupied" only with the deity and with nothing other than him is *not* to say that the commandments are simply the consequence of the divine will alone, the view of the Ash'arites.[12] For the kind of detachment and emptying that the commandments aim to achieve is not itself arbitrary or for no reason; it is a necessary condition for the person to achieve the perfection of an acquired intellect. However, according to this second account it is true that all the particular commandments have the *same* end or reason: detachment, emptying, occupying oneself only with that which is other than the world. Therefore "no cause will ever be found for the fact that one particular sacrifice consists in a lamb and another in a ram"; that is, no *differentiating* cause will be found for choosing one particular commandment rather than another; they "were all given merely for the sake of commanding something" (*Guide* 3.26: 508). The grain of truth in the kalam position is that there is no particular reason or end for each individual commandment, only one very general end that applies to all commandments and does not distinguish among them.

What, then, are the differences between these two accounts of *ta'amei mitzvot*? Both accounts are concerned with the *reasons of the legislator*—that is, the reasons or explanation why particular commandments, or the law as a whole, were legislated to Israel at the time of the Mosaic revelation—rather than with a reason for a *performer of the commandment*, a justifying reason, or more generally a *motive*, for a human agent at some particular time to perform that commandment, some end that would properly *motivate* one to do the act.[13] Both accounts also assume that the deity legislated the commandments for a reason, indeed an excellent reason. The main difference between the two accounts consists in the contents of their respective reasons. The reasons in the first account are anthropocentric, that is, oriented toward achieving human goods in this world. The reasons in the second account are theocentric, at least insofar as they are oriented toward denying everything other than the deity, everything material. Furthermore, the commandments according to the first account are attuned to achieving goods for the community as a whole; according to the second account, the commandments enable individuals, indeed a very select group of individuals, to achieve perfection.

How, then, should we characterize the relation between the two different accounts of *ta'amei mitzvot*? I propose that we understand it on the model of the different "levels" of meaning that Maimonides distinguishes in the interpretation of a parable. In the Introduction to the *Guide*, Maimonides tells us that one of the greatest sources of misunderstanding of prophetic texts, including the Torah, is the failure to recognize all of their meanings. In particular, the ordinary reader fails to realize that these texts contain parables "not explicitly identified there as such" (*Guide* 1, Introduction, p. 6). He fails to realize that these texts possess, in addition to their "vulgar" meaning—the meaning of their words, as the vulgar multitude (*Guide* 1, Introduction, p. 9) exclusively understands them—two other kinds or "levels" of meaning, what Maimonides calls *external* and *internal* meanings.[14] In contrast to the vulgar meaning of scriptural verses, which (at least sometimes) expresses beliefs that no reasonable person should hold (e.g., the corporeality of God or the belief that the highest perfection is moral rather than intellectual), both the external and internal parabolic meanings of the text express beliefs grounded in wisdom. The difference between the external and internal meanings of a parable is, as Maimonides explains in his interpretation of the rabbinic parable of "apples of gold in settings of silver," that the external meaning "contains wisdom that is useful in many respects, among which is the welfare of human societies," whereas its internal meaning "contains wisdom that is useful for beliefs concerned with the truth as it is" (*Guide* 1, Introduction, p. 12). That is, the external meaning of a parable communicates the beliefs necessary for the moral and political welfare of a community; its internal meaning communicates beliefs necessary for intellectual perfection, beliefs concerning physics and metaphysics.

This difference between the external and internal meanings of a parable is a function entirely of their *contents*. It is not a difference in respective intended audiences or in their literary forms of presentation, such as, whether the meaning is revealed or concealed, explicit or simply implied, intended for a select school or closed group or for the public at large. Of course, Maimonides also employs (as he states in the Introduction) various devices (deliberate contradictions, allusions, chapter headings, scrambling of passages, and the literary figure of the parable) to conceal the contents of some of his claims and interpretations. However, these means of concealment are *in addition to* his distinction between the external and internal meanings of parables, a distinction based on content. Rather than force Maimonides's hermeneutics into a dualistic schema like the exoteric/esoteric dichotomy, it would be more correct to view it as the product of a coordinate system with two axes, one for differences in content like the distinction between parabolic external and internal meaning, the other for differences in literary presentation that would differentiate concealed/secret and revealed/public information. Thus, not only its internal meaning but sometimes the external meaning of a parable, or parabolic passage, may be subject to literary concealment. The internal as well as external meanings of other parabolic passages may be openly, explicitly stated. Hence, the different possible combinations of these two interpretive axes allow for a much more subtle interplay of contents and forms of interpretation than can be achieved by the exoteric/esoteric dichotomy—which, to make matters worse, simply conflates differences of content with differences of form.

There is a second difference I should mention between the external/internal parabolic meaning distinction and the exoteric/esoteric distinction. The esoteric meaning of a text, in the received view, is typically presented as the "real" meaning of the text, the author's intended meaning, the meaning that expresses what the author himself believes. The exoteric meaning is the interpretation presented "merely" for public consumption, for the multitude or community-at-large, what must be said out of political, religious, or social necessity. The distinction I believe Maimonides draws between the external and internal meanings of a parable does not carry this contrast: both external and internal meanings are meanings expressed by or "contained" in the text. Both are intended by the author. The text, in other words, is genuinely polysemous, or systematically ambiguous. Both meanings express kinds of wisdom the author himself believes, intends to convey, and qua wisdom believes ought to be believed by his reader.

To be sure, apart from their external and internal parabolic meanings, texts also have their "vulgar" meaning, the meanings of their words. In some cases the vulgar meaning expresses the external or internal parabolic meaning; the words mean just what the text says, in whole or part. In other cases (say, where it describes God corporeally), it expresses neither kind of wisdom; instead it expresses harmful falsehoods that are the very opposite of wisdom, that the author does not believe and that he does not believe should be believed by any reasonable person, although it was absolutely necessary or unavoidable to use such language in its original context of utterance.[15] And in yet other cases, the "vulgar" meaning is innocuous: what it expresses is neither wisdom that ought to be believed nor falsehood that it is harmful to believe. At bottom, I would say that Maimonides is simply uninterested in such meaning, the meanings of words. He is concerned with what we ought to believe, and "belief is not the notion that is uttered but the notion that is represented in the soul" (*Guide* 1.50: 111). The vulgar meaning of the text aside, it is among the things that ought to be believed, and that the author intends to express, that Maimonides distinguishes the external and internal meanings of parables. Neither one of these to the exclusion of the other could be called the esoteric as opposed to exoteric meaning of the text.

Now, corresponding to this distinction between the external and internal meanings of a parable, Maimonides also distinguishes two analogous levels or kinds of *reasons* for the commandments. The first kind of reason is concerned with political or social wisdom; the second, with beliefs concerned with the truth, that is, physics or metaphysics.[16] With the commandments, however, Maimonides engages in this sort of parabolic interpretation, or explanation, with both microscopic and macroscopic units. At the microscopic level, he doubly explains certain individual commandments, or attributes to them two reasons, corresponding to the two parabolic levels of meaning. These particular commandments all appear to be concerned with the body; for example, the commandment to bury one's excrement (Deut. 23:14, see *Guide* 3.41 and 43), the commandment of circumcision (*Guide* 3.49), or the commandment to rest one's body, or refrain from work, on the Sabbath (*Guide* 2.31).[17] Maimonides's worry that the focus on the body will disengage the person from full, undivided concentration on the deity—who is separate from all matter—appears to be what motivates him to interpret these commandments as parables.

At the macroscopic level, Maimonides explains the totality of the law—"the practices of the worship, such as reading the Torah, prayer, and the performance of other commandments"—on the same two-leveled parabolic model. In 3.26-49 (or, in summary, in 3.27–28), the reasons given for the commandments of the law as a whole all serve the "welfare of human society," including the welfare both of the body and the soul, that is, political and social goods for the community and the inculcation of correct opinions by its members according to their respective capacities. Thus, the commandments explicitly cited as examples in the passage just quoted are said to "bring about useful opinions," that is, "beliefs concerning [God] as is necessary for everyone professing the law" (*Guide* 3.44: 574). These opinions and beliefs are not, to be sure, intellectually apprehended by everyone who is thereby led to profess them. And the way in which the commandments "bring about" these beliefs is not a way in which those who thereby hold them could be said to *know* them or to achieve intellectual perfection. Rather, the belief achieved in this way creates a community of a certain caliber that aims at the "welfare of the soul" as well as the "welfare of the body," the kind of community Maimonides says is created by a divine law.[18] Hence, in this first general explanation, the commandments serve to communicate "wisdom that is useful in many respects, among which is the welfare of human societies" (*Guide* 1, Introduction, p. 12). In short, this description is exactly how Maimonides characterizes the external meaning of a parable.

In 3.51–52, on the other hand, the reason given for the commandments—to train oneself to be occupied with [God's] commandments rather than with matters pertaining to this world—corresponds to the internal meaning of a parable. Here the substantive content of occupying oneself with the divine is primarily negative: one occupies oneself *with* God by detaching oneself *from* this world, from pursuit of material needs and desires. This, in turn, is a precondition for being an acquired intellect, an intellect engaged fully and exclusively in contemplation of truth within the limitations imposed by human capacities. Thus, the reason for the commandments on this second account is analogous to Maimonides's characterization of the internal meaning of a parable: "wisdom that is useful for beliefs concerned with the truth as it is" (ibid.). The commandments do not, strictly speaking, *contain* wisdom concerned with knowledge of physics and metaphysics. But their performance *enables* the individual to be engaged in such apprehension of truth in its highest form.

In sum, the general structure under which we might subsume Maimonides's two different explanations of the commandments, in 3.26–49 and in 3.51–52, seems to fit exactly the two-leveled structure of his idea of parabolic interpretation. As with the two meanings of parabolic texts, the commandments have both of these reasons and were legislated to achieve both of these different kinds of ends. At the external level, their reasons are oriented toward anthropocentric communal well-being; at the internal level, toward the theocentric (intellectual) perfection of individuals who are capable of such perfection.[19]

NACHMANIDES'S THEORY OF *TA'AMEI MITZVOT*

With the Maimonidean background in hand, I now turn to Nachmanides's conception of *ta'amei mitzvot*, which he lays out almost entirely in his commentary on Deut. 22:6 (*"Ki Yiqareh Qan Tzippur Lefanekha"*).[20] His choice of this verse, and the commandment of *shiluach ha-qen* as the locus for his most extensive discussion of this topic is determined entirely by its Maimonidean prehistory. Indeed Nachmanides opens his discussion by taking issue with Maimonides on two separate issues connected to this verse. Both of these disagreements are striking as much for what they omit as for what they say.

Nachmanides's first criticism of Maimonides is focused on the specific reason for the commandment of *shiluach ha-qen*, the commandment to send away the mother bird from the nest before taking her young. Nachmanides proposes two alternative explanations of his own. (1) The commandment is a means of moral education or character training: to instil in humans the trait of mercy rather than cruelty, even toward animals. (2) It inculcates belief in the doctrine of creation, by forbidding an act that, were one to perform it, could be construed "as if the [human agent] had destroyed a whole species," a consequence that, in turn, would contradict the account of creation in Genesis according to which species were created with "the power to reproduce: that they might exist in perpetuity [*a parte post*] so long as God wills the existence of the world."[21] By keeping the prohibition, the agent tacitly acknowledges this belief that it presupposes. Details aside, these two reasons are reminiscent of Maimonides's two aims for "the law as a whole . . . the welfare of the soul and the welfare of the body" (*Guide* 3.27: 510), the two aims that guide his first account of *ta'amei mitzvot* in 3.26–49. The only difference is that Nachmanides seems to interpret the Maimonidean dictum to mean that *each* commandment serves *both* of these ends.

Now, after stating these two reasons for *shiluach ha-qen*, Nachmanides contrasts them with Maimonides's explanation in *Guide* 3.48. Although Nachmanides correctly says that Maimonides's reason for this commandment is the same as his reason for the prohibition against slaughtering an animal "and its young on the same day" (Lev. 22:28), the specific reason for these two laws that Nachmanides attributes to Maimonides is incorrect. According to Nachmanides, Maimonides's reason for both is divine mercy for the parent animal or bird, whose love and concern for its young is based in the imagination (translated *koach ha-machashavah* in Al-Harizi's translation of the *Guide*, the text used by Nachmanides[22]) rather than intellect, and therefore, is no different from that of humans for their young.

However, this reason—mercy for the animal—is not Maimonides's true explanation for these commandments.[23] Most important, it explicitly contradicts his theory of providence according to which divine providence does not extend to the individuals of species other than the human.[24] Maimonides's actual view is the same as Nachmanides's: The commandment is meant to inculcate in *us* humans the appropriate moral character trait. Of course, to educate someone to act mercifully, one teaches the person to do so in circumstances that call for mercy. However, it does not follow that the legislator's reason for commanding *us* to be merciful in such circumstances as, say, that of *shiluach ha-qen* was *his* (or God's) mercy for the bird.

Nachmanides's misrepresentation, or misunderstanding, of Maimonides's reason in the *Guide* is complicated by an objection he raises against it. If the reason for *shiluach ha-qen* were mercy for the bird, as he alleges Maimonides holds, then all slaughter of animals for consumption as food ought to be prohibited. Now, as Nachmanides undoubtedly knew, this is an argument given by Maimonides himself in both his *Commentary on the Mishnah* and the *Mishneh Torah*. In the course of explaining the mishnaic decision to silence the one who says in his supplications, "May he who had mercy on the nest of the bird have mercy on us," Maimonides states, "these commandments are decrees of Scripture [*gezerat ha-katuv*] and [their reasons] are not mercy [for the creatures]; for if they were [legislated] because of mercy, [he] would not permit any slaughtering" (*Mishneh Torah*, "Laws of Prayer" 9.7). Therefore, Nachmanides's view on this question is in fact the true Maimonidean opinion, whereas his grounds for rejecting the position that he (mis)represents as Maimonides's is Maimonides's own argument in the *Mishneh Torah* for rejecting that very view.

This is not the only puzzling feature of Nachmanides's discussion. A second problem arises in the course of his own positive account of *taʿamei mitzvot* that, in turn, is built on a second criticism of Maimonides. Let me first describe the context for this second puzzle.

After discussing the specific reason for the commandment of *shiluach ha-qen*, Nachmanides cites two rabbinic passages quoted by Maimonides in the *Guide* that suggest that the commandments of the law were willed by God for no reason at all, a view that would evidently undermine all inquiry into *taʿamei mitzvot*. The first of these passages is quoted by Maimonides immediately following his own explanation of *shiluach ha-qen* in the *Guide*. He then adds that he should not be criticized for disagreeing with the rabbinic opinion, mentioned previously, according to which "We silence he who says: Thy mercy extends to young birds, and so on" (*Mishnah Berakhot* 5.3). "For this is one of the two opinions mentioned by us—I mean the opinion of those who think that there is no reason for the Law except only the will [of God]—but as for us, we follow only the second opinion."[25] Here Maimonides is referring back to his main discussion in the *Guide* 3.26, where, as we mentioned earlier, he rejects the Ashʿarite (as well as Muʿtazilite) view and argues that all commandments have reasons, the "second opinion" he mentions here.

The second passage cited by Nachmanides is the well-known midrash in *Bereshit Rabbah* quoted by Maimonides in *Guide* 3.26: 508. "What does it matter to the Holy One . . . that animals are slaughtered by cutting their neck in front or in the back? Say therefore that the commandments were only given in order to purify the people [*letzaref et ha-bri'ot*]. For it is said: The word of the Lord is purified [*tzerufah*]." It is, you will recall, in the wake of this midrash that Maimonides makes his (apparent) qualification that only the generalities of commandments and not their particulars have reasons, a qualification he claims is illustrated by the case of sacrifices—for which he then goes on to give his detailed historical reasons! However, as we mentioned earlier, these innovative explanations are Maimonides's most controversial *taʿamei mitzvot* and, because of their potential antinomian consequences (which he anticipates in his *Book of Commandments*), he may also have thought it best to conceal them. Nachmanides entirely omits this qualification in the Maimonidean position, as well as Maimonides's reinterpretation of the preceding midrash to suit his own theory of *ta'amei mitzvot*.[26] However, it is impossible not to read his citation of these problematic passages—loci classici for those who opposed inquiry into *ta'amei mitzvot* precisely because of its dangers—and his vigorous reaffirmation of Maimonides's view that every commandment has a reason as a reassertion of the legitimacy and indeed obligatoriness of inquiry into reasons for the commandments *even* in the face of its antinomian dangers.[27]

Furthermore, Nachmanides general conception of the project of *ta'amei mitzvot* follows Maimonides closely. For both, to say that every commandment has a reason (*ta'am*) is to say that none was *legislated* simply in virtue of divine will, *chefetz ha-boreh*, the kind of voluntaristic will that Maimonides associates with the kalam. For Nachmanides as for Maimonides, then, the project of *ta'amei mitzvot* is concerned with the reasons of the legislator, not reasons for the performer.[28] Following Maimonides's use of the term *gezerah* ("decree") in *Guide* 3.38: 550, Nachmanides also explains that it refers not to that which is arbitrary or without reason (as many thought) but to all commandments and especially to those whose good is not *immediately* recognizable to the *multitude*—for example, commandments whose purpose is moral discipline or character training, even when this is not readily apparent.[29] Also like Maimonides, Nachmanides emphasizes that each of these *ta'amim* is a "benefit (*to'elet*) and for the welfare of man (*tikun le'adam*)."[30] Indeed, because he does not make Maimonides's explicit qualification that only the generalities of commandments have reasons, and because he argues explicitly that the goods are only for humans—and not even for other nonhuman creations or creatures—Nachmanides seems to take the Maimonidean approach one step further than Maimonides himself did.[31]

At the same time, and perhaps to counterbalance his strong advocacy of the project, Nachmanides emphasizes the antiquity of the *ta'amei mitzvot*—that the reasons for the most obscure commandments were revealed to the ancient sages, Moses, Solomon, and R. Aqiba. Here he paints a much more conservative picture of the enterprise of *ta'amei mitzvot* than Maimonides, and one that would legislate against the innovative, naturalistic extremes of the *Guide*. In Nachmanides's conception, knowledge of the true reasons for the commandments must be by way of a tradition received from these earlier sages to whom they were divinely revealed.[32] As

he concludes, we do not know the reasons for certain commandments, not because they have no reasons or because of the nature
of the reasons, but because of only "blindness in our intellects"—
blindness that prevents the reasons from being revealed to us or
discovered through our autonomous intellects, as they were revealed to or known by the ancient sages of Israel.[33]

Now, having defended the legitimacy of inquiry into reasons
for the commandments while restricting the kinds of reasons one
might discover, Nachmanides next says that Maimonides misinter-
prets the passages quoted previously, which "he finds so difficult."
Maimonides took them to be saying that the commandments have
no reasons. Nachmanides wants to discredit this view entirely, so
much so that he is unwilling even to allow for a minority rabbinic
opinion supporting it. Instead, he argues, these passages advocate
the different claim that the goods, or utilities, because of which the
commandments were legislated *by* God are never goods or utilities
for God; they are goods only for their human agents. Notwithstanding the *peshat*, the literal, plain, or external meaning of
Scripture, God receives no benefit from the Temple candelabrum
as if he "needed" (*sheyitztareikh*) its light, nor does he "need" the
sacrifices for food or the incense for its fragrance.[34] Even the many
commandments that serve to commemorate God's miraculous acts
are not of value for or benefit to him; rather they enable "us to
know the truth and to be worthy of it." And the meaning of the
Bereshit Rabbah statement that the commandments "purify" us is
not, as Maimonides suggests, that they discipline people simply to
obey the divine will; instead it means that the commandments
cleanse humanity of ill traits and evil beliefs as one purifies a crude
metal of its impurities. Here, then, Nachmanides appears to take
a very strong line—more so than Maimonides—on the anthropocentric, even antitheocentric, character of the commandments.

It may not be entirely clear why Nachmanides argues this point
at such great length nor whom he is arguing against. However,
what is strangest about Nachmanides's vigorous refutation of this
view is that he does not even allude to the fact that he himself
elsewhere endorses a position at least superficially like it. In his
commentary on Exodus 29:46, following a hint by Abraham Ibn
Ezra, Nachmanides refers to the "great secret" (*sod gadol*) that
hashechinah beyisrael tzorekh gevoha velo tzorekh hedyot, that
the Shechinah—by which he seems to mean all aspects of divine

worship, and specifically the commandments, which cause the divine presence to dwell within Israel—satisfy "higher [i.e., divine] needs" (*tzorekh gevoha*) and not, as the literal meaning of Scripture (*peshat hadavar*) suggests, "ordinary [i.e., profane or human] needs" (*tzorekh hedyot*). The idea to which Nachmanides is referring here is a motif that becomes central to later kabbalistic theories of *ta'amei mitzvot*: that the human performance of the commandments serves to satisfy, complete, or perfect the deity or divine nature. As Moses de Leon describes this process of *hit'orerut* (arousal, awakening), "the event above [in the sefirotic realm] is 'stirred up' or 'aroused' by the event below."[35] That is, the commandments in this view are essentially theurgic in function. They were legislated to "satisfy" divine "needs," divine needs that can be fulfilled only by humans performing the commandments.

This theurgic explanation of the commandments is, of course, entirely foreign to the philosophical tradition and especially to Maimonides. However, what is more significant is that we now face in Nachmanides's writings, as in the *Guide*, two contrasting accounts of the reasons for the commandments, one highly anthropocentric, the other radically theocentric. According to the first account, which Nachmanides advances in his commentary on Deut. 22:6, the commandments were legislated to serve human needs and ends, explicitly not divine needs and purposes. According to the second account, hinted at in the commentary on Exodus 29:46, they do just the opposite: The commandments fulfill divine rather than human needs. What, then, is the relation between these two mutually incompatible explanations?

To resolve this contradiction in Nachmanides's writing, I wish to propose that the relation between his two almost diametrically opposed accounts of the reasons for the commandments—the one oriented toward human needs and ends, the other toward divine needs—is modelled by Nachmanides after Maimonides's idea of parabolic interpretation in general and, more specifically, after his 'parabolic'—that is, two-leveled—explanation of commandments. Although their accounts differ on the specific reasons they give for commandments, especially at the internal level, they both hold that the commandments should be explained on the two-leveled model of parables, that they have both internal and external reasons (in addition to their literal, or vulgar, meaning, the meanings of their words). Nachmanides's account of *ta'amei mitzvot* in Deut. 22:6

provides the external reasons for the commandments according to which they communicate or serve the ends of their human performers, social, moral, and intellectual. The account hinted at in his commentary on Exodus 29:46 provides the internal reason for the commandments—a theocentric account concerned with the truth or "according to the way of truth," as Nachmanides standardly refers to his kabbalistic traditions.

Nachmanides's general adoption, or adaptation, of the Maimonidean parabolic model of interpretation can be seen most clearly in the Introduction to his "Sermon on the Words of Kohelet." There he introduces his hermeneutical theory with Proverbs 1:6, the same verse with which Maimonides opens his discussion of the multiple levels of meaning of parables in the Introduction to the *Guide*:

> And it is said: He instructed the people [Eccl. 12:9]. For the parable (*mashal*) that Solomon spoke [served] to symbolize (*lermoz*) good character traits concerning one's behavior in this world and to symbolize the matter of the World to Come. And it symbolizes the higher [or divine] wisdoms [or sciences], concerning the [Account of the] Chariot, and the secrets (*sitrei*) of the Torah. Therefore he cautioned them to understand his words, and it is said: To understand a parable (*mashal*) and a figure (*melitzah*); the words of the wise and their riddles (*chidatam*). That is to say, they will understand the parable (*mashal*) and they will understand the figure (*melitzah*) that is the literal sense (*peshat*). And they will understand that which is wisdom (*chakhmah*) and riddle (*chidah*), that is to say, the secret (*sod*) that is forbidden to explain. And this is as the matter of the Chapter, "A capable wife who can find" [Prov. 31:10]. For the figure (*melitzah*), which according to its literal meaning (*peshuto*) is true, teaches knowledge concerning the good diligent wife, who acts with good ethics in her work and with her husband and all the members of her household and with the poor. And [the chapter] symbolizes (*termoz*) the act [or performance] of the Torah (*maaseih Torah*) with her husband, the teacher who engages in it [i.e., the Torah] for its own sake (*leshmah*) and with her sons the students and with the poor, i.e., the multitude (*hamon*). And it symbolizes the attribute called 'Atarah and to her actions in the governance of the world . . .[36]

Like Maimonides, Nachmanides here distinguishes three levels of meaning in the interpretation of a parable (*mashal*): (1) the *melitzah* (the external figure of speech), which he identifies with its *peshat*, its literal, plain sense—in the example of Prov. 31:10, the meaning according to which "the capable wife" signifies the knowledge of the diligent wife; (2) *chakhmah*, a kind of practical or moral wisdom, in this example, the wisdom concerned with performance of the Torah and its teaching; and (3) *chidah* (riddle), which he identifies with the *sod*, the kabbalistic significance of the verse—here the meaning that signifies the attribute '*Atarah*—which must be concealed and cannot be publicly revealed.[37] The first meaning of the verse—the *melitzah* or when it is taken simply as a *melitzah*—corresponds to Maimonides's vulgar (nonparabolic external) meaning of the passage, its interpretation according to the meanings of its words as they are understood by the vulgar or ordinary reader for whom such passages are not even taken to be parables but literally true narratives. This kind of meaning Nachmanides also labels *peshat*, adopting traditional terminology. The second and third of Nachmanides's meanings—the *chakhmah* and *chidah* contained in the verse—correspond respectively to Maimonides's two levels of external and internal meaning for the passage when it is recognized as a parable. *Chakhmah*, like Maimonides's external (parabolic) meaning, communicates wisdom concerning the welfare of the community, the kind of wisdom associated with the teaching of the law, or Torah, both practical and intellectual.[38] *Chidah*, or *sod*, like Maimonides's internal meaning, is concerned with metaphysics or divine science, be it philosophic or theosophic.

Of course, Maimonides and Nachmanides respectively assign different contents to the corresponding levels of meaning. Where, for example, Nachmanides takes the innermost meaning, the *chidah* or *sod*, of the phrase *capable wife* of Prov. 31:10 to be referring to the divine attribute '*Atarah*, Maimonides interprets it as referring in its internal meaning to matter (*Guide* 3.8: 433). However, what I wish to emphasize is, first, the common triadic *structures* of their two interpretive models: multilevel writing with two kinds of parabolic meanings in addition to a nonparabolic external or literal meaning, the meaning of the words used. Second, both see the parabolic model of multileveled interpretation extending from texts to commandments. Indeed Nachmanides continues the passage just quoted by explicitly applying his interpretive model to the commandments, which he says have both a literal meaning and an interpretation (*kepeshatah ukemidrashah*).[39] Third, for both thinkers the difference between the two parabolic reasons for the commandments is that one (the external meaning/reason) explains them in terms of human-oriented ends whereas the other (the internal meaning/reason) makes them instruments directed exclusively at the deity, either exercises designed to detach the person from everything other than God in order to worship him as a pure intellect or theurgic acts that affect him through concentration on his attributes.

There is, however, one significant difference between Maimonides's and Nachmanides's respective views about the 'structure' of explanation of the commandments. As we saw in the first section, Maimonides takes both the external and internal *parabolic* meanings/reasons to be ones that the author/legislator intended. Both can be said to be expressed as the meaning of the text/commandment. However, the same cannot be said for the external *non-*parabolic meaning, the vulgar meaning of the text. Although this is the (literal, historical, philological, narrative) meaning of the *words* used—the *peshat*, if you will—Maimonides does not believe that this meaning must express the author's intention or opinion or what he wishes his reader to believe. It does not follow, in other words, that the *peshat* is in any way meant by the text or its author. In some passages (for example, those presenting corporeal descriptions of God) the vulgar meaning, to the contrary, expresses what the author definitely does *not* intend for his audience to believe (although there is, of course, a story why this language was nonetheless adopted). And even when the vulgar meaning is not wrong or corrupt, Maimonides is simply uninterested in this level or kind of meaning; what he "aims at" and "investigates" is "what we should believe" and not "what we should say" (Maimonides, *Guide* 1.50: 111).

Nachmanides, on the other hand, *is* deeply interested in the literal meaning of the nonparabolic external utterance, its meaning as a *melitzah* or its *peshat*. Like Maimonides, he takes the interpretations of verses that constitute their *chakhmah* and *chidah/sod*—the practical and theoretical, or theosophical, truths they convey—as genuine meanings of the verses, as authorially intended meanings. But for Nachmanides, unlike Maimonides, these interpretations are always *in addition to* the literal meanings of their words, their *peshat*. All of these meanings—*melitzah/peshat* as well as *chakhmah* and *chidah*—are "borne by the words of the text" (*yisbol hakatuv et hakol*), and "included in its language" (*kulam belashon hakatuv nikhlalim*).[40] Similarly, for the corresponding kinds of reasons for commandments. Thus, although Nachmanides emphasizes the multiple parabolic meanings of the text, or multiple parabolic reasons of the commandments, in no way in his view does this displace, dislodge, or demote the place of *peshat*, the meanings of the words. In some cases, the *peshat* parallels the *chakhmah* or *chidah*, in other cases they may even be identified.[41] In either case, the two parabolic levels of meaning tend to enrich Nachmanides's notion of *peshat*. As he emphasizes in his notes on Maimonides's *Book of Commandments*, even in purely legal contexts the biblical text never loses its literal sense—*'ain miqra yotzei midei peshuto*—in the presence of a rabbinic derived interpretation. Rather "the scriptural text has its [nonliteral] interpretation (*midrash*) together with its *peshat*; it does not exclude either of them; but the text bears (*yisbol*) all of them and both of them are true."[42]

Nachmanides's restoration of cognitive value to *peshat* in the aftermath of its Maimonidean devaluation is, I would suggest, one of his most important and original contributions to medieval scriptural exegesis. Indeed many of the sharpest differences between Maimonides and Nachmanides in their approaches both to *parshanut* and to *ta'amei mitzvot* derive not from the philosophical vs. kabbalistic divide at the level of their respective internal meanings and reasons but from their opposing attitudes toward *peshat*.[43] For Maimonides, the *peshat*, or vulgar external meaning of Scripture, adds up to "many layers of rind" that have so obscured the "great roots of knowledge" that lie at the "core" of the Torah that people have "thought that beneath them there was no core whatever" (Maimonides, *Guide* 1.71: 176). For Nachmanides, in contrast, "all the [rabbinic] interpretations are included in the language of the text . . . because the Book of the Law of God is complete (*sefer Torat ha-Shem temimah*), it has no letter that is either excessive or lacking, everything in it was written in wisdom."[44]

The value and exegetical importance Nachmanides places on *peshat* in general may also help to solve one of the puzzling characteristics, mentioned earlier, in Nachmanides's commentary on Deut. 22:6: why he goes to such great lengths to show that the utility or benefits of commandments are never for God. The key word in his discussion is, I would suggest, *peshat*: God does not need the light of the Temple candelabrum or the food of the sacrifices and the fragrance of the incense, Nachmanides argues, "even though it would so appear from the literal meaning of the verses" (*kanereh mepeshutaihem*). As we have seen, Nachmanides does hold that the commandments, according to their parabolic internal meaning, "satisfy divine needs." But what he is intent on showing is that, despite the theurgic function of the commandments and despite the generally authoritative status of *peshat*, the way in which the commandments act on the deity is *not* according to the literal meaning of the text; that is, that the candelabrum fulfills a divine need for light, the sacrifices a divine need for nourishment, and so on.[45] In this exception to his rule, *peshat* is not a good guide toward discovering or understanding the theosophical significance of the commandments.

Finally, I would like to conclude with some brief comments on two aspects of Nachmanides's view of the obligatoriness of the commandments on which his multileveled parabolic conception of *ta'amei mitzvot* may throw some light.

A frequently recognized problem for naturalistic explanations of the commandments like Maimonides's and Nachmanides's—a problem that may also motivate one kind of philosophical antinomianism—is that they render the commandments at most reasonable but do not justify their obligatoriness. Even if they show that the commandments are sufficient to achieve certain ends, rarely if ever do they show that the particular commandments are necessary for those ends. In light of this problem, it is significant that Nachmanides locates the ground for the obligatoriness of the commandments at their internal, theocentric level of explanation rather than at the level of their external, naturalistic reasons. Thus, at the end of his commentary on Lev. 19:2, Nachmanides writes: "You should not serve God in order to receive a reward (*al menat leqabel peras*) because his simple will (*retzono hapashut*) is [the] proper [reason to serve him] and is what obligates [us to serve him] (*hu hara'u'i vehamechayeiv*)."[46] Now, Nachmanides's notion of divine will is not the kalam notion of an arbitrary, or absolutely unconstrained, voluntaristic divine will that legislates for no reason or utility. However, as with his internal reason for the commandments—*tzorekh gevoha*—this account makes their obligatoriness not only theocentric but dependent on a deity with quasi-personal characteristics: an active (though incomposite) will as well as passive needs that are satisfied by human acts. However reasonable it would be to perform the commandments because of the human goods for which they are means, it is only this divine will, manifest in the Mosaic legislation at Sinai, that renders the commandments obligatory. In his parabolic model, that is to say, the necessity of the law is a function of its internal rather than external significance.[47]

A second Nachmanidean doctrine may also be related to this idea of the theocentric grounds for the obligatoriness of the commandments. This is the opinion, apparently unique to Nachmanides, that *all* commandments—even those that are "obligations of the body" (*chovot ha-guf*) such as wearing phylacteries and fixing the *mezuzah* as opposed to "obligations of the land" (*chovot ha-qarqa*)—are to be *principally* performed only by those who dwell in the land of Israel (*ki iqar kal ha-mitzvot leyoshvim be-aretz ha-shem*). This is, to be sure, not a halakhically normative claim. Outside the land of Israel, Nachmanides continues, these laws must still be observed with the same strictness so that they will not be "novel to us" (*chadashim aleinu*) when we return to the land.[48] However, their performance in the diaspora is, in some sense, only to keep us in practice for their true observance, which is only in the land of Israel. Now, as long as we focus on the anthropocentric reasons for the commandments at their parabolic external level of explanation—the human goods for which they are means—it is difficult to see why we should differentiate between the land of Israel and other lands in evaluating the nature and domain of our obligation to perform the commandments. It is only when we turn to their parabolic internal explanation, their theocentric reason, that Nachmanides's distinction begins to make sense. The land of Israel, he argues, is under the direct, immediate governance of the deity, a governance not mediated by other celestial powers who have been "assigned" to the other lands and peoples and through whom, and only through whom, these others are governed. Hence, if the grounds for the obligatoriness of the commandments derive from their theurgic function as acts that satisfy *tzorekh gevoha*, the needs of the deity, then their principal, or primary, performance may only be in contexts like the land of Israel, which is directly governed by the deity whose needs they satisfy. Outside the land of Israel, they still serve as means to achieve the human goods that serve as their parabolic external reasons, their *chakhmah*, but their performance is only derivative from—at most training or practice for—their internal theurgic purpose. Only within the land of Israel do the commandments fulfill both their parabolic *taʿamei mitzvot*, their internal as well as external reasons. Hence, only within the land of Israel do the commandments achieve their principal (*iqar*) performance.[49]

NOTES

1. See, e.g., Baer 1966, vol. 1, p. 245. For this image in the context of *taʿamei mitzvot*, see Matt 1986, pp. 376, 379–382; Henoch 1978, pp. vii–xxiv, 65–69.

2. See, in particular, Septimus 1983; Idel 1983, 1990; Berger 1983; Wolfson 1989; Halbertal 1990.

3. See Wolfson 1989, p. 122.

4. One topic I shall not discuss here is the difference between Maimonides's and Nachmanides's concepts of a mitzvah, or biblical commandment. Suffice it to say that Maimonides draws a sharp distinction between scriptural mitzvot and all other obligations and prohibitions in the law, both scriptural and rabbinic, and that he explicitly states in the *Guide* that he gives reasons only for biblical commandments according to the "external meaning" of the biblical text (Maimonides, *Guide* 3.41: 567). Nachmanides, by contrast, has a much broader conception of the biblical commandments. In the same vein, he repeatedly includes among those acts for which he gives *taʿamei mitzvot* rabbinic as well as biblical prescriptions and prohibitions. For further discussion of Maimonides's and Nachmanides's conceptions of mitzvah, see Golding 1987 and Halbertal 1990.

5. See Galston 1978.

6. Stern 1986 and 1989; for an alternative explanation, see Frank 1993.

7. Elsewhere I intend to address in depth Maimonides's general arguments for grounds of obligation for the Mosaic commandments, including "obsolete" *chuqqim*.

8. See Heinemann 1954, pp. 97–128, although a comprehensive study of post-Maimonidean philosophical *taʿamei mitzvot* has yet to be written.

9. See Idel 1990, pp. 42–50. I cannot discuss here the interesting question, pursued by Idel, whether the Maimonidean 'revolution' caused the first kabbalists to create, or invent, new theosophical or theurgic

reasons to counter the philosophical ones of the *Guide* or whether it merely forced them to crystallize, systematize, and make public an older esoteric tradition of reasons for the commandments that they already possessed. It is also important to keep in mind, as Idel shows, that Maimonides's philosophical, naturalized Aristotelian reconstruction of the classical bodies of esoteric truth, *ma'aseh merkabah* and *ma'aseh bereshit*, elicited an analogous reaction from the kabbalists who viewed it as an innovation discrediting a tradition they inherited. The two topics must be evaluated conjointly.

10.   See my sequel to the present chapter, "Nachmanides's Maimonidean Idea of a *Choq*" (in preparation).

11.   Maimonides 1981, p. 394, based on BT *Sanhedrin* 21b. Compare also Maimonides's *Mishneh Torah, Me'ilah* 8:8; Maimonides, *Guide* 3.26: 507–508; and the discussion in Twersky 1980, pp. 391–401 and Stern 1986 and 1989. On Maimonides's use of the figure of Solomon, see Klein-Braslavy 1990.

12.   For an alternative, more Ash'arite, interpretation of this passage, see Leibowitz 1980.

13.   For discussion of this distinction, see Stern 1986 and Shatz 1991. Here I depart from Stern 1986 where I argued that Maimonides shifts in 3.51 from an account of reasons of the legislator to an account of reasons for a performer. Of course, to say that the account of 3.51–52 also concerns reasons of the legislator does not mean that such a reason, when known by the performer, cannot also serve as a (indeed *the* proper) motivating reason for performing the commandment.

14.   It should be added that Maimonides also sometimes, amphibolously, calls the vulgar meaning of a verse its *external meaning*; see *Guide*, Introduction, p. 11.

15.   See, e.g., *Guide* 1.26: 56f.; 1.36: 84.

16.   Apart from these two "wise" reasons, some individual commandments may also have what we might analogously call a "vulgar" reason; e.g. in the case of the commandments to bury one's excrement, the sanitary value of the act; in the case of the Sabbath, physical rest; in the case of circumcision, improvement of the physical organ. About the first two cases, Maimonides makes no explicit judgement; the third, he openly attacks, as I discuss in Stern 1991 and 1993.

17.   On the first example, see Stern Ms.; on the second, Stern 1991 and 1993. I intend to discuss the example of the Sabbath elsewhere.

18.   See *Guide* 2.40: 383ff.

19.   Two complicating qualifications do not, as far as I can tell, affect my general point. First, Maimonides's description of the class of commandments for which he intends his explanation in 3.51—"the practices of the worship, such as reading the Torah, prayer, and the

performance of the other commandments"—is left, apparently deliberately, open-ended. On the one hand, the specific examples he mentions all fall in the ninth class of commandments according to the categorization of the *Guide* or, as Maimonides himself adds (*Guide* 3.35: 537), in the Book of Adoration in the *Mishneh Torah*. On the other hand, Maimonides seems to be specifically concerned with them insofar as they involve "action" or performance "with one's limbs—as if you were digging a hole in the ground or hewing wood in the forest" (an allusion, I believe, to the commandment of Deut. 23:14), in other words, use of one's body (including the bodily organ of speech). This might suggest that the explanation ought to apply generally to all and only commandments that involve action or the body. Yet a third possibility, based on Maimonides's comparison of prayer to sacrifice in 3.32: 526, is that the explanation of 3.51 should be extended to all similar acts of worship—concerning the Temple, sacrifice, purity and impurity, and the other acts introduced to counter idolatry. In short, it remains open how broad a class of commandments should be explained under the parabolic structure of 3.26–49 and 3.51–52. The second qualification I would mention concerns the content of the internal meanings of parables and internal reasons of commandments. If, as some scholars (myself included) have argued, Maimonides's held a skeptical or limited view of the possibility of human knowledge of metaphysical truth or, more generally, of the possibility of human attainment of the status of an acquired intellect, then the requirement of disassociation from "this world" as a precondition for this kind of state must also be suitably qualified.

20.   Nachmanides, *Perush* Deut. 22:6; 448–451. (All translations from the Hebrew are mine.)

21.   For a full discussion of this reason, see Nachmanides, *Perush* Lev. 19:19, on the prohibition of interbreeding. Nachmanides states this reason in Deut. 22:6 in the briefest way, but it is clear that this is his intended argument.

22.   Or so at least it has been supposed by most scholars. For a dissenting opinion that Nachmanides himself knew Arabic and read the *Guide* in the original even though he may also have utilized translations like Al-Harizi's, see now Jospe 1987. On this particular mistranslation, see p. 93, n. 50.

23.   See Stern 1989.

24.   See Maimonides, *Guide* 3.17: 471–474. In a critique of Stern 1989, Weiss 1989 argues that Maimonides holds that, although divine providence does not extend to individual nonhuman animals, divine mercy does, on the assumption that "providence and mercy are not the same thing and do not necessarily imply one another" (p. 357). I would agree, but it is not at all clear that Maimonides distinguishes between

them in the case of the deity; see, e.g., his uses of the terms *mercy* (Hebrew *rachum* in the original), *providence* (Arabic, *'inaya*), and *governance* (Arabic, *tadbir*) in *Guide* 1.54 and 3.54. Furthermore, throughout her discussion, Weiss misidentifies Maimonides's references to "the Law" with references to the deity. Hence she writes that "Maimonides, in discussing the Law's exhortation to be merciful to animals, compares animals to human beings in respect of their common ability to experience pain . . . [e.g.,] 'If the Law takes into consideration these pains of the soul in the case of beasts and birds, what will be the case with regard to the individuals of the human species as a whole?' [*Guide* 3.48: 600]" (p. 357). Here "the Law" clearly cannot be interpreted as referring to the deity. Maimonides's point is rather that if the law requires *us* humans to take into consideration the pains of beasts and birds, surely it expects *us* to act with comparable mercy toward our fellow humans. This passage is irrelevant to the question whether or not God himself has mercy on bird or beast.

25.   Maimonides, *Guide* 3.48: 600. Note that the rejected rabbinic opinion here is not the mishnaic dictum itself but one of the amoraic explanations for the dictum in the Babylonian Talmud, that of R. Jose bar Zebida (BT *Berakhot* 33b). As we just saw earlier in the text, however, Maimonides himself appears to endorse this reason in the *Mishneh Torah* "Laws of Prayer" 9.7. Hence, Maimonides would *appear* to contradict himself in the *Guide* and *Mishneh Torah*. Note also that in his *Commentary* on the *Mishnah*, *Megillah* 4.7, Maimonides explicitly calls the commandment of *shiluach ha-qen* a *shim'it*, adopting the Saadianic terminology for a purely volitional revealed law. For extensive discussion of these apparently contradictory passages, see Stern 1989.

26.   He at most alludes to it by saying that Maimonides recognized that the midrash poses a difficulty for his view [*hukshah alav*].

27.   See especially his citation of BT *Sanhedrin* 21b, the same text about Solomon cited by Maimonides in the *Book of Commandments*, which Nachmanides cites to show that every commandment has a reason.

28.   Novak 1992, pp. 2–4 and 99–104, seems to hold that Nachmanides's project of ascertaining *ta'amei mitzvot* is to determine the content of the proper intentions (*kavvanot*) with which the commandments should be performed. Although there is surely a connection between *ta'amei mitzvot* and proper *kavvanah*, Novak's account does not, I think, pay sufficient attention to the distinction between reasons of a legislator and reasons for a performer.

29.   See also Nachmanides, *Perush* Lev. 19:19.

30.   Nachmanides distinguishes such benefits and goods from "rewards from the Legislator." Neither, it should also be noted, is a mystical

effect or a kind of kabbalistic significance that attaches to performance of the commandments. At the very end of the commentary, Nachmanides does allude [*romez*] to a kabbalistic reason, a *sod*, but this serves only to underscore its absence from the earlier part of his discussion. On kabbalistic, theurgic reasons, see later.

31.   Cf. Hyman 1979–1980, p. 343.

32.   On Nachmanides's conservativism and the essential role he gave to tradition in his conception of kabbalah, see Idel 1983 and 1990.

33.   Compare Nachmanides's statement on knowledge of esoteric, kabbalistic *ta'amei mitzvot* in his "Sermon on the Words of Kohelet," in Nachmanides, *Kitvei*, vol. 1, p. 190; see also Idel 1990, p. 45.

34.   Compare Nachmanides's remarks in his sermon "Torat ha-Shem Temimah," in Nachmanides, *Kitvei*, vol. 1, pp. 163 and 167.

35.   Quoted in Wolfson 1988, p. 226. See also Matt 1986, pp. 379–382, 394f.; and Faierstein 1983. The terminology, *tzorekh gevoha* and *tzorekh hedyot*, is, of course, talmudic in origin, where the former refers to the "needs of the Temple" and the latter to "lay or profane needs or uses." According to Faierstein, Nachmanides was the first to employ the phrases in their kabbalistic sense.

36.   Nachmanides, *Kitvei*, vol. 1, p. 180. On this passage and on Nachmanides's theory of interpretation in general, see Wolfson 1989, p. 122ff.

37.   Here I differ from Wolfson's 1989 interpretation of Nachmanides's terminology, according to which *mashal* and *melitzah* synonymously refer to "the external sense of that which is uttered or expressed, whereas *chakhmah* and *chidah* are used to connote the internal sense and hence the *sod* of the matter" (p. 124). In a recent paper, Wolfson, revising his earlier view, now claims that "*mashal* here, as elsewhere in Nachmanides' oeuvre, denotes the figurative or parabolic sense" (Wolfson 1993, p. 193, n. 29). In my interpretation of the passage, *mashal* does not denote any sense or meaning at all—either external or figurative—but the kind, or genre, of the passage or text to be interpreted, namely, that it is a parable. *Melitzah, chakhmah,* and *chidah* refer to the different kinds of meanings that can be given the passage.

38.   One wonders whether there is a deliberate play on the words *tzorfim* (the silversmiths who craft the "silver filigree-work" that figuratively represents Maimonides's external meaning) and *letzaraif* (the purification accomplished by the commandments according to Nachmanides's external explanation in Deut. 22:6).

39.   Note his example, the etrog and other members of the four species. Here, too, one wonders whether the example was deliberately chosen in light of Maimonides's disapproving statements about the

parabolic interpretation of this particular commandment in the Introduction to the *Guide*, p. 11, and in 3.43: 572–573.

40. Nachmanides (notes), in Maimonides, *Book of Commandments*,
pp. 44–45.

41. For many striking examples of these two phenomena, see
Wolfson 1989, pp. 129–153. For an intriguing discussion of the legal
implications (in their conception and enumeration of commandments) of
these hermeneutical differences between Maimonides and Nachmanides,
see Halbertal 1990, pp. 473–476.

42. Maimonides, *Book of Commandments*, with Nachmanides's
notes, p. 45. For discussion, see Wolfson 1989, p. 128.

43. As a consequence, Nachmanides's notion of *peshat* is, of course,
much richer than Maimonides's; see Septimus 1983, p 18.

44. Nachmanides (notes), in Maimonides, *Book of Commandments*,
p. 44.

45. One would think that this denial is based on opposition to
corporeal descriptions of the deity. However, Nachmanides's general
treatment of this issue is much more ambivalent and qualified than
Maimonides's rigorous denial of all such ascriptions; e.g. *Perush* Gen.
46:1, pp. 246–249 on Maimonides's interpretation of Onqelos on Gen.
1:26 on "tzelem." For a brief discussion, see Novak 1992, pp. 41–42.
The topic requires further evaluation.

46. Nachmanides, *Perush* 2, p. 117.

47. This passage also raises a different question. Performing a
commandment because it is the will of the deity is clearly a proper reason
to do so, whereas performing it simply to be rewarded is improper. But
where do the naturalistic external reasons of Deut. 22:6 stand in its
ranking of agents' reasons for performing the commandments? On the
one hand, because they aim at human goods or perfections, both practical and intellectual, they lack the theocentric condition Nachmanides
seems to require for *avodah me-ahavah*, service out of love of God. On
the other hand, they also do not fall under the low bill of *avodah shelo
leshmah al menat leqabeil peras*, service not for the sake [of heaven] but
[simply] to be rewarded, at least where such a reward is taken to be an
improper motive. I do not know whether, or how, Nachmanides resolves
this question concerning the normative status of the external reasons for
the commandments as motives for their performers.

48. See Nachmanides, *Perush* Lev. 18:25, pp. 110–111; Deut.
11:18, p. 394; "Sermon on the Words of Kohelet," *Kitvei*, vol. 1, pp.
200–201; "Sermon for Rosh Hashanah, ibid., p. 251.

49. I wish to thank David Shatz for suggesting this last implication,
and Moshe Idel and Martin Golding for very helpful comments on an
earlier version of this essay.

REFERENCES

Baer, Y. 1966. *A History of the Jews in Christian Spain*, 2 vols. Philadelphia: Jewish Publication Society.

Berger, D. 1983. "Miracles and the Natural Order in Nachmanides." In *Rabbi Moses Nachmanides (Ramban): Explorations in His Religious and Literary Virtuosity*, ed. I. Twersky, pp. 107–128. Cambridge, Mass.: Harvard University Press.

Faierstein, M. 1983. "God's Need for the Commandments in Medieval Kabbalah." *Conservative Judaism* 36: 45–59.

Frank, D. 1993. "*Ad Hoq.*" *S'vara* 3.1: 91–94.

Funkenstein, A. 1982. "Nachmanides' Symbolical Reading of History." In *Studies in Jewish Mysticism*, ed. J. Dan and F. Talmage, pp. 129–150. Cambridge, Mass.: Association for Jewish Studies.

Galston, M. 1978. "The Purpose of the Law According to Maimonides." *Jewish Quarterly Review* 69: 27–51.

Golding, M. 1987. "Maimonides: Theory of Juristic Reasoning." In *Maimonides as Codifier of Jewish Law*, ed. Nahum Rakover, pp. 51–59. Jerusalem: Library of Jewish Law.

Halbertal, M. 1990. "Maimonides' *Book of Commandments*: The Architecture of the Halakhah and its Theory of Interpretation" [Hebrew]. *Tarbitz* 59, nos. 3–4: 457–480.

Heinemann, I. 1954. *Ta'amei ha-Mitzvot be-Sifrut Yisra'el* [Hebrew], 3rd ed., vol. 1. Jerusalem: The Jewish Agency.

Henoch, C. 1978. *Nachmanides: Philosopher and Mystic.* Jerusalem: Torah Laam.

Hyman, A. 1979–1980. "A Note on Maimonides' Classification of Law." *Proceedings of the American Academy for Jewish Research* 46–47: 323–343.

Idel, M. 1983. "We Have No Kabbalistic Tradition on This." In *Rabbi Moses Nachmanides (Ramban): Explorations in His Religious and Literary Virtuosity*, ed. I. Twersky, pp. 51–74. Cambridge, Mass.: Harvard University Press.

―――. 1990. "Maimonides and Kabbalah." In *Studies in Maimonides*, ed. I. Twersky, pp. 31–81. Cambridge, Mass.: Harvard University Press.

Jospe, R. 1987. "Nachmanides and Arabic" [Hebrew]. *Tarbitz* 62, no. 1: 67–93.

Klein–Braslavy, S. 1990. "King Solomon and Metaphysical Esotericism According to Maimonides." *Maimonidean Studies*, vol. 1, pp. 57–86. New York: Yeshiva University Press.

Leibowitz, Y. 1980. *The Faith of Maimonides* [Hebrew]. Tel Aviv: Library of the IDF Broadcast University.

Maimonides. 1981. *Book of Commandments, with Nachmanides' Notes* [Hebrew], ed. C. Chavel. Jerusalem: Mossad ha-Rav Kook.

———. 1963. *The Guide of the Perplexed*, 2 vols., trans. S. Pines. Chicago: University of Chicago Press.

———. 1928. *Sefer Moreh Nevukhim* [Hebrew], trans. R. Judah b. Solomon Al-Harizi. Vilna: Katznelbogen. Reprint, London: L. Schlossberg, 1851, with notes by Scheyer.

Matt, D. 1986. "The Mystic and the Mizwot." In *Jewish Spirituality from the Bible through the Middle Ages*, ed. A. Green, pp. 367–404. New York: Crossroads Press.

Nachmanides. 1960. *Kitvei ha-RaMBaN*, 2 vols., ed. C. Chavel. Jerusalem: Mossad ha-Rav Kook.

———. 1959. *Perush ha-RaMBaN 'al ha-Torah*, 2 vols., ed. C. Chavel. Jerusalem: Mossad ha-Rav Kook.

Novak, D. 1992. *The Theology of Nahmanides Systematically Presented*. Atlanta: Scholars Press.

Septimus, B. 1983. " 'Open Rebuke and Concealed Love': Nachmanides and the Andalusian Tradition." In *Rabbi Moses Nachmanides (Ramban): Explorations in His Religious and Literary Virtuosity*, ed. I. Twersky, pp. 11–34. Cambridge, Mass.: Harvard University Press.

Shatz, D. 1991. "Worship, Corporeality, and Human Perfection: A Reading of *Guide of the Perplexed*, III:51–54." In *The Master as Exemplar*, ed. I. Robinson and L. Kaplan, pp. 77–129. New York: Edwin Mellen Press.

Stern, J. 1986. "The Idea of a *Hoq* in Maimonides' Explanation of the Law." In *Maimonides and Philosophy*, ed. S. Pines and Y. Yovel, pp. 92–130. Dordrecht: Nijhoff.

———. 1989. "On an Alleged Contradiction between Maimonides' *Guide of the Perplexed* and *Mishneh Torah*" [Hebrew]. In *Shenaton ha-Mishpat Ivri*, pp. 283–298. Jerusalem: Hebrew University Law School.

———. 1991. "Maimonides' Parable of Circumcision." *S'vara* 2.2: 35–48.

———. 1993. "Maimonides on the Covenant of Circumcision and the Unity of God." In *The Midrashic Imagination: Essays in Rabbinic Thought and Interpretation*, ed. M. Fishbane, pp. 131–154. Albany: SUNY Press.

———. Ms. "Excrement and Exegesis."

Twersky, I. 1980. *Introduction to the Code of Maimonides*. New Haven, Conn.: Yale University Press.

Weiss, R. 1989. "Maimonides on *Shilluah Ha-Qen*." *Jewish Quarterly Review* 79, no. 4: 345–366.

Wolfson, E. 1988. "Mystical Rationalization of the Commandments in *Sefer ha-Rimmon.*" *Hebrew Union College Annual* 59: 217–251.

———. 1989. "By Way of Truth: Aspects of Nachmanides' Kabbalistic Hermeneutic." *AJS Review* 14, no. 2: 103–179.

———. 1993. "Beautiful Maiden Without Eyes: *Peshat* and *Sod* in Zoharic Hermeneutics." In *The Midrashic Imagination: Essays in Rabbinic Thought and Interpretation*, ed. M. Fishbane, pp. 155–203. Albany: SUNY Press.

The Attitude Toward Democracy in Medieval Jewish Philosophy

Abraham Melamed

I

In his various writings D. J. Elazar characterizes the Jewish polity as a "republic with strong democratic overtones," which neverthe-less was in reality generally an "aristocratic republic in the classic sense of the term—rule by a limited number who take upon them-selves an obligation or conceive of themselves as having a special obligation to their people and to God." It is true that the Jewish polity is "rooted in a democratic foundation," in that it is based upon the equality of all (adult male) Jews and their basic right and obligation to participate in the establishment and maintenance of the body politic.[1] But this is as far as the "democratic overtones" of this republic went. It was a republic true enough, but no democ-racy. It did have some components of what is termed *communal democracy*, but it was not a liberal democracy. The various Jewish polities that existed over the centuries were generally very aristo-cratic in terms of their actual regimes. The idea of a democratic regime was alien to them and went against their basic political and theological premises. The idea of a liberal democracy was absent from the Jewish political tradition until modern times, and medi-eval Jewish political philosophy, which is the subject of this chap-ter, rejected its Greek variety outright.

Following the Platonic-Muslim political tradition, medieval Jewish philosophy held a basically monarchic conception of gov-ernment. By and large, medieval Jewish philosophers conceived the

173

ideal government to be that of a perfect philosopher-king in the Platonic mold, which acquired a distinct theological meaning through medieval Muslim intermediaries, especially Alfarabi and Ibn Rushd (Averroes). The Platonic philosopher-king was transformed into the prophet-legislator of the Jewish and Muslim monotheistic tradition. And halakhic thought too, for all its hesitations and reservations, finally accepted (limited) monarchy as the preferred kind of government.[2]

This situation is well illustrated by the fact that Muslim, and following it also Jewish, political philosophy—in contrast to all other branches of medieval philosophy—was squarely based upon the Platonic tradition, and not on Aristotle's *Politics*, the latter being almost unknown to them. The Aristotelian system did conceive the *politeia*, a kind of modified and moderate democracy ruled by the middle class, to be the preferred kind of government. But medieval Muslim and Jewish thinkers were hardly aware of the Aristotelian position. They, who so admired Aristotle and considered him "the philosopher," completely ignored his moderately democratic inclinations, as manifested in his *Politics*. For a variety of reasons, chance transmission of manuscripts as well as theological preferences, they directly followed the Platonic monarchist tradition.[3] In so doing they necessarily rejected democracy entirely and considered it one of the negative forms of government.

The kind of democracy they rejected was what we would term *liberal democracy* of the ancient Greek variety. This kind of government was based upon three premises: First, basic legal equality among the citizens (which means excluding most of the populace!), disregarding the differences in their potential and in their moral and intellectual perfection. Second, the acceptance of pluralism in opinions and ways of life as a basic norm of civic life (as long as this pluralism did not exceed certain basic *shared* norms!). Third, the election of temporary magistrates by some combination of majority vote and lot, based on the assumption that all citizens have the duty as well as the interest to participate actively in civic life.

Following an essentially monistic world-view, based, on the one hand, on Platonic philosophy, and on the other, on a divine revelation that posited the existence of one divine truth, known in its totality only to a few perfect individuals, Muslim and Jewish medieval political philosophers could not accept any of these premises. For them, only one who knows the one divine truth, through a combination of revelation and contemplation, could successfully rule human society.

It necessarily followed that men were unequal in their very nature. The differences in their potential and in the moral and intellectual perfection they were able to reach should also dictate differences in their legal, social, and political standing. Consequently, ruling society was not a matter for majority vote but for divine choice. Finally, because there was only one divine truth, manifest in a single, sacred and authoritative text, all other opinions were necessarily wrong. Pluralism was thus rejected and a basically monolithic world-view was adopted. The world-view of these philosophers was thus monarchic and antidemocratic in its very essence.

II

The fundamental classical formula for the rejection of liberal democracy appears in the eighth book of Plato's *Republic*. After describing the development of the perfect state ruled by the philosopher-king, its nature, structure, and its purpose, Plato proceeds in the eighth book to deal with the possible deterioration of the perfect state into a series of imperfect, bad, and erring states, in the following chronological order: timocracy, oligarchy (or plutocracy), democracy, and tyranny. Democracy is considered the necessary outcome of the failure of oligarchy. When the rule of the few bad rich deteriorates, the poor seize the opportunity to wrest power from the degenerate rich. For Plato, democracy is not rule by the people, but rule by the mob. For him, it violates the basic idea of justice; namely, that men, by nature having different capacities, should do only the work for which they are fit. Fitness to govern is regarded by Plato as the highest perfection of man, suitable for philosophers only. Most are by nature unfit to govern and so should freely accept rule by the perfect few. Equality means the rule of the lowest common denominator, that is, the appetites of the lowest part of the soul. This is summed up by Plato when he says, "These then, and such as these, are the features of a democracy, an agreeable kind of anarchy with plenty of variety and an equality of a peculiar kind for equals and unequals alike."[4] His cynical rejection of democracy is clear. It is a kind of hedonistic and pluralistc anarchy, based on a profoundly distorted conception of human equality.

Because, according to the famous parable of the small and large letters (368d), the state is only a macrocosm of the people who rule it, Plato goes on to describe the nature of the democratic man on the microcosmic level. Plato's vivid description, which was the basis for the medieval Muslim and Jewish descriptions of the democratic condition, merits lengthy quotation:

> In his life thenceforth he spends as much time and pains and money on his superfluous pleasures as on the necessary ones. If he is lucky enough not to be carried beyond all bounds, the tumult may begin to subside as he grows older. Then perhaps he may recall some of the banished virtues and cease to give himself up entirely to the passions which ousted them; and now he will set all his pleasures on a footing of equality, denying to none its equal rights and maintenance, and allowing each in turn, as it presents itself, to succeed, as if by the chance of the lot, to the government of his soul until it is satisfied. When he is told that some pleasures should be sought and valued as arising from desires of a higher order, others chastised and enslaved because the desires are base, he will shut the gates of the citadel against the messengers of truth, shaking his head and declaring that one appetite is as good as another and all must have their equal rights. So he spends his days indulging the pleasure of the moment, now intoxicated with wine and music, and then taking to a spare diet and drinking nothing but water; one day in hard training, the next doing nothing at all, the third apparently immersed in study. Every now and then he takes a part in politics, leaping to his feet to say or do whatever comes into his head. Or he will set out to rival someone he admires, a soldier it may be, or, if the fancy takes him, a man of business. His life is subject to no order or restraint, and he has no wish to change an existence which he calls pleasant, free, and happy.
>
> That well describes the life of one whose motto is liberty and equality.
>
> Yes, and his character contains the same fine variety of pattern that we found in the democratic state; it is as multifarious as that epitome of all types of constitution. Many a man and many a woman too, will find in it something to envy. So we may see in him the counterpart of democracy, and call him the democratic man.[5]

The characteristics of the democratic man in the microcosm are completely equivalent to those of the democratic state in the macrocosm. The democratic man is one who is driven by passion to satisfy all his most bodily desires. Holding a subjectivist, hedonistic, and pluralistic world-view, he deems all appetites and all opinions to be of equal value. This is why he is characterized by instability, ever-changing interests, opinions, and occupations, an inclination to extremes, without order or restraint in his life.

This is how "democratic" liberty and equality are considered by Plato. When liberty is defined negatively, according to the liberal tradition as the extreme absence of constraints, and all are considered equal, it creates, according to Plato, total anarchy in the sphere of the behavior of each individual, and consequently in society at large. This goes against the very premises of his idea of justice upon which the ideal state is erected. The Platonic idea of justice is based on a positive definition of liberty, by which freedom means the suppression of one's lowly appetites through free will: to rule them rather than be ruled by them. By Platonic standards, freedom means the acceptance of the role designated for one in the perfect social fabric, according to natural capacities and social needs.

III

Plato's rejection of liberal democracy was transmitted to medieval thought mainly by two major Muslim philosophers, Alfarabi and Ibn Rushd (Averroes). Through them it also reached and influenced medieval Jewish thinkers. Alfarabi's discussion in his *Book of Principles* (or *The Political Regime*) was translated into Hebrew in the thirteenth century by Moses Ibn Tibbon under the title *Sefer ha-Hatchalot*. In Ibn Rushd's writings we find two discussions of democracy, both directly following Plato, one in his commentary on Plato's *Republic*, the other in his commentary on Aristotle's *Rhetoric*. The commentary on Plato's *Republic* was translated into Hebrew in the early fourteenth century by Samuel ben Judah of Marseilles under the title *Sefer ha-Hanhagah le-Aplaton* and exerted a great influence on subsequent generations of Jewish scholars. The commentary on Aristotle's *Rhetoric* was translated into Hebrew, also in the fourteenth century, by the Spanish Jew Todros Todrosi, under the title *Sefer ha-Halatzah*, and was popular with later medieval and Renaissance Jewish scholars. One of them, the Mantovan Jew Judah Messer Leon, inserted long passages from this translation, including the discussion of democracy, in his rhetorical tract *Nofet Zufim*, written in Italy in the late fifteenth century.

What interests us now is the way in which Jewish scholars transmitted these texts into Hebrew, coined, for the first time, Hebrew terms for *democracy* and related terms, and inserted Jewish motifs into their translations from the Arabic texts. All this would, in turn, also reveal their attitude toward democracy.

After discussing the nature of the perfect state, Alfarabi goes on in his *Book of Principles* to differentiate among the various kinds of imperfect state. The fourth kind is democracy, which is defined as "free association in the democratic city and the city of the free." The term *kibbutz* (in Ibn Tibbon's Hebrew translation), which usually designates the general political term *association* (*kibbutz medini*, political association), is used here also to designate a particular kind of regime, that is, democracy—*medinah mekubbetzet*, or *kibbutzit*, that is, "an associated state", and also *kibbutz ha-cherut*, "the association of the free."[6] Ibn Tibbon chose to use these terms for democracy to indicate that this kind of regime is a free association of equals. Indeed, Moses Ibn Tibbon was the first to coin in Hebrew terms for democracy.

In translating the discussion of the nature of the democratic state, Ibn Tibbon closely follows Alfarabi's text. This kind of state is characterized by full legal equality of natural equals and non-equals alike, total freedom of action that is practically anarchic, unlimited pursuit of material desires, private and public instability, the rule of the mob, and extreme pluralism in opinions as well as in action.[7] Following Alfarabi, Ibn Tibbon transmitted to Hebrew Plato's beautiful parable of the embroidered garment, full of many different colors and shapes, which the common people like too much. The democratic state, with all its variety and its appeal to the lowest common denominator, resembles that embroidered garment.[8]

Besides coining Hebrew terms for democracy, and transmitting the aforementioned Platonic parable into Hebrew literature, Ibn Tibbon inserted into his discussion allusions to two specific Hebrew motifs. He closely, almost literally, translated Alfarabi's opening statement: "The democratic city (*medinah kibbutzit*) is the one in which each one of the citizens is given free rein and left alone to do whatever he likes."[9] This translation is indeed literal. But the phrase "do whatever he likes," echoes the biblical phrase in the last verse of the book of Judges: "In those days there was no king in Israel, every man did what was right in his own eyes" (Judges 21:25). The biblical source is very critical of this kind of anarchy, where a stable centralized government did not exist and each individual did whatever he pleased. By inserting an allusion to this verse Ibn Tibbon only reinforced the Platonic-Farabian criticism of democracy, in which freedom meant the freedom to pursue one's lowest appetites, and social order was reduced to anarchy.

The same phenomenon is also found in his father's, Samuel Ibn Tibbon's, translation of Maimonides's *Guide of the Perplexed*, 3.27. Discussing the conditions for achieving welfare of the body, Maimonides says, "One of them is the abolition of their wrongdoing to each other. This is tantamount to every individual among the people not being permitted to act according to his will . . ."[10]

Maimonides's phrasing here is strongly reminiscent of Alfarabi's definition of democracy quoted previously. Although Alfarabi opened his discussion with a seemingly "objective" definition of democracy, and only then went on to criticize it, Maimonides's description is, of course, subjective and critical outright. Freedom to act according to one's will, that is, democracy, is described as the source of all wrongdoing. The solution Maimonides proposes is, of course, life according to the law of the Torah, which is by no means a liberal democracy. Samuel Ibn Tibbon translated Maimonides's words quite literally here, but invested them with an allusion to the same biblical verse from Judges.[11] In both cases, by infusing the text with the biblical allusion, father and son intensified the rejection of this kind of freedom, which is so essential to liberal democracy. For them, as for Plato, Alfarabi, and Maimonides, such freedom is nothing but anarchy of the worst kind. Like Maimonides's phrasing, so reminiscent of Alfarabi's definition of democracy, the Ibn Tibbons' translation of these two texts is also very similar.[12] In both translations they inserted the allusion to the same biblical text. It is no accident either that Maimonides's phrase "the abolition of their wrongdoing to each other" was translated by Ibn Tibbon in a manner that alludes to another biblical text—"and the earth was filled with violence" (Gen. 6:11). It is significant that this kind of democracy is identified by Ibn

Tibbon with the most extreme case of anarchy and violence in human history. The original Maimonidean text does not imply these verses, although Maimonides did insert, on various occasions, biblical verses into his text. In this case it was Ibn Tibbon's independent allusion that was superimposed on the original Maimonidean text. By doing so, Ibn Tibbon, again, only reinforced the rejection of liberal democracy. For the Ibn Tibbons, as for their three "masters," Plato, Alfarabi, and Maimonides, true freedom did not mean the unlimited right to do whatever one pleased, but rather to accept, through one's free will, the rule of the one divine law, and of those authorized to apply it.

The other Hebrew motif inserted into Moses Ibn Tibbon's translation of Alfarabi's negative description of democracy is the use of the term *am ha-aretz* (people of the land) for "the multitude of this city."[13] This too is an obvious choice, but it is also infused with a powerful antidemocratic sense. The term *am ha-aretz* is used by Maimonides in the introduction to his commentary to *Zeraim* and in his commentary to *Avot* to designate the multitude. The meaning he attributes to the term is as follows: "the sages, of blessed memory, called a person who has no wisdom an *am ha-aretz*, that is, the purpose they serve is the settlement of the earth. Therefore they associated their name with the earth."[14] Maimonides argues that the common people, who are unfit to fulfill the intellectual end of human existence, were created to serve the material and emotional needs of the few wise men, so that these few would have the leisure to contemplate and thus to fulfill the ultimate purpose of the whole species.[15] This is an explicitly elitist, Platonic-Farabian idea. By inserting the term *am ha-aretz*, which is so charged with antidemocratic meaning, into his translation, Ibn Tibbon, once more using Maimonidean terminology, fortified the initial negative description of democracy of Plato and Alfarabi. Although in Maimonides's Platonic scheme the *am ha-aretz* fill their proper function and thus contribute to the general well being of society, in Ibn Tibbon's description of democracy, they rule the land, with all the ensuing negative consequences.

IV

The other avenue by which Platonic political ideas were transmitted into medieval Jewish thought is Ibn Rushd's commentary on Plato's *Republic*, which was translated into Hebrew in the fourteenth century by Samuel ben Judah of Marseilles.[16] This very literal translation is extremely important because the Arabic original is lost and the Hebrew translation is the only extant evidence of the lost original.

Following Plato, Ibn Rushd deals with the imperfect states (*hanhagot asher einan meulot*) in the third part of his commentary, after discussing the nature of the perfect state (*hanhagat ha-medinot ha-meulot*) in the first two parts of his commentary. Democracy is listed fourth among the five kinds of imperfect state, which are themselves listed in chronological order. The establishment of a democracy is a necessary consequence of the deterioration of a timocracy, and its own deterioration would necessarily give rise to despotic rule, illustrative of *its* negative character.

Democracy is here termed *rashiyut ha-kibbutz ha-hamonii*, translated by Rosenthal from the Hebrew as "the leadership of the people's community."[17] Lerner translated a little differently: "the primacy of the assembly of the multitude."[18] I prefer Rosenthal's "leadership" to Lerner's "primacy," for *rashiyut*. On the other hand, Lerner wisely inserted the term *multitude* for *ha-hamonii*, which is absent from Rosenthal's translation. The term *hamonii* ("of the multitude" or "mob") indicates the popular nature of this kind of government. Other variations used by Samuel ben Judah are *medinah kibbutzit* (or *medinat ha-kibbutz*) and *ha-kibbutz ha-kehilii* (or *medinah kehiliit* [*madina jimaiyya* in Arabic]).[19] Both Rosenthal and Lerner, although they literally translated ben Judah's first term for democracy, decided to translate all other variations of the term as "democracy."[20] The terms ben Judah used here, *medinah kibbutzit* and *medinah kehiliit*, both refer to the fact that democracy is the rule of the whole community; *kibbutz* and *kehillah* both indicate association or community in Hebrew. In fact, the term *kibbutz kehilii* literally means "an associated association." The term *medinah kibbutzit* was initially coined by Moses Ibn Tibbon, as noted previously, and ben Judah repeats it here. Another variant ben Judah uses is *ha-adnut ha-kibbutzi* or *ha-adnut ha-kehilii*. Both refer to the kind of authority (*adnut*) that exists in a democratic state. Thus, ben Judah uses two basic Hebrew terms for democracy. One is the initial *rashiyut ha-kibbutz ha-hamonii* and the other is *medinah kibbutzit*, or *kehiliit*, in different variants. These two terms refer to the same basic feature of democracy, which is rule of the state by the multitude, in which the whole community participates equally. It is interesting that in contrast to Ibn Tibbon before him, and to his contemporary Todrosi, ben Judah did not choose also to use the term *kibbutz ha-cherut* ("the association of the free"), or any of its variants, for democracy. This was probably because Ibn Rushd did not use this phrase. By this omission he neglected the other major feature of democracy, which is freedom of action and thought. The latter, nevertheless, was referred to in the body of the text.

After listing the different kinds of imperfect state Ibn Rushd presents two separate discussions of the nature of the various kinds of imperfect regime. First he defines them individually, and then he considers the way each evolves as a necessary consequence of the disintegration of the previous kind of imperfect regime.

As for democracy, this is defined just as Alfarabi, following Plato, defined it: "The democratic association (*ha-kibbutz ha-kehilii*) is the community in which everybody is free from restraint. This means that a man does whatever his heart desires and he takes himself toward every enjoyment to which his soul leads him."[21]

All the basic components of liberal democracy, which Plato so despised, are indicated here: legal equality, freedom from restraint, pluralism, and hedonism. For this reason this kind of government is also termed by him *hanhagah ta'anugiit* ("hedonistic constitution"), at least in its initial transformation from a plutocracy into a democracy.[22] The expression "that a man does whatever his heart desires" (*ma shelibo chafetz*) again echoes the words of the last verse of the book of Judges, with all its negative implications.

The pluralistic nature of democracy creates a situation, unique to this particular kind of regime, that all different kinds of people are represented in its social fabric—lovers of honor, property, or tyranny. This is why different kinds of regime could potentially develop out of democracy, even a virtuous state (*medinah meulah*), because among all kinds of regime, democracy can, theoretically at least, give rise even to virtuous people.[23] The democratic man is described as he who occasionally behaves in a philosophical manner.[24] The problem is that this happens only occasionally, and therefore it is advisable for the philosophers to focus their attention particularly on this kind of state that, among others, produces people who could be good raw material for the creation of the ideal state.[25] However, as we shall see, it was generally considered that tyranny was the kind of government into which democracy was most prone to deteriorate.

Another aspect of democracy treated here is the nature of authority (*adnut*). In a democratic regime authority is based on the will of the citizenry and because the will, or rather the whims, of the citizens are accidental and ever changing (*kibbutz be-mikreh*), authority will be in a similar condition (*adnut be-hizdemen*); but this is contrary to the very nature of authority, and therefore in a democratic state there will be no real authority.[26] However, without any authority, no state, not even a democracy, could survive, because men are driven by their natural inclinations to kill and plunder one another. Such a "Hobbesian" condition would eventually ruin the state. For this reason even a democracy cannot tolerate the complete absence of laws, that is, total liberty. Even this kind of government has to create some minimal authority, as well as a government to implement them, to prevent complete anarchy and consequently self-annihilation.[27] This is the kind of authority that exists in a democratic state. It is what ben Judah termed *ha-adnut ha-kibbutzi* or *ha-adnut ha-kehilii* ("the democratic authority").[28] This entails that to ensure its existence a democracy is in fact obliged to deviate from its basic principles, a proof of its basic deficiency.

Ibn Rushd's other discussion of democracy concerns the way it necessarily evolves out of the disintegration of plutocracy and itself disintegrates into tyranny. Following Plato, Ibn Rushd offers a complete parallelism between the way a plutocratic man disintegrates into a democratic one, and consequently the way a plutocratic state disintegrates into a democracy.[29] Because authority in a plutocratic state is based on ownership, its laws are designed to increase the rulers' property as much as possible. People would not only be allowed but actually urged to follow their desires and spend as much money as possible on fulfilling them. Laws of temperance would be unheard of in such a state. Consequently, most people in a plutocratic state would lose all their possessions to the ruling plutocrats. The rich would become richer and fewer in number, while the poor would become poorer and more miserable, and increase in number. The gap between the ruling few and the impoverished majority would grow ever wider. This majority would become increasingly angry and envious of the ruling few. Finally, a moment would come when the impoverished masses would realize the potential of their sheer numerical majority and the "invaluable" services they render to the plutocratic state in war and other civic services. When the poor realize their power, they would rebel against their oppressors and the plutocratic state would eventually crumble. Following Plato, Ibn Rushd compares the poor to drones born in a beehive, who would ruin the existing structure from within.[30]

On the ruins of this plutocratic state a democracy would be established. The regime, based on the dominion of the majority of the poor, is defined here, for the second time, by Ibn Rushd, in ben Judah's Hebrew rendering, as follows: "As this is so, and as such men rule over the State, every one of the free poor will do what is right in his own eyes. Rule among them will be maintained in a haphazard fashion. Every kind of men will no doubt be found in this State, and there will not be among them a rank at all for any one. Their law will be an equal law, that is, no one among them will be excellent."[31]

This definition of democracy is essentially the same as Ibn Rushd's first one, discussed earlier, but it is more detailed. Democracy is again defined as the rule of the multitude, based upon the principles of liberty, authority by chance, legal equality, and the rule of the lowest common denominator. As indicated previously, democracy, like its predecessor, is a "hedonistic form of government" (hanhagah ta'anugiit), as ben Judah phrased it. The only difference between plutocracy and democracy is that the first strives to fulfill the desires of the ruling few, whereas the second strives to fulfill the desires of the multitude as a whole.

Ben Judah's Hebrew text brings to a culmination a tendency we found in previous Hebrew texts. In Ibn Tibbon's translation from Alfarabi and also in his own translation from Ibn Rushd, we discovered allusions to the last verse of the book of Judges superimposed upon the text. What we find here is no hint or allusion, but a full direct quotation of the text: "every man did what was right in his own eyes."[32] The negative attitude toward the kind of liberty democracy offers, which is nothing more than sheer anarchy, is again only strengthened by the Hebrew translators' superimposition of the biblical verse upon the Platonic-Averroist definition. Ben Judah's translation is reputedly literal. He was a translator in the strictly limited sense of the term and not a commentator. But he was not impartial. By inserting the biblical allusions and by the choice of Hebrew terms, he also expressed his own opinions. He wholeheartedly concurred here with Plato and Ibn Rushd.

Tyranny (*medinat ha-nitzuach*) is the form of regime into which democracy is most likely to deteriorate, because democracy is based upon an excess of liberty. Like every excess, this one too is bound to have negative consequences. It would enable the development of a kind of person, sick in body and soul, who would pursue the most bestial desires without limit and would use a boundless freedom of action to enslave other people.[33] The pluralistic nature of democracy can in theory create different kinds of people, even philosophers. However, considering democracy's basic characteristics, it is most likely to create tyrants who would transform the democratic regime into a tyranny. The fact that democracy is most likely to deteriorate into tyranny also proves, according to Plato and Ibn Rushd, its inherent deficiencies. It is a kind of government that, in fact, combines the worst tendencies of what it developed from and into which it deteriorates.

V

A variant of the same theme can be found in *Sefer ha-Halatzah*, a fourteenth century Hebrew translation by the Spanish Jew Todros Todrosi of Ibn Rushd's commentary to Aristotle's *Rhetoric*. In his commentary, Ibn Rushd superimposed Platonic ideas on the original Aristotelian text and thereby also introduced a strong anti-democratic component into his classification of regimes.[34]

In this work Ibn Rushd treats the theory of government, democracy in particular, in connection with the knowledge that the perfect orator should have in political matters. To be persuasive the orator must have a thorough knowledge of the kinds of government that exist and the laws proper for each of them. Although he is commenting upon Aristotle, Ibn Rushd makes the basic *Platonic* distinction between the ideal state (*ha-hanhagah ha-meshubachat* in Todrosi's translation) and all the imperfect regimes. These latter are represented here by democracy.[35]

The terms Todrosi chooses for democracy here are *ha-hanhagah asher tikareh ha-cherut* ("the regime that is called liberty"), or *hanhagat ha-cherut* ("the regime of liberty").[36] Another variant he uses later is *ha-medinah ha-kibbutzit* ("the associated state") and *ha-hanhagah ha-kibbutzit* ("the associated leadership").[37] We have already noted such variants in Ibn Tibbon's and ben Judah's translations. They all refer to the definition of democracy as a free association of equals.

Democracy is taken here as an example of the various kinds of imperfect regime. Whereas the perfect state is based on an exact and well-balanced system of justice, all imperfect regimes, including democracy, are based on different degrees of unjust and unbalanced laws, too strict or too weak. Each of these systems of law is a byproduct of the nature of a particular kind of imperfect regime, and it is supposed to serve its needs and safeguard its continuous existence. The problem with democracy is that it employs a distinctly weak system of law. The difference among the legal systems of the various kinds of imperfect state is illustrated here by the contrast between democracy and tyranny. Each of these represents one extreme of the legal system. The democratic legal system is too weak, because every man is allowed to do whatever he pleases, without any restraints, while the tyrannical legal system is too strict, because it is based upon total subordination to an unjust rule. Ibn Rushd illustrates this contrast with a nice example, which sounds almost comical in Todrosi's medieval Hebrew translation: "For example, in a tyrannical government (*hanhagat ha-nitzachon*), justice (*yosher*) means that no harm should be done to a guard who hit somebody under his jurisdiction, while in a government of liberty (*hanhagat ha-cherut*, democracy), justice requires that the person who was hit by a guard has the right to retaliate accordingly."[38] The anarchic nature of democracy, based upon the ideal of full equality and total liberty, is well illustrated here. For this reason, as we have seen, real authority cannot exist in a democratic state. Consequently, democracy, like all other imperfect states, is bound to deteriorate. Generally, it was assumed that democracy would deteriorate into tyranny. Here, however, it is asserted that democracy would likely deteriorate into some kind of plutocracy. This is explained by the weakness of its legal system, which enables everyone to pursue freely his material desires to the extreme, without any restraint.[39] Although in most variants plutocracy is the kind of government democracy developed from, in this case the situation is the reverse. Plutocracy is described as the government into which democracy is most likely to deteriorate.

Later, the commentary distinguishes among the various kinds of imperfect state and defines each. Democracy is concisely defined in Todrosi's Hebrew translation as follows: "The associated state (*ha-medinah ha-kibbutzit*) [i.e., democracy] is such [a regime] in which leadership (*rashut*) is accidental (*be-hizdemen*) and by lot (*mazal*), and not in accordance with any appropriate law (*choq*), since in this [kind of] state, no one has any advantage upon another."[40] Directly following Aristotle, Ibn Rushd defines the end of democracy as follows: "The end of associated leadership (*hahanhagah ha-kibbutzit*) [i.e., democracy] is freedom (*cherut*)."[41]

This again is a definition that contains all the ingredients of the classical Platonic definition of the Greek variety of liberal democracy. It is important to note here that in the Aristotelian source democracy is defined as "a form of government under which the citizens distribute the offices of state among themselves by lot."[42] There is no value judgment here, only a description of the facts. Ibn Rushd's commentary and its Hebrew translation, however, give us a more elaborate definition with negative overtones. Ibn Rushd's commentary superimposes a Platonic meaning upon the Aristotelian text, and thereby transforms the whole structure of the Aristotelian theory of government. Whereas Aristotle distinguishes four basic kinds of government—democracy, oligarchy, aristocracy, and monarchy (kingship and tyranny)—Ibn Rushd's commentary distinguishes between the ideal state, on the one hand, and all other kinds of government, which are deficient, on the other. Hence, although in Aristotle democracy appears as a legitimate form of government, one among others, in Ibn Rushd, following Plato, it is described as one of the deficient kinds of government. This is yet another example of how medieval Muslim and Jewish political philosophy followed Plato, even when it was interpreting an *Aristotelian* text. Its negative attitude toward democracy was the result of this.

VI

Medieval Jewish political philosophy generally considered (limited) monarchy to be the preferred form of government, albeit with a great deal of suspicion and hesitancy. This was the combined effect of the Platonic tradition and halakhic norms. Don Isaac Abravanel, writing at the end of the Middle Ages, is the only major Jewish thinker who openly opposed monarchy and followed rather the Aristotelian tradition.

Abravanel's democratic leanings were influenced by a combination of factors, mainly by late medieval scholastic political philosophy, which was based upon Aristotle's *Politics*, his own devastating personal experience with Iberian monarchies, and the very positive impression the Italian republics of his day, especially Venice, made upon him after he settled in Italy in the last decade of the fifteenth century. In the first place, however, it was the result of his theological views, which aspired for direct divine rule over humankind, and thus considered any kind of human rule a usurpation of divine rights. His theocratic world view necessarily led to a more "democratic" attitude in earthly affairs.[43]

Although Abravanel's antimonarchist inclinations are strongly indicated in his commentary to Deut. 17 and 1 Samuel 8, his republican tendency is illustrated in his commentary on the two biblical versions of Jethro's advice to Moses (Exodus 18 and Deut. 1), in which the Mosaic constitution, created under his wise father-in-law's advice, is described according to the lines of the Venetian constitution, considered at that time to be the embodiment of the perfect republic. The Mosaic constitution is described as a mixed constitution, according to the Aristotelian-Polybian line, creating the perfect balance among the three positive kinds of government: monarchy, aristocracy, and democracy. In this system, the rulers of thousands, being the largest representative assembly in this governmental system, represent the democratic element.[44]

According to Abravanel's interpretation of the biblical text, Moses improved upon his father-in-law's advice and imposed a stronger democratic component. In the first version (Exodus 18) Jethro advised Moses to appoint the various rulers himself, according to his own superior judgment: "thou shalt provide . . . and place over them" (v. 21). According to this version of the story, Moses did exactly what his father-in-law advised: "And Moses chose able men out of all Israel and made them heads over the people . . ." (v. 25). In the second version of the story (Deut. 1), however, we find a different picture altogether. Here Moses transferred the election of the various officers to the people themselves: "Get you, from each one of your tribes, men who are understanding, and full of knowledge, and I will make them heads over you" (v. 13).[45] According to Abravanel, Moses did not accept Jethro's advice on this point, so that it would not be said that he behaved like Korah, who appointed his relatives to official duties and was punished accordingly.

Even Abravanel's Moses, however, was no wild democrat. Moses did not simply transfer the election of the officers to the people. He gave them clear instructions to choose appropriately, according to the candidates' virtues and their suitability to fulfill judicial, political, and military duties. Abravanel indicates that Moses directed the people to choose officials according to their virtues, not their lineage; nevertheless, he hastens to add—no doubt considering himself a good example—virtuous and able men will generally be found among distinguished families.[46] Although Moses gave to the people the power to choose, he kept the final approval of the elected officials in his own hands: "and I will make them heads over you." (v. 13). This is how far his trust in the people went. His "democratic" tendency was mitigated by a strong aristocratic flavor. Still, Abravanel's Moses chose to act in a more democratic manner than was counselled. Jethro advised him to create a system that would be a combination of monarchy and aristocracy. Moses added to it a democratic element.

To sum up, medieval Jewish thought, following Platonic and Muslim political philosophy, on the one hand, and halakhic norms on the other, was basically, although reluctantly, monarchist, and inherently antidemocratic. It rejected outright the ancient Greek version of liberal democracy. Even Abravanel, for all his clear antimonarchic tendencies, showed democratic, or republican, tendencies only to a very limited degree. His antimonarchism was not the consequence of any liberal tendencies, but rather of his professed theocratic views. There were various manifestations of "communal democracy" in the premodern Jewish experience, but liberal democracy was totally rejected in Jewish philosophy. Jewish political experience with liberal democracy is a phenomenon of modern times.

NOTES

This chapter originated with my discussion in the workshop on Liberal Democracy and Communal Democracy in the Jewish Political Tradition, at the International Center for University Teaching of Jewish Civilization, Jerusalem (July 14–19, 1991). A version of it has already been published in the *Jewish Political Studies Review* 5, nos. 1–2 (Spring 1993). It is reproduced here, slightly revised, by permission of the publisher.

1. See Elazar 1993 and many of his other writings. For the development of medieval communal democracy, see Agus 1953; see the author's conclusion, p. 157: "We encounter in the communities of the thirteenth century a government, democratic in form, based on ideals of justice, freedom and equality." I would be more cautious in applying modern terms to medieval systems of government. In any case, if the political order really was some kind of "democracy," it was communal democracy and not liberal democracy of the Greek or modern variety.

2. See Melamed forthcoming a, especially chapter 1, and with additional bibliography.

3. See Melamed 1992.

4. Plato, *Republic* 8 (558c).

5. *Republic* 8 (561a–e). On the theory of liberal democracy in Greek thought, see Havelock 1964.

6. Lerner and Mahdi 1967, p. 42; cf. the Hebrew translation: Alfarabi, *Sefer ha-Hatchalot*, p. 47.

7. For the English translation, see Lerner and Mahdi, ibid., pp. 50–53; cf. the Hebrew translation: Alfarabi, *Sefer ha-Hatchalot*, pp. 56–58.

8. For the English translation, Lerner and Mahdi, ibid., p. 51: "It looks like an embroidered garment full of colored figures and dyes." For the Hebrew text, Alfarabi, ibid., p. 57. The Platonic source is *Republic* 8 (557c): "Many people may think it [i.e., democracy] the best [government] just as women and children might admire a mixture of color of every shade in the pattern of a dress." Compare Rosenthal 1969, p. 93, and his English translation, pp. 229–230: "Therefore this state, that is, the democratic one, resembles a garment woven in many colors. Just as women and youths may think that such a kind of garment is good because of the variety of its colors, so seems to be the idea about this state at first thought."

9. Lerner and Mahdi, ibid., p. 50; cf. the Hebrew text, Alfarabi, ibid., p. 56.

10. Maimonides, *Guide* 3.27: 510.

11. Maimonides, *Moreh Nevukim with Commentaries*, trans. Samuel Ibn Tibbon, 3.27, p. 41.

12. See notes 9 and 11.

13. Alfarabi, *Sefer ha-Hatchalot*, p. 57.

14. Maimonides, *Commentary on the Mishnah*, pp. 128–129 (Rosner trans.). See also commentary to *Avot*, pp. 32–33 (David trans.): "The ignorant man [i.e., *am ha-aretz*] is one who does not have intellectual virtues but has some moral virtues."

15. See Melamed forthcoming a; also, Melamed forthcoming b.

16. For Rosenthal's translation, see Rosenthal 1969. For Lerner's translation, see Lerner 1974. On Ibn Rushd's commentary, see Rosenthal's and Lerner's introductions; also Rosenthal 1968, pp. 175–209, Mahdi 1978, Butterworth 1985, 1986. On the Hebrew translation, see Berman 1967.

17. Rosenthal 1969, p. 80 [Hebrew], p. 207 [English].

18. Lerner 1974, p. 105.

19. Rosenthal 1969, pp. 85, 88, 92, 93 [Hebrew].

20. Ibid., pp. 227, 229–230. Rosenthal translates all the variants as "the democratic state." Lerner 1974 translates *medinah kibbutzit* as "democratic association," p. 110, and "democratic city," pp. 113, 125, 127, 130.

21. Rosenthal 1969, p. 83 [Hebrew], pp. 212–213 [English]. See also Lerner 1974, p. 110: "It is the association in which everyone in it is unrestrained. He does what his heart desires and moves toward whichever of the pleasing things his soul leads him." On Ibn Rushd's discussion of democracy, see also Butterworth 1986, pp. 75–76.

22. Rosenthal 1969, p. 94 [Hebrew], p. 230 [English]. Lerner 1974 translates as "hedonistic governance," p. 128.

23. Rosenthal 1969, p. 83 [Hebrew], p. 213 [English].

24. Ibid., p. 94 [Hebrew], p. 231 [English].

25. Ibid., p. 83 [Hebrew], pp. 213–214 [English].

26. Ibid., pp. 83–84 [Hebrew], pp. 213–214 [English].

27. Ibid., p. 83 [Hebrew], p. 213 [English].

28. Ibid., p. 94. Rosenthal translates as "democratic rule," p. 232; Lerner 1974 translates as "democratic leadership," p. 130.

29. Rosenthal 1969, pp. 92–95 [Hebrew], pp. 227–233 [English]; Lerner 1974, pp. 125–131.

30. Plato, *Republic* 7 (555e). Compare Rosenthal 1969, p. 92 [Hebrew], p. 228 [English]; Lerner 1974, p. 126.

31. Rosenthal 1969, p. 93 [Hebrew], p. 229 [English]; cf. Lerner 1974, p. 127 and see note 34.

32. Neither Rosenthal nor Lerner refer at all to the possible usage of the biblical text by the Hebrew translator, although elsewhere Rosenthal does refer to the usage of biblical phrases; see, for example, p. 230, n. 1.

33. Rosenthal 1969, p. 95 [Hebrew], p. 232 [English]; Lerner 1974, p. 130.

34. Ibn Rushd 1842. On Ibn Rushd's rhetoric, see Butterworth 1972. Butterworth makes clear Ibn Rushd's departure from an Aristotelian position to a more Platonic one. With respect to the present issue, however, he says merely that unlike Aristotle, "Averroes did not hesitate to discuss the best regime in his rhetorical treatise" (ibid., p.

195). Butterworth does not refer to the fact that in content, too, the discussion is more Platonic in nature. On the other hand, in his commentary on Plato's *Republic*, Ibn Rushd presents, at various points, an "Aristotelian" interpretation to the Platonic text; see Butterworth 1986, pp. 48, 72, 89. Butterworth argues that, in the theory of regimes, Ibn Rushd adopts an "Aristotelian" position by indicating the possibility of more than one positive kind of government (ibid., p. 72); see also Lerner 1974, p. 104. Ibn Rushd, however, did not attenuate Plato's negative view of democracy by adopting a more moderate, "Aristotelian" interpretation, and that is what is most important as far as my discussion is concerned. The general position indicated here—namely, to attenuate the differences between Plato and Aristotle—is very typical of Ibn Rushd and other Muslim philosophers; on this, see Rosenthal 1968.

35. Ibn Rushd 1842, p. 31.

36. Ibid. See also the Latin translation of the Hebrew version by the Italian Jewish humanist Abraham de Balmes, in Aristotle 1562. Balmes incorrectly translated "*hanhagut ha-cherut*" as "*politia nobilitatis*," pp. 79, 86.

37. Ibn Rushd, 1842, pp. 53–54. Balmes translates (correctly, this time) as "*civitas popularis*," p. 87. In Judah Messer Leon's rhetorical treatise *Nofet Zufim*, written in the Italian Renaissance, long segments of Todrosi's translation are inserted, including the discussion of the theory of government; see Messer Leon 1983. Rabinowitz translates *ha-hanhagah ha-kibbutzit* as "collective government," p. 305, n. 2.

38. Ibn Rushd 1842, p. 53, and see Balmes's translation, p. 86.

39. Ibn Rushd 1842, p. 31, twice.

40. Ibid., pp. 53–54. Messer Leon copies the text from Todrosi almost verbatim; see Messer Leon 1983, p. 306, and Rabinowitz's English translation, p. 307: "A democratic state is one in which headship is achieved through chance or luck, not through being really deserved, since in this sort of state no one individual has superiority over any other." My translation is different in various points. Rabinowitz is mistaken when he translates *ha-mazal* as "luck." In the context of the electoral system of the Athenian democracy, and the original Aristotelian text (see n. 42), the correct translation is "lot." The same goes for Balmes's Latin translation where *ha-mazal* is translated as "*fortuna*," p. 86.

41. Ibn Rushd 1842, p. 54; compare Aristotle, *Rhetoric* 1.8 (1366a).

42. Aristotle, *Rhetoric* 1.8 (1365b).

43. For Abravanel's political philosophy in general, see Netanyahu 1972 and note 44.

44. See in detail Melamed 1990.

45. Abravanel, *Perush al ha-Torah* 2.157; compare Aquinas's identical commentary, in Melamed 1990.

46. See in detail Melamed 1990; compare Nachmanides's even more "democratic" interpretation, in ibid., p. 32, n. 24.

REFERENCES

Abravanel, I. 1969. *Perush al ha-Torah*. Jerusalem: Torah ve-Daʿat.

Agus, I. A. 1953. "Democracy in the Communities of the Early Middle Ages." *Jewish Quarterly Review* 43: 153–176.

Alfarabi. 1349. *Sefer ha-Hatchalot*, trans. Moses Ibn Tibbon. In *Sefer ha-Asif*, ed. Z. Filipowsky, pp. 1–64. Leipzig: K. F. Köhler. Photoreproduced in Israel, 1970.

Aristotle. 1966. *The Basic Works of Aristotle*, ed. R. McKeon. New York: Random House.

———. 1562. *Aristotelis Opera cum Averrois Commentariis*. Venice. Photoreproduced at Frankfurt am Main, 1982, vol. 2.

Berman, L. V. 1967. "Greek into Hebrew: Samuel ben Judah of Marseilles, Fourteenth Century Philosopher and Translator." In *Jewish Medieval and Renaissance Studies*, ed. A. Altmann, pp. 289–320. Cambridge, Mass.: Harvard University Press.

Butterworth, C. E. 1972. "Rhetoric and Islamic Political Philosophy." *International Journal of Middle East Studies* 3: 187–198.

———. 1985. "Ethics and Classical Islamic Philosophy: A Study of Averroes' *Commentary on Plato's Republic*." In *Ethics in Islam*, ed. R. G. Hovannisian. Malibu, Calif.: Undena Publications.

———. 1986. "Philosophy, Ethics and Virtuous Rule: A Study of Averroes' *Commentary on Plato's Republic*." *Cairo Papers in Social Sciences*, Vol. 9, Monograph 1.

Elazar, D. J. 1993. "Communal Democracy and Liberal Democracy in the Jewish Political Tradition." *Jewish Political Studies Review* 5: 5–31.

Havelock, E.A. 1964. *The Liberal Temper in Greek Politics*. New Haven and London: Yale University Press.

Ibn Rushd. 1842. *Biur Sefer ha-Halatzah le Aristo be-Ha'atakat Todros Todrosi*, ed. J. Goldenthal. Leipzig.

Lerner, R. (trans.). 1974. *Averroes on Plato's Republic*. Ithaca, N.Y., and London: Cornell University Press.

———, and M. Mahdi (eds.). 1967. *Medieval Political Philosophy: A Sourcebook*. New York: The Free Press.

Mahdi, M. 1978. "Alfarabi et Averroes: Remarques sur le *Commentaire* d'Averroes sur la *République* de Platon." In *Multiple Averroes*, ed. J. Jolivet, pp. 91–101. Paris: Les Belles Lettres.

Maimonides. 1960. *Moreh Nevukim with Commentaries*, trans. Samuel Ibn Tibbon. Jerusalem.

———. 1963. *The Guide of the Perplexed*, 2 vols., trans. S. Pines. Chicago: University of Chicago Press.

———. 1968. *The Commentary to Mishnah Aboth*, trans. A. David. New York: Bloch Publishing Company.

———. 1975. *Commentary to the Mishnah: Sefer Zeraim*, trans. F. Rosner. New York: Feldheim Publishers.

Melamed, A. 1990. "Jethro's Advice in Medieval and Early Modern Jewish and Christian Political Thought." *Jewish Political Studies Review* 2: 3–41.

———. 1992. "Aristotle's *Politics* in Medieval and Renaissance Jewish Thought" [Hebrew]. *Pe'amim* 51: 27–69.

———. Forthcoming a. *The Philosopher King in Medieval and Renaissance Jewish Political Thought*. Atlanta: Scholars Press.

———. Forthcoming b. "Maimonides on the Political Nature of Man: Needs and Responsibilities." In *Festschrift for S. O. Heller Wilensky*, ed. D. Dimant and M. Idel.

Messer Leon, J. 1983. *The Book of the Honeycomb's Flow*, ed. and trans. I. Rabinowitz. Ithaca, N.Y.: Cornell University Press.

Netanyahu, B. 1972. *Don Isaac Abravanel: Statesman and Philosopher*. Philadelphia: Jewish Publication Society of America.

Plato. 1967. *The Republic of Plato*, trans. F. M. Cornford. New York and London: Oxford University Press.

Rosenthal, E. I. J. 1968. *Political Thought in Medieval Islam*. Cambridge: Cambridge University Press.

———. (ed. and trans.). 1969. *Averroes' Commentary on Plato's Republic*. Cambridge: Cambridge University Press.

Abravanel and the Jewish Republican Ethos

Reuven Kimelman

The two most influential medieval Jewish political theorists, Maimonides and Abravanel, are deeply divided on the nature and structure of government. Whereas Maimonides appears to champion monarchy, Abravanel appears as an advocate of republicanism. Many assume that Maimonides represents the normative tradition and Abravanel the exception. Accordingly, treatments of Maimonides frequently start with his treatment of the biblical commandment to appoint a king,[1] whereas treatments of Abravanel oftentimes focus on external influences.

One of the best known efforts at uncovering the external influence on Abravanel is that of Fritz Baer. After placing Abravanel within the contemporary world of Renaissance humanism, he goes on to attribute Abravanel's politics to his humanism. For him, Abravanel's republicanism is simply a correlate of his humanism.[2] Baer's position has been countered by B. Netanyahu who shows the lack of correlation between the humanists of the day and any specific political position. Netanyahu also discounts the alleged influence of the Greco-Roman political tradition, including Plato, Aristotle, and Cicero. Moreover, he rejects any strict correlation between Abravanel's experiences with the monarchies of his day and his own republicanism.[3] Instead, he holds that Abravanel's "attack on monarchism . . . lies . . . in his conception of the dual government: the secular-human and the spiritual-divine" and his goal of constructing a complete theocracy under the rule of God alone. The source for these ideas, according to Netanyahu, was the

Augustinian division between the City of God and the City of Man and its goal of eliminating "the City of Man . . . to establish the sole reign of the City of God."[4] The major contemporary influence, according to Netanyahu, was the Florentine leader and martyr against tyranny Girolamo Savonarola.[5]

A more recent effort at accounting for Abravanel's position has been that of Aviezer Ravitsky. In underscoring the commonality between the political thinking of Aquinas and Abravanel he points out that both Aquinas and Abravanel compared the transition from the period of the Judges to the monarchy with that of the transition from the Roman Republic to the Roman Empire. In both cases, the change to either monarchy or empire was viewed negatively. As Ravitsky notes, however, Aquinas does not draw the antimonarchic conclusions that Abravanel does. Indeed, by refuting Aquinas's analogies from theology and nature for government by an autocrat, Abravanel undermines the argument put forward by Aquinas for monarchy.[6] Not being able to explain Abravanel's position by reference to Aquinas, Ravitsky suggests that Abravanel's deviation from the Maimonidean model of monarchy can be attributed to the influence of Nissim of Gerondi, whose claim to fame is his doctrine of the separation of judicial from monarchic powers.[7] Gerondi's position on the separation of powers, however, explains little of Abravanel's absolute antimonarchic position. Indeed, as Ravitsky points out, Abravanel actually reverses Gerondi's position to highlight the arbitrariness of royal power. Abravanel's position is even more problematic in the light of a recent study by Abraham Melamed that concludes that Abravanel probably never read Aristotle's *Politics* directly and was influenced only minimally by Christian political thought.[8]

The real issue, however, is not whether Augustine, Savonarola, or someone else enunciated ideas similar to those of Abravanel, but rather what made Abravanel so receptive to this agenda. It is my contention that it was precisely the republican tradition *in* Jewish political theory that accounts for the receptivity. This chapter seeks to show the degree to which Abravanel's position is consonant with a long-standing reading of Jewish political history. The approach consists in surveying those trends in classical Jewish thought that could serve to ground a republican political philosophy and thus could have served as the soil from which Abravanel's theory sprouted or at least from which it was nourished.

The point is to underscore how representative of Jewish political theory Abravanel is and how subsequent readings of the tradition have been skewed by the Maimonidean reading. Maimonides is such a commanding figure in the history of Jewish law that his rulings cast long shadows over subsequent deliberation. Nevertheless, if it can be shown that Abravanel's position is rooted in pre-Maimonidean thought, then a strong case is made for Jewish republicanism, however theocratic.

There are two focused discussions of kingship in the Bible, one in the book of Samuel, the other in Deuteronomy. The Samuel discussion appears in a context of the prophet Samuel seeking to dissuade the people from having a king. In doing so he lists the following norms of kingship:

> This will be the practice of the king who will rule over you:
>
> 1. He will take your sons and appoint them as his charioteers and horsemen, and they will serve as outrunners for his chariots.
> 2. He will appoint them as his chief of thousands and of fifties; or they will have to plow his fields, reap his harvest, and make his weapons and the equipment for his chariots.
> 3. He will take your daughters as perfumers, cooks, and bakers.
> 4. He will seize your choice fields, vineyards, and olive groves, and give them to his courtiers.
> 5. He will take a tenth part of your grain and vintage and give it to his eunuchs and courtiers.
> 6. He will take your male and female slaves, your choice young men (or cattle—*Septuagint*) and your asses, and put them to work for him.
> 7. He will take a tenth part of your flocks, and you shall become his slaves. (1 Samuel 8:11–17)

The second is the laws of kingship in Deuteronomy. The first part mentions the request for a king along with the conditions, qualifications, and restrictions on an Israelite monarch: "If, when you have entered the land that the Lord your God has given you, and have occupied it and have settled in it, you decide, 'I will set a king over me, as do all the nations about me,' you shall be free to set a king over yourself, one chosen by the Lord your God. Be sure to set as king over yourself one of your own people; you must not set a foreigner over you, one who is not your kinsman. More-over, he shall not keep many horses, or send people back to Egypt to add to his horses, since the Lord has warned you, 'You must not go back that way again.' And he shall not have many wives, lest his heart go astray; nor shall he amass silver and gold to excess" (Deut. 17:14–17).

The second part stipulates the conditions for dynastic perpetuation: "When he is seated on his royal throne, he shall have a copy of this Torah written for him by the levitical priests. Let it remain with him and let him read from it all his life, so that he may learn to revere the Lord his God, to observe faithfully every word of this Torah as well as these laws. Thus he will not act haughtily toward his fellows or deviate from the *mitzvah* to the right or to the left, to the end that he and his descendants may reign long in the midst of Israel" (17:18–20).

Although these two passages have proved seminal for the biblical understanding of government, there is disagreement on their thrust. With regard to Samuel, the question is whether the prophet Samuel is laying out the legitimate prerogatives of monarchy or just deterring the establishment of monarchy by underscoring its excesses. One of the more recent attempts to understand the material as antimonarchic is that of Baruch Halpern. He construes the material as an "effort to dissuade the assembly from adopting monarchy." According to him, Samuel "adopts the subtle strategy of formulating a proposal stronger than the proponents of change would like. . . . Concentrating on the economic costs of kingship, he suggests that the government will burgeon, . . . [and that] central government could grow only at their expense."[9] Nonetheless, Halpern points out that in accommodating to this change, Samuel took safeguards to prevent the process from running amok. Thus the king must secure divine approval and consent of the assembly. The fact that the king must secure divine approval and that the law of kingship was written down and deposited before God (1 Samuel 10:25) seems to confirm, following Halpern, that the preceding list was intended to delimit regal prerogatives and place them under the oversight of prophets or priests. Recent literary analysis of 1 Samuel 8–12 has shown that the various units alternate between affirming and negating monarchy. The result, it claims, is that the four chapters together constitute a literary effort at exploring the problematics of kingship.[10]

At any rate, there are contemporary readings of Samuel that parallel the position of Abravanel. In arguing against monarchy, Abravanel adopted scare tactics similar to those of Samuel. He adapted the theory of Nissim of Gerondi: the "great authority" granted to the monarch becomes for Abravanel "absolute authority." He also eliminated the right of rebellion. Both moves absolutized royal authority. Through such absolutization of monarchic power Abravanel endeavored to quash the desire for monarchy.[11]

This oscillation between pro and antimonarchic stances in Samuel can be detected as well in the book of Judges. Gideon's reply to the request that he become king, saying, "I will not rule over you myself, nor shall my son rule over you; the Lord alone shall rule over you" (Judges 8:23), clearly reflects antimonarchic sentiments, as do Jotham's fable and the story of Abimelech in Judges 9. Judges 17–21, however, reflects the opposite tendency.

Indeed, pro and antimonarchic sentiments run through the classical biblical literature. Much of the focus of the debate revolves on whether the establishment of an Israelite monarchy is a commandment or an option. The basis for the debate is the verse "And you shall say, I will set a king over me" (Deut. 17). The *Sifre* (156) comments:

> R. Nehorai says: This is to Israel's discredit, as it says: ". . . for they have not rejected you but they have rejected Me, that I should not be king over them" (1 Samuel 8:7).
> Said R. Judah: But is it not a command of the Torah that they should request a king, for it says: ". . . you shall surely place a king over you" (Deut. 17:15).[12]

It is clear that what R. Judah sees as a positive commandment, R. Nehorai sees as a condemnation.[13] As he says elsewhere, the monarchy is nothing more than an accommodation to the anticipated insistence of the people. For him, Deuteronomy 17:14 reflects the same grudging concession to the popular demand for a monarch based on the models of the surrounding gentile nations as found in Samuel. Nonetheless, based on this statement of R. Judah and another of his that says: "Israel was commanded three commandments upon their entry to the land: to appoint a king . . . ,"[14] Maimonides concluded that monarchy is a biblical mandate.[15] Among those who followed the Maimonidean reading are Moshe of Coucy, Joseph Bekhor Shor, Menachem ha-Meiri, Nissim of Gerondi, and Joshua Ibn Shu'ib.[16]

Despite the impact of the Maimonidean reading, the notion that monarchy is (biblically) optional or concessive runs through the literature from the first through the twentieth centuries. It is already found in Josephus,[17] and supported by the commentaries to Deuteronomy 17:14 of Saadia Gaon, Abraham Ibn Ezra, Abravanel, Sforno, David Zvi Hoffmann, and others. If there is a mandatory element at all, according to Abravanel, it is to abide by the restrictions of consanguinity and divine selection if the people initiate a request for a king.[18] In this sense, notes Abravanel, the concession of monarchy is comparable to that of the captive woman in Deuteronomy 21:10–14.[19] Between the positions of Maimonides and Abravanel are the mediating positions of Gersonides, Nachmanides, Bachya ben Asher, possibly Rashi, and the ambivalent positions of R. Samuel b. Eli and R. Samuel b. Chofni.[20]

Even though much of subsequent legal opinion followed Maimonides, he has been taken to task for deviating from the normal rules of codification that would have decided with R. Nehorai or at least against R. Judah.[21] If R. Nehorai is representative of talmudic opinion, then Abravanel is not that exceptional. As such, the explanation for Abravanel's position given by Netanyahu could apply equally well to that of the Talmud. According to Netanyahu, "The democratic features of his [Abravanel's] government must be viewed merely as part of his theocratic concept of government, since theocracy agrees to a great extent with democratic principles and practices. His opposition to monarchy was radical because nothing could symbolize more vividly for him the reign of man with his man-made law, with his tyranny and injustice, than the reign of a king. The monarch was for him the embodiment of anti-divine rule, of a regime in which people must pay obedience to man instead of paying obedience to God."[22]

The reading of the Nehorean position as reflecting the idea that human sovereignty implies a rejection of divine sovereignty is supported by the midrash that spells out the contrast between divine and human kingship. The midrash glosses the verse "I will set a king over me," saying, "Our Rabbis said: The Holy One, blessed be He, said: 'In this world you asked for kings, and kings arose in Israel and caused you to fall by the sword.'" It then goes on to enumerate the national tragedies precipitated by the kings Saul, David, Ahab, and Zedekiah, and concludes with a denigration of human kingship in favor of divine sovereignty: "When

Israel saw what befell them on account of their kings they all began to cry out: 'We do not desire a king, we desire our first king,' (as it is said), 'For the Lord is our judge, the Lord is our law-giver, the Lord is our king; He will save us' (Isaiah 33:22). Whereupon God replied: 'By your life, I will do so.' How do we know this? For it is said, 'And the Lord shall be king over all the earth' (Zechariah 14:9)."[23]

This idea that human sovereignty is contrasted negatively with divine sovereignty is also indicated in the eleventh benediction of the daily 'Amidah prayer, albeit in a more subtle form. Concerned with the theme of the restoration of political sovereignty, this benediction peculiarly lacks any reference to monarchy. Instead, rephrasing Isaiah 1:26, it says, "Return our judges as of old." The simplest form of the full version as found in the *Siddur* of R. Saadiah Gaon reads: "Return our judges as of old and our counselors as of yore. Praised are You, O Lord, King, who loves righteousness and justice." Other early medieval versions, such as that of the Genizah, a version of the *Seder* of Rav Amram Gaon, *Machzor Vitry*, and Maimonides all insert in the middle the request "You (O Lord—just the *Seder* of Rav Amram Gaon) reign over us by Yourself." Not only is there no mention of kings, there is explicit mention of judges. They are the ones to mediate divine rule. This downplaying of monarchy is borne out by the rest of the "political" benedictions of the 'Amidah in which the Davidic messiah plays no role in the redemption except to mark "the culmination of the process."[24]

Josephus also sees a collective leadership of the best, limited by law, as most consonant with divine rulership. A monarchy is permissible only as a response to popular demand. In such a case, its occupant must be one of their own, committed to promoting virtue, especially justice, and subject to the laws of God. He is also enjoined from initiating policy without prior consultation with the high priests and elders.[25]

There is not a large gap between these sources and Abravanel's outright rejection of monarchy. For him, monarchy entails absolutism and absolutism entails tyranny. Although under certain conditions he is willing to tolerate a constitutional monarchy, he clearly prefers the vesting of authority in judges.[26] In his commentary to Deuteronomy 17 and 1 Samuel 8:7, he expounds the grounds for his principled antimonarchism:

Even if we should admit that a king is beneficial and necessary for other peoples for the improvement and maintenance of political order—which actually is contrary to the truth—such reasoning does not make kingship necessary for Israel. The general proposition advances three arguments in favor of kingship:

1. As supreme commander of the armed forces, the king provides people with help and comfort against the enemy, and leads them in the fight for their country;
2. As supreme legislative authority, he provides his people with a constitution and laws as the occasion warrants;
3. As supreme judicial tribunal, he sentences and punishes often against the law if called for by the circumstances.

Abravanel counters all three arguments for the necessity of a king to maintain security, initiate legislation, and adjudicate conflict by holding that (1) God is Israel's help against their enemies and judges like Joshua, Gideon, Samuel, and others were sufficiently competent to lead them to battle; (2) the Torah and not the king is the source of legislation; and (3) the supreme court or Sanhedrin is authorized to administer judicial function and not the king. There is no greater recipe for tyranny than granting extra-legal power to an absolute monarch.[27]

His argument for the superiority of judges over kings is made by reviewing the historical experience of Israel during the biblical period, colored by citations from Job and Hosea:

Experience teaches us that we can even more forcefully point to the lesson of the kings of Israel and Judah about whom it is said, "They were rebels against the light" (Job 24:13). They turned Israel's heart backward, as you know of Jereboam, the son of Nebat, as did all the other kings of (the northern kingdom of) Israel, as well as most of the Judean kings, who brought about the Judean exile. Such was not the case with Israel's judges and prophets, who were all competent rulers who feared God, all men of integrity, who hated unjust gain. . . . All this demonstrates that the leadership of judges is a good thing, whereas the leadership of kings is bad, harmful and extremely dangerous. This accounts for Hosea prophesying in God's name, "I give you kings in my ire . . ." (Hosea 13:11).[28]

According to Abravanel, it is precisely the political pluses of monarchy that are its moral minuses. The advocates of monarchy praise it for its unity or singular leadership, cross-generational stability, and absolute power. Abravanel, on the other hand, advocates limited powers and collective leadership, subject to limited terms. Collective leadership will promote mutual scrutiny and monitoring. It also allows the deficiencies of one to be made up by the other. Rotational leadership allows subsequent administrations to check the probity of their predecessors, thereby holding them accountable for any wrongs committed under their administration.[29]

This concern with the abuse of power is also the focal point of the biblical discussion. It constitutes the organizing idea behind chapter 17 of Deuteronomy, which is, following the biblical order, the first mention of the institution of monarchy for Israel. Its strangeness lies in its complete focus on the limits of the monarch. Unlike Samuel, there is a total absence of an outline of regal power. The absence of any mention of regal power makes the document concerned rather with the prevention of despotism than with the establishment of monarchy. The limitations of Deuteronomy enjoin the monarch from multiplying horses, wives, silver, and gold, while obliging him to be an Israelite and have his own copy of the Torah. There are two major schools of thought on this effort to circumscribe royal power. One school of thought takes the limitations as intended primarily to limit the excesses of the king, the other to limit the excesses of government.

The first position as propounded by Maimonides views the restrictions as safeguards against the moral dissolution of the king. It argues for the impropriety of a king being involved in nonfunctional ostentation, or vainglorious acquisition of possessions, or indulgence in sexual excess, "so that his heart turn not away" (Deut. 17:17), "for his heart is the heart of the whole community of Israel."[30] Being preoccupied with the heart of the people he will, as the verse says, "turn not away," that is, not be diverted from the affairs of state.

This concern with the moral and political stature of kingship induces Maimonides to append to the Deuteronomic restrictions one regarding intoxication. He states: "The king is forbidden to drink to the point of intoxication as it is written: 'It is not for kings to drink wine' (Prov. 31:4). He shall be occupied day and night with the study of the Law and the needs of Israel, as it is said: 'And it shall be with him, and he shall read therein all the days of his life' (Deut. 17:19)." The connection between the moral life and political duty is here tied tightly. Incapable of attending to the needs of people, a sottish monarch becomes a political liability. Maimonides lines up with earlier Gaonic thought in grasping the prohibitions as a means of preventing the ruler from being distracted from the responsibilities of leadership.[31]

Maimonides prefers to deal with the threat of the abuse of power by cultivating a king more resistant to the enticements of power than by infringing on the authority of the king. By relying on the cultivation of a philosophic spirit in the king through constant study he hoped to balance the corrupting influences inherent in the office. His tactic is twofold: On the one hand, he grants the king wide-ranging authorities, among which is responsibility for the security of the realm including that of initiating defensive wars and, with proper approval, even engaging in economic and political expansion by military means.[32] He may even exceed the limits of legality in capital punishment to maintain the social order.[33] On the other hand, he stresses the moral role of kingship and makes the king responsible for the propagation of justice and religion. He thus concludes his presentation of royal prerogatives with the following charge: "Whatever he does should be done by him for the sake of Heaven. His sole aim and thought should be to uplift the true religion, to fill the world with righteousness, to break the arm of the wicked, and to fight the battles of the Lord."[34] This last rhetorical flourish is made all the more poignant by echoing motifs found in the Isaianic description of the messianic king.[35] There is nothing like a sense of mission to abate the cravings of power.

Abravanel also explains the restriction imposed on the king as directed at containing royal excesses. For him, the prohibition against multiplying horses counters the royal drive for self-glorification that is frequently promoted by military exploits. The limitation on the number of wives corresponds to the temptation of royalty to overindulgence and the sating of lust to utter distraction. And finally, to thwart the royal proclivity of becoming immersed in amassing great wealth, there is the rule against the excessive acquisition of gold and silver. Indeed, Abravanel believed that a monarch engrossed in the pursuit of wealth will come to acquire it illegally, oppressively, and violently.[36] Abravanel maintains that the power and visibility of the king imposes upon him a special obligation to serve as moral exemplar. A king must appear reluctant to resort to violence, be above self-indulgence, and not be enmeshed in the pursuit of self-aggrandizement. As subject to the commandments, he is not only to commission his own copy of the Torah, but to make provision to be in possession of one in all of his endeavors.

Abravanel supplies three considerations for the special role of the king as religious paradigm. As the most visible and admired person in the realm, both his virtues and defects will be magnified among the people. As a public figure, his position becomes a public trust. Abravanel realized that whatever a king does, for good or for ill, takes place on a grand scale. Secondly, as subject to the temptations and vertigo of power, he is in need of edification and restraint. Long-term, intensive character education is a royal prerequisite. Last, as the most exalted of men in this world, he should cultivate those spiritual qualities that will allow him to be and remain above the transience of this world.[37] If a ruler cannot remain above the fray, the exigencies of the moment will preclude the possibility of far-sighted statesmanship.

The other school of political philosophy holds that the limitations on the king are aimed less at his personal development than at inhibiting the arrogation of power that leads to tyranny. Because this phenomenon is so often associated with warfare, the limitations are seen as impeding any rush into war.

The prophet Isaiah was one of the first to link up the limitation on horses with a limitation on war. He understood that horses meant chariots and that chariots are for offensive purposes. It follows for him that the acquisition of horses belies any reliance on divine protection.[38] By impeding the accumulation of military might, the restriction places brakes on the militarization of society, thereby minimizing the potential for dragging the people into war unnecessarily. For an ambitious king, a large standing army may prove irresistible.[39]

The limitation on wealth follows similar lines. As the medieval Bible commentator Abraham Ibn Ezra noted,[40] it keeps the king from exacting oppressive taxes. Moreover, such a limitation can dampen the king's desire to drag his people into war for the sake of accumulating spoil. The link between these considerations is made three centuries later by Joseph Albo, who explains that the king is prohibited from gathering "gold and silver even from enemies lest he fail and take from his people."[41] Philo, over a millennium earlier, also noted that such measures serve "to prevent him from . . . storing up great wealth all unjustly wrung from the poverty of his subjects."[42] Burdensome, especially military, taxation is particularly prone to promote the malignant growth of an imperial monarchy.

Finally, the limitation on wives can arrest the formation of entangling alliances, which were often sealed through marriage.[43] This consideration may also be behind the extra restrictions of the *Temple Scroll* (57:15–17), which not only prohibit a foreign wife but limit the king to only one wife who must be of his clan. In any event, the widespread practice of marital diplomacy facilitated not only the importation of foreign practices,[44] but also the forging of intergovernmental ententes for mutual support. Such alliances are helpful in the event of popular uprisings. How often are security forces created under the guise of protection from foreign incursion, only to be deployed to suppress internal dissension? Such unholy alliances are not rare in the history of politics. Because security alliances can increase the chances of going to war for others, the prohibition serves to counter also the strong correlation between alliance involvement and proneness to war.[45] Furthermore, the limitation on wives limits the number of contenders to the throne. Wars of succession, like all civil wars, take the greatest toll in human life.

Whereas these considerations see the limitations on the king aimed at restraining the growth of oppressive government power, Josephus specifically views the prohibitions against amassing wives, possessions, and horses as stemming the royal bent to spurn the law. He apparently believes that a government of law is the best bulwark against despotism. For him, the polity must possess the means to govern effectively without the excess that paves the way for oppression.[46]

The special injunction of commissioning a copy of the Torah, or, as some say, a summary of it such as Deuteronomy, concretizes the idea of the ruler as servant of the law rather than its master. Both Philo and the Rabbis view the purpose of a royal Torah as a way of lending prominence to the idea of royal authority as derivative of, and subject to, the Torah.[47] The constant intercourse between king and Torah was meant to produce a law-abiding king. As Joshua was told upon being installed as Moses' successor, "Let not this Torah book cease from your lips, but recite it day and night, so that you may observe faithfully all that is written in it" (Joshua 1:8). By pronouncing this admonition, Joshua is functioning in a manner that seems to fulfill the Deuteronomic requirement for the king. Although Joshua is described more as a successor of Moses than as a predecessor of Saul, he nevertheless served in several roles that were subsequently ascribed to kings. He led in war, he divided up the land, he administered and enforced the covenant, he studied the law from which he deviated neither to the right or the left, and he is called "servant of God." In this sense, Joshua, especially in chapters 1 and 23–24, is more of a link between Moses and Saul than between Moses and the Judges.

The link between Torah and the king is further promoted by the mishnaic requirement upon the king to read prescribed selections of the Torah before the whole people at the septennial national assembly.[48] These many links between the law and the king exist precisely because of his broad discretionary powers. The king must be inculcated in the rule of the law, lest he forget the true sovereign and lord it over the people. Such is the paradox of authority: The more power, the less freedom there is to follow one's whims.

Cognizant of the connection between the rise of authority and the pathology of power, a midrash underscores the need for a heightened awareness of royal limitations and responsibilities upon each assumption to the throne. It pictures a herald reminding the king of each as he ascends the six steps of the throne.[49] At the first three steps, the herald proclaims: "He shall not have many wives." "He shall not keep many horses." "Nor shall he amass silver and gold in excess" (Deut. 17:17). At the last three steps, the herald announces: "You shall not judge unfairly." "You shall show no partiality." "Neither shall you take bribes" (Deut. 16:19). Finally, as the king is about to take his seat on the throne, the herald cries out, "Know before whom you sit."[50] By combining the prohibitions against the amassing of monarchic power of the first three steps with those against judicial turpitude of the last three steps, attention is drawn to the links between governmental draining of the economy and militarization, on the one hand, and the corruption of the rule of law, on the other.[51]

Following the second school of thought that the regal directives are aimed at tempering the potential abuse of monarchy, the biblical idea of postponing the appointment of a king until after the conquest of the land takes on added sense. Normally it would be strange to make provisions for a king only after residence in the land that God had granted was secured. Indeed, the timing of the request is so strange that Abravanel considers it, "Idiocy, for you should have requested a king upon your entry into the land to fight your wars. That was the proper time for his need, not after the conquest, the division, and the dwelling in security in the land." [52]

Apparently in an effort to counter Abravanel's criticism, the sixteenth century Italian exegete Abraham Menachem Porto explains the provisions as aimed at preventing the ruler from being accredited with the conquest of the land.[53] The natural propensity of a people to attribute their security and domestic tranquillity to the military genius of the king will thus be blunted. Since the king had neither conquered nor parcelled out the land, they would not have become accustomed to total submissiveness or indebtedness. Were the king to lead the people in the conquest, they might become prone to render him absolute fealty. Were he subsequently to oversee distribution of the land, they might become totally beholden to him. Such habits of obeisance and feeling of gratitude to one who has exercised absolute authority in time of war have all the markings of tyranny in time of peace. There is nothing like imperial responsibility for creating imperial rule. Precluded from laying title to the land, a nonconquering king would be hard-pressed to exercise economic control. Moreover, the biblical perception of God as sole proprietor of the land[54] precludes any comparable claim by the king. A healthy distance between the locus of political power and that of economic power thwarts the temptation for abuse that is well-nigh irresistible when the two coincide.

Concerned with the capricious use of power, this school of thought holds that the biblical moves to limit royal power are also intended to curb the natural bent of the people to relinquish their power to the king. The problem is twofold: the usurpation of power by the king, and the unconditional renunciation of power by the people. The temptation to exchange responsibility for tranquillity or to barter freedom for security is everpresent.

The argument that the balance between the need for adequate power to govern and the need for safeguards against its arbitrary use can best be maintained through the separation of powers was developed and popularized by Montesquieu. The institutionalization of the distribution of power limits the latitude for abuse by any single person or branch of government without diluting the total power available to government as a whole. Dispersing sovereignty over several institutions of government enables them to monitor each other, thereby containing each other's excesses.

The idea that members of government would monitor each other was one of Abravanel's arguments for collective leadership. As noted previously, because he advocated such clear demarcations between the military, legislative, and judicial functions of government, he saw no need for a king. This is in contradistinction to Nissim of Gerondi who advocated a separation of powers only between judges and the monarch who has responsibility for the stability and security of the political order.

The twentieth century biblical commentator David Zvi Hoffmann[55] has argued that a similar concern with the abuse of power accounts for the ruling on kingship in Deuteronomy 17:14–20 appearing in the midst of the whole corpus of ancient biblical officialdom. Prior to the rule of monarchy, the ruling on the judicial and legislative offices appears in Deuteronomy 16:18–20 and 17:8–12. Afterward comes the rulings on priests and levites (18:1–9), prophets (18:10–22), and war leaders (20). The king thus is not to function as priest, prophet, or general. By separating the judiciary from the monarchy, the system minimizes the identification of the monarch with the law, thereby enhancing his susceptibility to legal accountability.[56] By distinguishing the priesthood from the monarchy, the system guarantees the separation of the aura of the cult from the authority of the king, thereby preventing the sacralization of kingship.[57] By having separate personnel for the conduct of war, the system decreases the chances for the militarization of government, thereby reducing the conceptualization of the monarch primarily as commander-in-chief. Through such diffusion of authority, the separation of powers seeks to minimize the abuse of office. Hemmed in by the "constitutional" functions of others, the king is directed to his primary responsibility of enforcing the law. The result is that coercive sovereignty is not confused with legislative or other types of sovereignty.[58]

Finally, Abravanel's republican tendency can account for the history of Jewish leadership precisely where Maimonides's monarchic position falters. As already noted, the sine qua non of monarchism is the hereditary principle. Yet it is widely held that dynastic succession is not the only method for producing chief executives. Even Maimonides understood Joshua to be serving as a king,[59] considered the Hasmoneans to be legitimate kings,[60] and had no reservation in designating Bar-Kokhba "a great king."[61] R. David Ben Zimra, in his commentary to Maimonides's *Code*, states explicitly that when Maimonides mentions *king*, it denotes not only one crowned by a prophet, but anyone who rules by consent of the people.[62] Long before, Philo has already understood the biblical injunction of "you shall establish a ruler over yourself" to entail "appointment by election . . . made by the whole people."[63] Indeed, from Philo[64] to Rashi[65] the qualification of popular approval and that of merit has served to circumscribe the hereditary principle.

A good example of the executive = king equation is the case of the aforementioned public reading of the Torah by the king at the septennial assembly. According to 2 Kings 23:1–3, King Josiah performed this role. According to several commentators, Joshua was viewed as performing the role in Deuteronomy 31:11. Afterward when the kings had ceased to rule Israel, a somewhat similar ceremony was carried out by the Persian king's emissary, Ezra the Scribe (Nehemiah 8). Thus it is not surprising that in the postbiblical period Josephus reports that the public recitation of Scripture was a function of the high priest.[66]

Once the overlap of functions between regal and executive authority is established, one can, as Nachmanides did, conclude that war may be undertaken not only by a king, but also "by a judge or whosoever exercises jurisdiction over the people."[67] Even monarchists agree that, in the absence of a king, authority may be assumed by the consent of the governed.[68] It follows that since the king represents sovereign authority, an executive who duly assumes the reins of power is entitled to those powers of kingship that express such authority.[69]

In the twentieth century, Abraham Kook, the former Chief Rabbi of (pre-state) Israel, was most influential in promoting the idea of a king as chief executive. He saw the monarch as the embodiment of national sovereignty in whose absence sovereignty reverts back to the people. For him, a leader who represents the people and administers their affairs for the general well-being assumes the authority of a king.[70] Rabbi Kook's position on the nature and authority of the chief executive has achieved such acceptance that it serves as a halakhic basis for legitimating the security decisions of the Israeli government.[71]

By now it should be clear that Abravanel's republicanism is not so exceptional. Indeed, it may have as much right to claim to represent Jewish political theory as Maimonides's monarchism, if not more.

NOTES

1. See, e.g., Girshuni 1984 and Blidstein 1983.
2. Netanyahu 1968, p. 183.
3. Ibid., pp. 184–186.
4. Ibid., pp. 189f.
5. Ibid., p. 193.
6. Ravitsky 1989, pp. 476–479.
7. Ibid., pp. 472f.
8. Melamed 1992, pp. 27–69.
9. Halpern 1981, p. 80.
10. See Gerbrandt 1986, p. 150. On the history of the discussion of 1 Samuel 8–12 as antimonarchic, see pp. 143–154.
11. See Ravitsky 1989, pp. 472–475, 480f., who contrasts Abravanel 1964 (Commentary on Deuteronomy), pp. 170b–171a, with Maimonides (*The Laws of the Temple Utensils* 4:21) and Radak (ad 1 Kings 21:10), who allow for the removal of the monarch on grounds of moral turpitude. Nonetheless, these cases are quite exceptional; see Blidstein 1991, pp. 295–304.
12. The three loci for this debate are *Sifre Deuteronomy* 156, *Tosefta Sanhedrin* 4:5, and B. *Sanhedrin* 20b. The cited *Sifre* passage presents the clearest version of the disagreement.
13. For a discussion of their positions within rabbinic literature and culture, see Blidstein 1982–1983, pp. 15–39.
14. See note 12 and parallels in amoraic literature.
15. Maimonides, *The Laws of Kings and Their Wars* 4:1 and Maimonides 1981, Positive Commandment no. 20.
16. See Blidstein 1983, p. 21, n. 5.
17. Josephus, *Antiquities* 4.8.17 (223).
18. Abravanel 1964 (Commentary on Deuteronomy), p. 167a. Similar analyses appear earlier in Josephus and later in Chatam Sofer, *Choshen Mishpat*, no. 19; Luzzatto 1965, p. 534; and Naphtali Zvi Berlin (Netziv), *Ha'ameq Davar* (ad Deuteronomy 17:14). According to the latter, if there is a commandment, it devolves on the Sanhedrin and

only then upon the request of the people after an assessment by the Sanhedrin that neighboring monarchies are superior at maintaining the social order. Thus, for Netziv, the desirability of a monarchy is contingent upon the success of foreign models and upon popular will.

19. Abravanel 1964 (Commentary on Deuteronomy), p. 167a; Abravanel 1955 (Commentary on Samuel), p. 208a. Sforno (ad Deut. 18:14), in comparing the two, notes the disastrous results of the latter.

20. See Blidstein 1983, pp. 21f. and notes; and for Rashi, Blidstein 1986, pp. 138f.

21. Perla 1973, vol. 3, p. 230.

22. Netanyahu 1968, p. 193.

23. *Deuteronomy Rabbah* 5:11.

24. Kimelman 1988–1989, p. 177.

25. Josephus, *Antiquities* 4.8.17 (223–224).

26. Abravanel 1955 (Commentary on Samuel), pp. 204a–205a; see Funkenstein 1991, pp. 182–187.

27. Abravanel 1955 (Commentary on Samuel), pp. 206b–207; and Abravanel 1964 (Commentary on Deuteronomy), pp. 165b–166.

28. Abravanel 1964 (Commentary on Deuteronomy), p. 166b; see Abravanel 1955 (Commentary on Samuel), p. 207a.

29. Abravanel 1955 (Commentary on Samuel), pp. 205b–206b; Abravanel 1964 (Commentary on Deuteronomy), p. 165a.

30. Maimonides, *Laws of Kings* 3:6

31. *Otzar ha-Geonim, Sanhedrin*, no. 329, p. 159.

32. See Kimelman 1992, pp. 312f.

33. See Maimonides, *Laws of Kings* 3:10 with Ravitsky 1989, p. 474, n. 15 and Elon 1973, 1:43f.

34. Maimonides, *Laws of Kings* 4:10.

35. See Isaiah 11:14.

36. Abravanel 1964 (Commentary on Deuteronomy), pp. 168b–169.

37. Ibid., p. 170, For Abravanel's ambivalence about the requirements of practical politics, see Ravitsky 1989, p. 487, n. 59.

38. See Isaiah 31:1 with 2:7, along with Joshua 11:6 and 2 Samuel 8:4 and Zachariah 9:10.

39. For the social-military context, see Ikeda 1982, pp. 215–238.

40. Ibn Ezra, ad Deuteronomy 17:17; see also Abulafia 1953, ad *Sanhedrin* 21b, p. 22b.

41. Albo, *Sefer ha-Ikkarim* 4:26.

42. Philo, *The Special Laws* 4:158

43. This theory of the sixteenth century commentator, Jacob Kuli, in *Yalqut Me'am Lo'ez, Deuteronomy* 2:721, was confirmed by Malamat 1963, pp. 8–10, and Malamat 1982, pp. 198f.

44. This seems to be the major fear of Isaiah, for instead of berating the amount of silver and gold, horses, and wives as does Deuteronomy, he decries the excess, indeed unlimited, amount of silver and gold, horses, and instead of wives, idols (Isaiah 2:7–8).

45. As shown by Singer and Small 1968, and Singer and Wallace 1980, pp. 520–547.

46. Josephus, *Antiquities* 4.8.17 (223–224).

47. Philo, *The Special Laws* 4:160, 161, and 164; *Genesis Rabbah* 6:9.

48. *M. Sotah* 7:8, based on Deuteronomy 31. Bächli 1962, pp. 88–92, argues that Deuteronomy 17:18–19 also requires the king to conduct a public reading.

49. Based on 1 Kings 10:19 and 2 Chronicles 9:18.

50. *Numbers Rabbah* 12:17.

51. Philo holds out social immortality for "a law abiding ruler who honors equality, who is impervious to bribes and gives just judgements justly and ever exercises himself in the laws" (*The Special Laws* 4:169). The *Temple Scroll* 58:19b–21 also emphasizes that the king "shall not pervert justice and he shall not accept bribery to pervert the righteous administration of justice. And he shall not covet fields, vineyards and any property, houses and anything valuable in Israel so that he steals it."

52. Abravanel 1964 (Commentary on Deuteronomy), p. 167a.

53. Porto 1972, ad Deuteronomy 17; see Hoffmann 1961, vol. 2, p. 332.

54. So Leviticus 25:23.

55. Hoffmann 1961, vol. 2, p. 329.

56. As opposed to those kings who did exercise judicial functions; see 2 Samuel 8:15, 15:2–7; 1 Kings 3:9, 16–28; 7:7; 2 Kings 8:3, 15:3; Jeremiah 22:15–17.

57. As opposed to those kings who did exercise priestly functions; see 1 Samuel 13:9–16; 2 Samuel 6:14–18; 24:18–25; 1 Kings 8:25; 12:28–35; 2 Kings 16:12–16. However, 2 Chronicles 26:17–20 does share a concern with protecting hieratic prerogatives from royal encroachment.

58. The tendency to restrict the exercise of royal power reaches its extreme in the *Temple Scroll*; see Hengel, Charlesworth, and Mendels 1986, pp. 28–38.

59. *Commentary on Mishnah, Yoma* 7:5; *Laws of Kings* 3:8; *Laws of Terumah* 1:2.

60. *Laws of Chanukkah* 3:1.

61. *Laws of Fasts* 5:3.

62. Ad *Laws of Kings* 3:8.

63. Philo, *The Special Laws* 4:157.

64. See Wolfson 1968, vol. 2, pp. 328–333.
65. See Blidstein 1986, pp. 138f.
66. Josephus, *Antiquities* 4.8.12 (209).
67. Nachmanides's addenda to Maimonides 1981, p. 409.
68. See Elon 1973, vol. 1, pp. 46f. and n. 143.
69. See Meiri, *Beit ha-Bechirah, Sanhedrin* 52b.
70. Kook 1966, section 144, pp. 336f.
71. See, e.g., Yisraeli 1966, chapter 9, especially pp. 76–81;
Waldenberg 1952, 1:175f.; Magence 1979, pp. 252–263; and Goren
1982, p. 451. Chazon Ish 1957 (*Hilkhot Eruvin, siman* 114, letter *alef*),
p. 332, allows even nondefensive warfare to be conducted by a nonroyal
executive.

REFERENCES

Abravanel, I. 1964. *Commentary on the Torah* [Hebrew]. Jerusalem:
B'nei Abre'al.
———. 1955. *Commentary on the Former Prophets* [Hebrew]. Jeru-
salem: Torah ve-Da'at.
Abulafia, M. 1953. *Sefer Yad Ramah Al Massekhet Sanhedrin*. New
York: Chayil.
Bächli, O. 1962. *Israel und die Völker: Eine Studie zum Deuteronomium.*
Zürich: Zwingli Verlag.
Blidstein, G. 1991. "On Political Revolution in the Jewish Tradition." In
*Authority, Power, and Leadership in the Jewish Polity: Cases and
Issues*, ed. D. Elazar, pp. 295–304. New York: University Press of
America.
———. 1986. "Studies in the Commentaries of Rashi: Issues of Leader-
ship and Government" [Hebrew]. In *Eshel Beer-Sheva* 3:137–148.
Beer-Sheva: Ben-Gurion University Press.
———. 1983. *Political Concepts in Maimonidean Halakha* [Hebrew].
Ramat Gan: Bar-Ilan University Press.
———. 1982–1983. "The Monarchic Imperative in Rabbinic Perspec-
tive." *AJS Review* 7–8: 15–39.
Chazon Ish. 1957. *Sefer Chazon Ish, Orakh Chayyim*. Bnei-Brak.
Elon, M. 1973. *Jewish Law: History, Sources, Principles*, 3 vols. Jeru-
salem: Magnes Press.
Funkenstein, A. 1991. "The Image of the Ruler in Jewish Thought at
the End of the Middle Ages" [Hebrew]. In *Image and Historical
Consciousness in Judaism and its Cultural Environment*, pp. 182–
187. Tel Aviv.
Gerbrandt, G. 1986. *Kingship According to the Deuteronomistic History.*
Atlanta: Scholars Press.

Girshuni, Y. 1984. *Sefer Mishpat ha-Melukhah.* Jerusalem: Moznaim.

Goren, S. 1982. *Torat ha-Shabbat ve-ha-Moed.* Jerusalem: WZO Dept. for Torah Education and Culture in the Diaspora.

Halpern, B. 1981. "The Uneasy Compromise: Israel Between League and Monarchy." In *Traditions in Transformation: Turning Points in Biblical Faith,* ed. B. Halpern and J. Levenson, pp. 59–96. Winona Lake, Ind.: Eisenbrauns.

Hengel, M., J. H. Charlesworth, and D. Mendels. 1986. "The Polemical Character of 'On Kingship' in the Temple Scroll: An Attempt at Dating 11Q Temple." *Journal of Jewish Studies* 37: 28–38.

Hoffmann, D. Z. 1961. *Sefer Devarim,* 2 vols. Tel Aviv: Nezach.

Ikeda, Y. 1982. "Solomon's Trade in Horses and Chariots in Its International Setting." In *Studies in the Period of David and Solomon and Other Essays,* ed. T. Ishida, pp. 215–238. Winona Lake, Ind.: Eisenbrauns.

Kimelman, R. 1988–1989. "The Daily 'Amidah and the Rhetoric of Redemption." *Jewish Quarterly Review* 79: 165–198.

———. 1992. "War." In *Frontiers of Jewish Thought,* ed. S. Katz, pp. 309–332. Washington, D.C.: B'nai Brith Books.

Kook, A. 1966. *Mishpat Kohen.* Jerusalem.

Luzzatto, S. D. 1965. *Commentary on the Pentateuch* [Hebrew]. Tel Aviv: Dvir.

Magence, Z. 1979. *Sefer Qedushat ha-Arets.* Jerusalem: Gross Brothers.

Maimonides. 1981. *Sefer ha-Mitsvot,* ed. C. Chavel. Jerusalem: Mossad ha-Rav Kook.

Malamat, A. 1963. "Aspects of the Foreign Policies of David and Solomon." *Journal of Near Eastern Studies* 22: 1–17.

———. 1982. "A Political Look at the Kingdom of David and Solomon and Its Relations with Egypt." In *Studies in the Period of David and Solomon and Other Essays,* ed. T. Ishida, pp. 189–214. Winona Lake, Ind.: Eisenbrauns.

Melamed, A. 1992. "Aristotle's *Politics* in Medieval and Renaissance Jewish Thought" [Hebrew]. *Pe'amim* 51: 27–69.

Netanyahu, B. 1968. *Don Isaac Abravanel.* Philadelphia: Jewish Publication Society.

Perla, Y. F. 1973. *Saadiah ben Joseph Gaon, Sefer ha-Mitsvot,* 3 vols. Jerusalem: Keset.

Porto, A. 1972. *Minchah Belulah.* Jerusalem.

Ravitsky, A. 1989. "On Kings and Statutes in Jewish Thought in the Middle Ages: From R. Nissim Gerondi to R. Isaac Abravanel" [Hebrew]. In *Culture and Society in Medieval Jewry: Studies Dedicated to the Memory of Haim Hillel Ben-Sasson,* ed. M. Ben-Sasson, R. Bonfil, and J. Hacker, pp. 469–491. Jerusalem: Zalman Shazar Center.

Singer, J. D., and M. Small. 1968. "Alliance Aggregation and the Onset of War, 1815–1965." In *Quantitative International Politics: Insights and Evidence*, ed. J. D. Singer. New York: Free Press.

Singer, J. D., and M. Wallace. 1980. "Intergovernmental Organization and the Preservation of Peace, 1816–1964: Some Bivariate Relationships." *International Organizations* 24: 520–547.

Waldenberg, E. 1952. *Sefer Hilkhot Medinah*. Jerusalem.

Wolfson, H. A. 1968. *Philo*, 2 vols. Cambridge, Mass.: Harvard University Press.

Yisraeli, S. 1966. *Yad Yemini*. Tel Aviv.

Spinoza's Challenge to the Doctrine of Election

David Novak

SPINOZA'S INVERSION OF THE DOCTRINE

No authentically philosophical attempt to recover the doctrine of the election of Israel and thereby explicate its truth for our time can hope to begin rigorously without first confronting Spinoza and then overcoming him. For it was Spinoza who presented what is still the most profound rejection of the traditional meaning of this doctrine. His rejection of the traditional meaning of the doctrine greatly influenced almost every subsequent modern thinker who dealt with it. This was the case with those Jewish thinkers who chose to remain part of the Jewish people, even as Spinoza had chosen to leave the Jewish people. It was the case with those thinkers who were very much opposed to just about everything else in Spinoza's philosophy. It was the case with those thinkers who probably never read Spinoza carefully or even read him at all. The power of this rejection is that it was not a simple dismissal of the doctrine. Instead, it was a radical inversion of its traditionally accepted meaning, a deconstruction of it, if you will. In the traditional version of the doctrine, it is God who elected Israel and instituted the covenantal relationship with her. Spinoza, conversely, inverts this relationship and asserts that in truth it was Israel who elected God and instituted the covenantal relationship with him.

This inversion of meaning was accomplished by an explicit reading of the doctrine's biblical sources, a reading he thought far more convincing than that of the Jewish tradition theretofore.

However, the real power of the inversion is that it is based on the very foundation of Spinoza's whole philosophy, his intellectual vision of God. Any philosophical attempt to recover the doctrine for out time cannot be truly cogent if it does not confront and overcome Spinoza's inversion of its meaning at its very roots and then proceed from them along Spinoza's own trajectory. Even Jewish thinkers who opposed Spinoza's rejection of Judaism and defection from the Jewish people did not go far enough in their confrontation with the philosophical foundation of all this. As such, because they did not fully confront him, in the end they were not really able to overcome his rejection of what lies at the very core of Judaism.

THE GOD OF SPINOZA AND HIS RELATIONS

It is clear why the God of Spinoza cannot possess the capacity for election in general and the actual election of Israel in particular. Election is the choice by one person of another person out of a range of possible candidates. This choice then establishes a mutual relationship between the elector and the elected, in biblical terms a *covenant* (*berit*). Election also promises its ultimate purpose will be fulfilled, which is to bring finally the whole world into the covenant, that is, "redemption" (*ge'ulah*). Election is much more fundamental than just freedom of choice in the ordinary sense, where a free person chooses to do one act from out of a range of possible acts. Instead, the elector chooses another person *with whom* he or she will both act and elicit responses, and then establishes the community *in which* these acts are to be done, and then promises that *for which* the election has occurred. The content of these practical choices is governed by law (*Torah*), but there could be no such coherent standards of action without the prior context of election, the establishment of covenantal community, and the promise of ultimate purpose.[1] Covenantal election, therefore, requires an ontology that can constitute possibility, mutual relationship, and purpose. All three of these modes, however, are precluded from the ontology of Spinoza. All of them as external relations intend transcendence, something that Spinoza's immanence of internal relations cannot bear.

For Spinoza, God is the foundation of a system of complete necessity. On the purely ontological level, there is no contingency at all. Everything is exactly as it must be. Accordingly, God is *causa immanens*, which is to be understood as a cause totally correlated with all its effects necessarily.[2] The effects inhere within the cause as much as the cause inheres within the effects. Neither of them has any reality apart from this nexus. There being no gap at all between them, there is no possibility. Without possibility, it is meaningless to talk about election.[3] Even when Spinoza uses the term *choice*, which we shall see is in fact a metaphor, he does not mean that God has any other option. God himself is free only *from* any outside influences because in truth there are none. But God is not free *for* anything other than ultimately immutable eternity.[4]

It is even more meaningless to talk about a mutual relationship emerging from election on the ontological level. For mutuality presupposes that not only is the elector free to elect anyone, it also presupposes that the elected have the capacity to respond to being elected, that they have the power to themselves contribute to the ongoing relationship. But for Spinoza, if the cause is bound by necessity, a fortiori so is the effect.[5] Here there is no mutuality, only subordination. Neither causes nor effects in any way choose their status. All ontological relations are those of cause and effect.

Finally, Spinoza cannot admit any purpose on the ontological level, inasmuch as purpose presupposes a radical gap between the past, the present, and the future. What is yet to come is not simply the inevitable outcome of what has already come to be. Instead, it lies beyond what has ever been as its hidden horizon. In the biblical sense, it can only be promised by God and hoped for by humans. As for the past, because it does not inevitably and unilaterally lead into the future, those in the present cannot look to it as an unambiguous prediction of what is yet to come. Only part of the past can even be recovered, namely, that part which is revealed to those in the present as precedent for what is to be experienced and done here and now and which is to lead the elect somehow or other into the promised future.

Purpose involves an essential temporality that Spinoza cannot admit. As it was for the medieval Aristotelians, so it was for Spinoza: Time is a form of change, and what is eternal cannot by definition change.[6] To do so would fatally compromise God's total perfection. Even causality, which as Kant later showed presupposes the irreducibility of time (a *then* b, the *then* signifying the temporal gap between cause and effect), is for Spinoza to be understood *more geometrico*, namely, as the atemporal relation between lines and figures in geometry or the equally atemporal relation of ground and consequent in formal logic.[7] To use Kantian terms, the relation is analytic not synthetic.

Election itself presupposes not just possibility, which can be mathematically conceived, but *historical* possibility; that is, it takes place within distinct temporal events. In a system of thought where what is real can be seen only *sub specie aeternitatis*, the essential temporality presupposed by covenantal election, revelation, and redemption is necessarily precluded. They can be seen only *sub specie durationis*.[8] Thus in his discussion of election Spinoza wants to separate totally the eternal "word" of God—a word not uttered in literal words—from anything pertaining to history, which is the only realm where eventful words can be uttered.[9] Being unable to provide us with immutable definitions, history cannot be known by deductive means, that is, *more geometrico*.[10] Hence it is not a science, but only a form of practical surmisal, something useful (as opposed to veridical) in the active pursuit of political ends, rather than in the knowledge of natural causes. It deals with plausible meaning, not clear and distinct truth.[11]

THE POLITICAL ESSENCE OF ELECTION

If one remains at the level of Spinoza's ontology alone, it would be impossible to think even about the biblical doctrines of election, covenant, and redemption. Yet Spinoza has a good deal to say about them when he is not discussing ontology. How then does he make this considerable transition? How are ontology and history related?

In his *Tractatus Theologico-Politicus* Spinoza deals with these doctrines and carefully shows how his interest in them is not divorced from his ontological concerns. For even though reality conceived *sub specie aeternitatis* is wholly determined by prior causes, with no room at all for temporality and its possibilities, most of human reality cannot be so conceived. This is due to human ignorance. As long as humans are ignorant of the true sequence from cause to effect in their own lives, living in noetic gaps as it were, they will have to invert the ontological order when ordering their own lives. That is, they will have to look upon

the anticipated results of their actions as the determining teleological principle of them, rather than looking upon their actions as
part of a causal chain from which the results are subordinate
effects inevitably. In other words, considerations of *for which* take
practical precedence over considerations of *from which*.[12] In the
realm of human action, consideration of final causes is simply
unavoidable.

This is especially the case in the political realm. When it comes
to the fulfillment of human political needs, humans must have
purposes in mind if they are to accomplish anything in concert.
This is because Spinoza believes that human societies, unlike
individual human bodies and individual human minds, are not
natural entities.[13] Instead, they are human inventions; they are
essentially artificial constructs created by human imagination for
certain previously conceived purposes. That is why they cannot be
conceived in the perspective of strict causality (*causa sui*), namely,
sub specie aeternitatis. Therefore, ignorance of ontological causality in the political realm is not just temporary, something that
further research could eventually uncover. Such noetic progress
could be the case only in the actions of certain enlightened individuals.[14] The permanent ignorance of ontological causality is the
very presupposition of a society truly in keeping with the human
condition and its political contingencies. That is why political
knowledge cannot even have mathematical certainty.[15] Spinoza
seems to be saying that it would be folly to allow political decisions to wait for the mathematical demonstration appropriate
to the study of nature. Its very subject does not allow any such
precision.[16]

This also seems to be why Spinoza can be a determinist in the
ontological realm and a democrat in the political realm. Contemporary determinisms, on the other hand, seem to entail a much less
democratic, if not even antidemocratic political philosophy. Many
of them assume that the hierarchy we can perceive in nature now
can soon be paralleled in human society through scientific advance.
They can make this assumption, with which Spinoza would seem
to very much disagree, only because they believe that human
societies are just as natural, if not more natural, than human
individuals. As such, human societies, and for some of them even
all of human history itself, can be understood from the perspective
of strict causality of some sort.

It is the fundamental confusion of natural causality with human purposiveness that Spinoza sees at the heart of religious thinking stemming from the Bible, thinking that assimilates human choice to the will of God. For Spinoza, this is the great error of anthropomorphism; it is the confusion of God with humanity. Instead of believing that God *chose* this or that effect to happen, one should attribute to God's inalterable being the primary power that empowered those who brought about beneficial results to human individuals in society.[17] Moreover, although the affirmation of final causality qua human purposiveness is a political require- ment, the philosophical recognition of the primacy of what Spin- oza insists is *efficient* causality should keep a tight lid on the temptation to project final causality any further than is minimally required in the ordering of society. There is no more an ultimate end in history than there is an ultimate end in nature. For Spinoza, there is no eschatology. Spinoza is therefore highly critical of the Jews who still see their chosenness as having a divinely intended cosmic purpose rather than as being merely a metaphor for their own unique polity. Chosenness qua distinctiveness is only the effect, not the telos, of divine causative action.[18] And the same fascination with final causality, unchecked by a truly critical phil- osophical perspective, also led the Jews to emphasize miracles, "whose cause cannot be explained on scientific principles known by the natural light of reason."[19]

The most immediate and pervasive purpose of society is to provide its citizens with order and a greater sense of safety than they would have if they lived as lone and isolated individuals. Accordingly, when one is pleased with the function of one's own society, as the ancient Jews seem to have been with theirs, one retrospectively projects the source of this success back to an origi- nal divine plan. This is what Spinoza calls God "acting through hidden external causes."[20] One goes through the particularities of nature as experienced (*natura naturata*) back to nature per se as known directly by the mind (*natura naturans*).[21] What he means by this is that one infers from the effect back to the cause. In a true ontology, however, one deduces from the cause to its effects. This is the case when one discerns the power of God acting directly within oneself so that one knows oneself to be part of it. At this level, for Spinoza, one is happily knowledgeable and just as happily aware of being part of the divinely determined order of nature.

About this Spinoza says, "whatever human nature can effect solely by its own power to preserve its own being can rightly be called God's internal help."[22]

It is at the level of external causes that Spinoza understands the first meaning of the idea of election. It is seeing one's own chosen way of life as being consistent with "the predetermined order of nature."[23] In other words, being chosen by God is a metaphor for what human beings have chosen for themselves and believe is part of the eternal cosmic plan of God. One's work, when successfully carried out, retrospectively implies one is designated for it, rather than one's (divine) chosenness establishing the community in which one is to do one's work. In retrospect, however, the "choice" could not have been other than it was. That it is why it can only be metaphorical to attribute election or special vocation to God. Only human beings really choose anything, and those choices are significant only in the political realm.[24]

THE COVENANT AS SOCIAL CONTRACT

In the classical biblical presentations of election, the event of election is concretized in the covenant. The covenant (*berit*) is not a contract negotiated between two equal parties that can be terminated by mutual consent. Instead, the covenant is a relationship offered by God to some of his creatures and it is one they cannot finally refuse. Sooner or later they are convinced to accept it.[25] Because it is founded by God's promise, it is also interminable. "My covenant of peace shall never depart, says the Lord who loves you" (Isaiah 54:10).

For the reasons just discussed, it is clear why Spinoza cannot accept this idea of covenant as authentic. God does not make agreements with anyone. Only humans make agreements among themselves. The question is just what sort of interhuman agreement the covenant really is. Spinoza defines it as follows:

> For if men were by nature bound by the divine law, or if divine law were a law by nature (*ex natura*), there would have been no need for God to enter into a contract (*contractum*) and to bind them by a covenant (*pacto*) and by oath (*juramento*). Therefore we must concede without qualification that the divine law began from the time when men by express covenant promised to obey God in all things, thereby surrendering, as it were, their natural

freedom and transferring their right to God in the manner we described in speaking of the civil state.[26]

Although Spinoza rejects the primary biblical sense of covenant precisely because it designates a divinely elected and structured relationship with a particular people, he has, nevertheless, skillfully appropriated the secondary biblical sense of covenant. Covenant in this sense is an agreement initiated by humans among themselves and placed within the context of the primary covenant between God and his people. For example, "All of the elders of Israel came to the king at Hebron, and David made a covenant with them (*lahem*) in Hebron before (*lifnei*) the Lord" (1 Chron. 11:3). Here it is clear that the covenant between the human parties is only possible because these respective parties have a prior covenantal relationship with God. Accordingly, no human covenant is valid if it contradicts the primary covenant established by God.[27] That is why when it comes to the incorrigibly idolatrous Canaanite nations, the Bible states, "you shall not make a covenant with them" (Deuteronomy 7:2).[28]

This secondary sense of covenant becomes more fully developed in the Talmud's concept of rabbinic law (*derabbanan*). (It should not be forgotten that Spinoza was not only a student of the Bible, but also that he studied Talmud with the learned rabbis of Amsterdam.) This law is based on a covenant made between the people and their leaders *before* God.[29] The law of this covenant is made *for the sake of* enhancing the primary covenantal relationship between God and Israel.[30] It is also made *for the sake of* the common good of the people themselves and it must assume at least their tacit consent.[31] Although itself not directly revealed, it is *sanctioned by* revelation. It is observed *as if* revealed by God, even though directly revealed law (*d'oraita*) retains its normative priority.[32] For this reason, rabbinic law may not directly contradict the primary revealed law.[33]

Spinoza, of course, does not recognize the primary biblical sense of covenant because it follows from a literal acceptance of the divine election of Israel. Therefore, for him, it seems that the old secondary meaning of covenant becomes its new primary meaning; indeed, its only meaning. This covenant, then, must be *for the sake of* an ultimately noncovenantal, nonhistorical, *natural* relationship between God and any rational person. Nature has now replaced the old primary covenant of the Bible and the Rabbis.

What has not been replaced, however, is the notion that the stability and permanence of interhuman agreements require a divine referent.

With this biblical and rabbinic background of Spinoza's political theory in mind as well as his basic ontology, it is now more evident that Spinoza is not describing a contract in the way we understand that term in our secularized societies. (He was no more a "secularist" in the contemporary sense than he was an "atheist" in the contemporary sense.) For Spinoza, God plays no role in our contracts at all. Instead, he is describing a contract between humans, one whose purpose is ultimately for the sake of knowledge of God. Only at this level can God's "laws" be disobeyed because these laws are only human surmisals of what the divine plan for humans actually is. On the level of strict causality, however, where God's laws are truly operative, nothing can be disobeyed because disobedience presupposes a nonexistent mutability. Obedience or disobedience presumes a realm of possibility that Spinoza's ontology, as we have seen, cannot admit.[34]

In Spinoza's constitution of the social contract made for the sake of God two things are accomplished that could not be accomplished in an ordinary interhuman contract.

The first thing such a contract accomplishes is to affirm politically that every citizen is directly related to God.[35] The contract, precisely because it is artificial and not natural, involves no causal series. The individual's relation to God, then, is not mediated by any political structure because political structure itself is logically subsequent to it; it is not its precondition. Religion, then, begins with the individual citizen, not with any ecclesiastical-political institution, however exalted.[36] Although most people do not seem interested in being related to God for its own sake, Spinoza still insists that "the supreme good" is "the true knowledge and love of God."[37] The purpose of divinely directed law is to make society receptive and supportive of those individuals who are interested in God as he truly is, that is, as the *causa sui*, rather than as a personal and selective benefactor.

This end is what characterizes a law as "divine," a point Spinoza clearly learned from Maimonides.[38] But he also explicitly asserted that the origin of all law is human, and that the law is "divine" if concerned with the human relation to God, "human" if concerned with the relationship among humans themselves.[39]

This is a far more radical notion than Maimonides would allow because he still affirmed the traditional Jewish doctrine that all true law comes *from* God (*min hashamayim*) as well as being *for the sake of* God (*leshem shamayim*), either immediately or ultimately;[40] only rabbinic law is human-made.[41] For Spinoza, however, law in the sense of a promulgated statute could not come directly from God, because God does not speak in words. Therefore, the words of revelation are human projections, "statute[s] (*jus*) which men ordain for themselves."[42] They are responsible human attempts to promulgate laws that are intended to be consistent with the true human relation to God. They are spoken *as if* they were the direct decree of God; in Spinoza's terms the law is "referred to God."[43] But, in truth, Spinoza is convinced that "the idea and nature of God [is] not indeed in words, but in a far superior way and one that agrees excellently with the nature of mind."[44] In this refusal to admit directed verbal revelation to man, let alone philosophically constitute it, Spinoza was followed by most modern Jewish thinkers.

By connecting human political equality directly to the human relation to God, Spinoza provides a far more effective ontological orientation for democracy than the totally anthropocentric views of later social contract theorists.[45] Also, by his reinterpretation of the biblical covenant, which he doubtless believed really did take place in history, Spinoza does not have to invent the fiction of the transition from the "state of nature" to the state of society as the social contract theorists from Hobbes on had to do.[46] Thus ancient Israel, at least as described in the Bible, becomes for Spinoza a forerunner (although not a literal model) of democracy that is neither theocratic nor atheistic. This was an important political concern of Spinoza in seventeenth century Holland, where Calvinistic appropriations of the biblical doctrine of election were used to ground a theocratic polity from which Spinoza and other liberals of the time sharply differed.[47] And, although he was accused of atheism both during his lifetime and after his death, it seems clear that Spinoza would have been opposed to an atheistic society because such a society would demand a total diremption between politics and ontology. It would not allow the individual to pursue his or her true happiness, which is the knowledge and love of God—a point that the atheistic regimes of this century have made all too clearly and painfully. Spinoza would have no doubt seen their invented mythologies, which inevitably deify the state or its leader, to be idolatrous.

The second thing that the biblical covenant qua social contract accomplishes is to provide a highly effective means for the end of human law, "whose sole aim (*quae ad*) is to safeguard life and the commonwealth."[48] Now those who are philosophically astute clearly understand the benefit of social order and tranquillity as ends in themselves. They need no further goad to uphold laws designed for the sake of these ends. For them, true knowledge is sufficient. Virtue is its own reward.[49] Such persons do not need any historical revelation. The good is already theirs through what Spinoza calls "natural knowledge."[50] However, Spinoza is convinced that the vast majority of people, acting as they do for the sake of external benefits (and even conceiving God as an external benefactor), require external constraints to act in their own best interests. Here again, the biblical teaching of divine reward and punishment helped the citizens of ancient Israel become virtuous in a way that they could not if simply left to their own individual devices. So when communal religion, which is the religion of revelation, performs this function, reason is to "respect" it.[51]

The most immediate purpose of revealed law is to ensure the obedience to rightful authority that the virtue of ordinary people requires.[52] That is why revealed law is practical and not theoretical, primarily constraining rather than edifying.[53] In the realm of nature, conversely, being related to God is not an act of obedience, inasmuch as God no more commands than he elects a particular group of people.[54] Yet by referring these constraints directly to God, this system of human law avoids the arbitrary constraints of human authorities, acting only to enhance their own self-conceived political power. As Spinoza puts it, "Since the Hebrews did not transfer their right (*suum jus*) to any man, but, as in a democracy, they all surrendered their right on equal terms, . . . it follows that this covenant (*ab hoc pacto*) left them all completely equal, and they all had an equal right to consult God; . . . they all shared equally in government of the state. . . . Therefore, if one of them transgressed against religion and began to violate individual rights given by God (*jusque divinum*), the others could treat him as an enemy and lawfully subdue him."[55] By directly relating everything to God, rather than proceeding through a chain of intermediate causes, the ancient Hebrews could function without the elaborate hierarchy that usually entails tyranny. Israel's choice to covenant with God led to the establishment of a society where both the needs of the body for sustenance and safety and the needs of the soul for knowledge and love of God were well served.

In this new constitution of the covenant, Spinoza has seemingly retained the classical Jewish distinction between the relationship of man and man (*bein adam lechavero*) and the relationship of man and God (*bein adam lemaqom*).[56] The relationship of man and man is seen as a mutual covenant between free persons, who equally refer this relationship to God and thus ensure their own political equality. It is political obedience that is protected from the inequality of tyranny. Thus it is primarily practical.[57] The relationship of man and God is seen as an insightful individual's awareness of being part of the *causa sui*.[58] It is the knowledge of the individual's true cosmic status, one that is elevated from the insignificance of mutable history. Thus it is primarily theoretical. And, whereas the practical relationship is explicitly set forth in Scripture, the theoretical relationship is only implicitly alluded to there. Indeed, being based in nature rather than in human society, it cannot be the direct subject of ordinary social discourse. It is a good available only for gifted individuals. Society can only "allow freedom to philosophize (*libertatem philosophandi*) for every individual."[59] Social discourse, on the other hand, is concerned not with eternity, but rather with the historical human good, with the "sure dictates of our reason . . . which aim only at the true good of man."[60]

The covenant, then, has both practical criteria and theoretical criteria. Both these criteria are, however, universal. They could apply anywhere anytime. As such, they both preclude that aspect of the covenant most closely connected with the event of Israel's election by God, namely, the laws whose function is commemorative, the "testimonies" (*edot*). These laws, like the commandment to celebrate Passover annually, are designed "that you remember the day you went out from Egypt all the days of your life" (Deut. 16:3). Spinoza calls these laws *ceremonial observances*. And, to eliminate particular history from being a realm where humankind is related to God, he sees their sole function to be "to strengthen and preserve the Jewish state."[61] In other words, their function is now seen as essentially political in the sense of serving the universal human need for a well-ordered society.

By this reduction of the historical-ritual realm to the political-moral realm, rather than accepting it as the unique celebration of the elect of God in their election, Spinoza has inverted the classical Jewish relation of general morality and the singular covenant. For in this relation, as I have argued and presented evidence elsewhere, universal morality is seen as the precondition for the historical covenant between God and Israel.[62] The latter, in Maimonides's words, "completes" the former.[63] This universal morality is put forth in the rabbinic doctrine of the Noachide laws, that is, the laws (such as the prohibitions of idolatry, bloodshed, incest, and robbery) that pertain to the descendants of Noah, to humankind per se.[64] However, the historical revelation of God, which is the covenantal context and its normative content, is put forth as the direct relationship between God and humans for which the indirect Noachide relationship is only preparatory. It is its background not its ground. Conversely, Spinoza has made historical revelation and its most singular "ceremonial" content a historically contingent means to an essentially moral end.[65] This too was an assumption accepted by most modern Jewish thinkers, most of whom only differed from Spinoza on the degree of contingency and dispensability these ceremonies now had.

In this new elevation of practices that are essentially moral laws over practices that are more immediately "religious" laws, Spinoza was following a lead established by his famous heterodox predecessor in Amsterdam Uriel da Costa. In his rejection of much of Jewish law as morally and religiously cumbersome, da Costa saw the Noachide laws as not only necessary but sufficient as well for a fulfilling human life.[66] Furthermore, in a famous critique of Maimonides's connection of full moral sufficiency with an affirmation of revelation, Spinoza argues that "a true way of life," that is, natural morality, does not depend on specifically "prophetic inspiration."[67] In other words, practical excellence (virtue) is not at all subordinate to a historical relationship with God. Indeed, morality is the criterion of the validity of revealed law, rather than revealed law being the criterion of morality, as it is in the classical Jewish sources.[68]

For this reason too I think Spinoza frequently invokes Christianity against Judaism in the *Tractatus Theologico-Politicus*. Christianity's practical value seems to be that it stressed the minimal morality necessary for human flourishing, and it rejected

Pharisaic Jewish tradition with its numerous particularistic accretions to that minimal morality.[69] And despite his usual insistence that philosophy and theology be kept apart in their respective realms, Spinoza makes an important exception when it comes to political philosophy. Being the study of a human artifact, society, as opposed to metaphysics, which is the study of nature in toto (*natura naturans*), political philosophy is related to theology. In fact, it determines the very validity of theology. He writes that "we can use judgment before we accept with at least moral certainty that which has been revealed."[70] But, even at the level of morality, not to speak of ontology, the doctrine of election plays no constitutive role. Such a role could be played only by a doctrine that Spinoza could reconstitute as a rational idea in his system. God's election of Israel in the literal, nonmetaphorical, sense could never become any such idea.

To many readers Spinoza's subordination of Jewish ceremonial law to Jewish moral law seems to reflect classical Christian teaching about Judaism. Had not Christianity historically relativized Jewish ceremonial law by insisting that it applied to the Jewish people only before the coming of Christ, something it had just as strongly insisted was not the case with the basic precepts of Jewish moral law?[71] Nevertheless, a closer reading of the *Tractatus Theologico-Politicus* leads one to conclude that Spinoza's treatment of Jewish ceremonial law is much more radical than that of any of the classical Christian theologians. Although they replaced Jewish ceremonial law with the Christian sacraments, which were now seen as being the true content of the covenantal relationship with God,[72] Christian theologians did not propose a moral justification of religious practice; rather, they, like their Jewish counterpart, included morality within the historical covenant between God and his people.[73] Christian theologians insisted that the ceremonial law pertains to the true relationship with God, and that it is to be distinguished from the moral law, which pertains only to human society.[74] As such, the former is clearly superior to the latter by virtue of its direct object: God rather than other humans.

The difference between Judaism and Christianity, then, is *what* constitutes the full covenant, not *that* the covenant is foundational. And the covenant, for both Judaism and Christianity, is initiated by God's election of Israel. Jews and Christians differ—and the difference is crucial—as to the extent of that initiating election.

Christians affirm that this election begins with Israel and extends to the incarnation, God's coming to dwell within the body of the Jew Jesus of Nazareth as the Christ. Jews refuse to accept this. Hence, for Christians, Judaism is deficient; for Jews, Christianity is redundant.

With all of this in mind, Spinoza cannot be taken as simply an elaboration of the old Christian critique of Jewish "ceremonialism." Spinoza has gone beyond that critique radically, for he has deconstructed Christianity every bit as much as he has deconstructed Judaism. In this sense, both Jews and Christians have more in common with each other than either of them has in common with Spinoza.

THE TERMINATION OF THE COVENANT

Because Spinoza sees the covenant presented in the Bible as an essentially human device designed by the Jews to relate properly their society to God and to each other, it cannot be eternal.[75] As such, it is not the subject of truth whose proper object is nature as a whole and in its parts. The covenant is something created within time, and it is thus subject to historical judgment, whose criteria are evaluative rather than veridical.[76] At this level, Spinoza's question about the covenant is whether its original purpose is still being served. If it is, then the covenant is still valuable because, as we have just seen, Spinoza approves of the covenant, including what he considers the historical myth of its origin in divine election. If this is the case, the covenanted society is something that ought to be preserved. However, if that original purpose is not still being served, then the covenant is not still valuable, and hence it is something that ought not to be preserved. And, if it is still being preserved by the Jews anyway, then it can be preserved only in some perverted form. That the latter is Spinoza's historical judgment we shall soon see.

As a former rabbinical student, Spinoza knew quite well that in the traditional Jewish understanding of the covenant the Law is its primary content. However, he added to that traditional understanding the modern notion that law is essentially the rule for a sovereign state living in its own land and functioning as a "social body."[77] Thus Spinoza writes that "the Hebrews were called God's chosen people . . . for no other reason than that God chose for them a certain territory where they might live in security and wellbeing. . . . [T]he law of the Hebrew state . . . was therefore binding on none but the Hebrews, and not even on them except while their state still stood."[78]

Along these lines, of course, the loss of their own sovereign state in their own land should have convinced the Jews that their election had come to an end and that they should assimilate into whatever sovereign states they happened to find themselves living. Indeed, Spinoza saw the covenant being annulled already during the Babylonian exile when the Jews had to recognize the king of Babylon rather than God as their sovereign.[79] The very reality of the covenant and not just its subsequent confirmation depended on the transfer of individual natural powers qua rights to one's present sovereign. Thus no human contract, even a covenant with God, is in principle everlasting or nonnegotiable.

For Spinoza, the separate existence of the Jews no longer served a positive purpose. Even their ceremonial law, which for the most part could be observed by individual Jews anywhere at any time, seemed to Spinoza to be so communal in its character that its viability too was ultimately connected with the question of statehood.[80] Revealed religion and its morality have meaning only within a polity.[81] Only rational apprehension of God and the natural world is a proper individual concern. In contrast to the Rabbis, Spinoza did not see ceremonial law as a personal obligation (*chovat haguf*), something that relates individual Jews to God in such a way as to remain viable with or without a state of their own.[82] For him, a stateless society and its cultural-religious practices could be only some sort of historical perversion in which the individual pursuit of truth and virtue would have to be thwarted. Spinoza was convinced that the perpetuation of these ceremonies after the loss of statehood was separation for separation's sake. It is a negation serving no positive purpose, something that could not be related to God who is the positive foundation of existence itself. Accordingly, Spinoza is very harsh with the Jews' insistence on perpetuating their unique ceremonial practices, and he accuses them of profaning what was originally sacred, thus severing it from any relation to God at all.[83]

For Spinoza, then, a stateless society can justify its continued existence only on negative grounds. Instead of its difference being for the sake of its unique sovereignty, which is a positive historical reality, its difference becomes an end in itself. In Spinoza's opinion, such a stateless society determined to persist inevitably incurs "the hatred of all . . . [and] that they are preserved largely through the hatred of other nations is demonstrated by historical fact."[84] In other words, whereas the members of one sovereign nation-state can well understand and respect the desire of the members of another sovereign nation-state to remain separate and independent of others, they cannot well understand much less respect the re- fusal of a stateless community to remain separated from others. Thus they inevitably attribute to the Jews a xenophobic hatred, a hatred the Jews return in kind. So it seems from Spinoza's analysis of the reasons for Jewish survival that Jewish separatism as an end in itself led to the hatred of the Jews by the nations among whom they lived, and that this very hatred now keeps the Jews in their unhealthy isolation. At the bottom of all this, then, the fault clearly lies with the Jews themselves. It is they who originally "vaunted themselves above all men—indeed, despising all men."[85]

THE FUTURE OF ISRAEL

After his discussion of how hatred of the Jews has actually led to their survival long after their loss of political sovereignty, Spinoza makes a remark, seemingly *en passant*, that has had, nevertheless, a profound effect on many modern Jewish thinkers who came after him. He writes, "Indeed, were it not that the fundamental prin- ciples of their religion discourage manliness (*effoeminarent*), I would not hesitate to believe that they will one day, given the opportunity—such is the mutability of human affairs—establish once more their independent state (*imperium*), and that God will again (*de novo*) choose them."[86]

I think the reason for the subsequent Jewish interest in this rather cryptic passage is that it seemed to offer a way to resolve the great ambivalence many modern Jewish thinkers felt toward Spinoza. On the one hand, they much admired what we might now call Spinoza's "demythologization" of Jewish tradition. Spinoza showed them how the tradition could be still appreciated even when severed from the supernaturalist theology that had previously undergirded it. On the other hand, they could not identify with the fact that Spinoza had clearly separated himself from the Jewish people and her community and not just from what they too regarded as antiquated Jewish theology. Therefore, what this passage suggested to many modern Jewish thinkers was that Spinoza had not totally or irrevocably separated himself from his own people after all.[87] He seemed to be suggesting here that if the state of Jewish belief were different, if it were made consistent with what Spinoza thought was the irrefutable new physics (the science of *natura naturata*) and metaphysics (the science of *natura naturans*), an ontology and epistemology in which there was surely no place for a transcendent God, then he too could perhaps return home.

Spinoza seemed, therefore, to be offering the Jews a "naturalist" solution to their problem of homelessness.[88] And, although he thought that many aspects of the ancient covenant (as he had reconstituted its meaning, of course) were "quite profitable to imitate," he was explicit in his judgment that the covenant itself could not be reinstated in the modern world.[89] By reason of factors both spiritual and historical, Spinoza concluded that any such reinstitution was impossible. For even in the ancient world, it was the Jews who had elected God, rather than being elected by God. And in the modern world that election could be the affair only of private individuals, not of the state. All the state should now do is to respect such individual human choices, as long as they are not disruptive of "the peace and welfare (*paci et utilitati*) of the commonwealth."[90]

Spinoza thought that the external event of the founding of the covenant between God and man could be better seen as the internal awareness of rational persons. Here he invoked the New Testament's great emphasis on inwardness in the relationship with God.[91] Now it is clear from his use of the New Testament that he was not advocating conversion to Christianity as a solution to the political problems of the Jews—or anyone else for that matter. Instead, he saw Christianity as a step away from Judaism toward the rational religion he called *religion universal* or *catholic religion*.[92] This latter term, of course, does not designate the Catholic Church (or any religious body), which Spinoza regarded as irrational and oppressive.[93] Instead, the term *catholic* is being used in its original Greek meaning of universal (*kata holos*), a universal religion of reason, a novum in human history. The symbiosis of this rational religion—maintained privately by the philosophically insightful—and the liberal state—maintained publicly by every citizen—can be seen as Spinoza's combining what he saw as the political strengths of Judaism with the spiritual strengths of Christianity. This combination is meant to herald a new entity in human history. As Leo Strauss so well put it, "Spinoza . . . was both a Jew and a Christian and hence neither." [94]

Spinoza thought too that the ancient covenant was suited only for a society separated from the rest of the world, living in splendid isolation.[95] But in the world in which he lived, especially the Netherlands whose very survival and prosperity depended on international commerce, Spinoza concluded that the reinstitution of such an ancient covenantal polity was not only highly improbable but, also, highly undesirable.[96]

The willingness of many modern Jewish thinkers to accept Spinoza's general premises, even if they would not accept his own particular religio-political conclusion, meant that they had to alter radically the classical Jewish doctrines of creation, election, revelation, and redemption to ideas of origin, destiny, insight, and progress. As we shall see, creation was changed from the founding cosmic event to the perpetual origin of cosmic process; election was changed from external choice to an intuition of one's own destiny; revelation was changed from the voice of God to human beings to the human insight about God; and redemption was changed from an apocalyptic event to the culmination of historical progress. This radical alteration is especially evident when one looks at modern Jewish transformations of the doctrines of election and redemption. Indeed, these two classical doctrines and the modern ideas of destiny and progress are the most closely similar.

It seems most likely that Spinoza himself was suggesting this naturalistic solution to the Jews' religious-political problem only as a hypothetical possibility. There is no evidence that he had any interest in the Jews after his departure from the Sephardic Jewish community of Amsterdam in 1656.[97] But many modern Jewish thinkers saw it as the suggestion of something historically probable for the Jews. For them, Spinoza seemed to be advocating that the Jews once again take charge of their own lives and their own future. And clearly their consciousness of their own historical continuity required that they not totally sever their ties to their past. Most modern Jewish thinkers accepted this, differing only as to what this transformation of the Jewish people and Judaism was to be. Those Jewish thinkers who saw the future of the Jews and

Judaism to be within modern secular Western nation-states generally thought that the Jews had to become a faith community of like-minded individuals and that Judaism had to become a religion like Protestant Christianity—in form, that is, but not in substance. Those thinkers who, conversely, saw the future of the Jews within their own nation-state generally thought that the Jews had to become a modern ethnic entity and that Judaism had to become a national culture. Some thinkers tried to combine both perspectives in one way or another. But for all of them, if there was to be any election in the real, nonmetaphorical sense, it had to be the election of the Jews of themselves and their God by themselves. In other words, these modern Jewish thinkers followed Spinoza's philosophical reconstitution of the covenant, while simultaneously rejecting his permanent relegation of it to the irretrievable past. At the deepest philosophical level, then, they accepted his general premises, and actually built upon them, while at the same time refusing to draw his own particular historical conclusions.[98]

The loss of the classical doctrine of election, that Spinoza so powerfully advocated, entailed a considerable lowering of the eschatological horizon. By abandoning the hope for the heretofore elusive messiah and world to come, many modern Jews felt they could now at long last gain control of their own destiny. The loss of the transcendent mystery of their beginning brought with it the loss of the transcendent mystery of their end. This, more than anything else, appears to be Spinoza's legacy to modern Jewish thought. Yet I believe it must be overcome if the classical doctrine of election is to be philosophically recovered. But that recovery cannot be truly effective until we see the varied fruit that grew out of the seeds Spinoza planted at the very beginnings of Jewish modernity.

NOTES

1. For the inclusion of the meaning of *Torah* within that of *berit*, see Heschel 1962, p. 230.

2. Note, "Except for God, there neither is, nor can be conceived, any substance. . . . [M]odes can neither be nor conceived without substance. . . . [E]xcept for substances and modes there is nothing" (*Ethics*, 1, prop. 15, 1:420) [trans. Curley]. And "outside God there can be no substance, i.e., thing which is in itself outside God . . . God,

therefore, is the immanent, not the transitive cause of all things, q.e.d."
(*Ethics*, 1, prop. 18, 1:428). And "God was not before his decrees and
cannot be without them" (*Ethics*, 1, prop. 33, schol. 2, 1:437). See *The
Correspondence of Spinoza*, p. 343.

    3. See Zac 1979, p. 179; 1978, p. 553.

    4. See *Ethics*, 1, def. 7 and prop. 32.

    5. See Wolfson 1934, vol. 1, pp. 319–322, 422.

    6. Note, "By eternity I understand existence itself . . . Exp.: For
such existence, like the essence of a thing, is conceived as an eternal
truth, and on that account cannot be explained by duration or time, even
if duration is conceived to be without beginning or end" (*Ethics*, 1, def.
8, 1:409.) For a critique of Spinoza's denigration of time, written by a
thinker influenced by Einstein's revolution in physics, see Alexander
1921, pp. 21ff. Yet it should be noted that Einstein himself considered
himself a Spinozist. As he stated in response to a query from a prominent
New York rabbi in 1929: "I believe in Spinoza's God who reveals himself
in the orderly harmony of what exists, not in a God who concerns himself with the fate and actions of men" (quoted in Clark 1971, pp. 413–
414). Thus, although an affirmation of historical reality presupposes an
affirmation of the reality of time, the latter does not necessarily entail the
former.

    7. See *Ethics*, 3, pref.; see also, Hampshire 1987, pp. 39ff; Allison
1975, pp. 69ff. Cf. Kant, *Critique of Pure Reason*, B248ff.; Cohen 1968,
p. 70.

    8. See *Ethics*, 5, prop. 23.

    9. Note, "The common people, prone to superstition and prizing
the legacy of time (*quod temporis*) above eternity itself, worship the
books of Scripture rather than the Word of God" (*Tractatus Theologico-
Politicus*) (hereafter TT-P), pref., pp. 54–55 [trans. Shirley]; (Latin text:
Opera, ed. J. van Vloten and J. P. N. Land (The Hague, 1914), 2:90). See
also, chap. 1, p. 60; chap. 15, p. 230.

    10. See *Ethics*, 1, App., 1:441; 2, prop. 47; 3, pref. Cf. TT-P, chap.
7, p. 141: "Scripture frequently treats of matters that cannot be deduced
from principles known by natural light; for it is chiefly made up of
historical narratives and revelation."

    11. Note, "For the point at issue is merely the meaning of texts
(*sensu orationum*), not their truth. . . . All these details . . . should be
available from an historical study of Scripture" (TT-P, chap. 7, p. 144);
see also chap. 15, p. 232. For the distinction between the *vera ratio* of
philosophy and the *sensus* of theology, see ibid., p. 228; and Strauss
1979, p. 113.

    12. Note, "But the means that serve for the attainment of security
and physical wellbeing . . . mainly depend on the operation of external

causes of which we are in ignorance. . . . Nevertheless, much can be effected by human contrivance (directio) and vigilance. . . . To this end (Ad quod), reason and experience have taught us . . . to organise a society" (TT-P, chap. 3, p. 90 [Latin, 2:124]). Cf. Ethics, 1, App., 1: 443–444.

13. Note, "But surely nature creates individuals, not nations" (TT-P, chap. 17, p. 267); see chap. 4, p. 101.

14. This distinction between natural, individual action, based on scientia, and artificial, human action, based on teleological imagination, comes out of the following observation by Spinoza: "Still, it rarely happens that men live according to the guidance of reason. . . . They can hardly, however, live a solitary life; hence that definition which makes man a social animal [e.g., Aristotle, Politics, 1253a3; Seneca, De Clementia, 1.3.2] has been quite pleasing to most" (Ethics, 4, prop. 35, schol., 1:564). Therefore the individual morality (pietas) of philosophically blessed individuals like Spinoza himself, based as it is on apprehension of internal causality, is essentially different from ordinary political morality, based on the teleological imagination of political leaders. For these leaders often have to coerce those living under their authority to obey the law (obidientia) because these ordinary people often do not understand the teleology of political order, much less true ontological causality. See Ethics, 4, prop. 36, schol. 1 et seq., 1:565ff.

15. TT-P, chap. 15, pp. 233–234. Cf. Aristotle, Nicomachean Ethics, 1094b13ff.; also, Rawls 1971, pp. 136–137.

16. This sounds somewhat like Saadiah Gaon's decision to practice the commandments on the authority of Jewish tradition until he can discover for himself their true teleological reasons (Book of Beliefs and Opinions, intro.). For Saadiah, though, this is only tentative, inasmuch as he believes there are real final causes in created nature and they are simply awaiting discovery. But for Spinoza, because final causes are not natural but only imagined by humans in their construction of society, they can never be discovered as one would discover natural (i.e., efficient) causes. Final causes will never admit such certainty. That is why causal ignorance in the practical-political realm is permanent.

17. See TT-P, chap. 3, p. 91.

18. Concerning efficient causality, see Ethics, 1, prop. 25. Concerning the overextension of final causality, see TT-P, chap, 6, p. 125.

19. TT-P, chap. 6, p. 127. The less prophets relied on miracles, the closer they came to philosophical knowledge. See TT-P, chap. 11, p. 199.

20. TT-P, chap. 3, p. 91.

21. See Ethics, 1, prop. 29.

22. TT-P, chap. 3, pp. 89–90.

23. Ibid.

24. See Gelhaar 1987, p. 167.

25. See B. *Shabbat* 88a–b.

26. TT-P, chap. 16, pp. 246–247 [Latin, 2:267]. See chap. 17, p. 255 concerning the transfer/limitation of natural power to a sovereign in the founding of a human polity.

27. See, e.g., M. *Baba Batra* 8.5; B. *Baba Batra* 126b.

28. Cf. Y. *Shevi'it* 6.1/ 36c; Maimonides, *Mishneh Torah: Melakhim*, 6.5.

29. See Ezra 10:3 and Neh. 10:1; B. *Yevamot* 89b.

30. See, e.g., M. *Avot* 1:1; B. *Berakhot* 26b.

31. See, e.g., B. *Gittin* 36a–b; Maimonides, *Mishneh Torah: Sanhedrin*, 24.9; B. *Avodah Zarah* 36a and parallels; *Mishneh Torah: Mamrim*, 2.6–7.

32. See B. *Shabbat* 23a re Deut. 17:11 and 32:7; B. *Betzah* 3b.

33. See, e.g., B. *Berakhot* 19b re Prov. 21:30; B. *Yevamot* 90b.

34. Note, "A law (*lex*) which depends on nature's necessity is one which necessarily follows from the very nature of the things, that is, its definition; a law which depends on human will . . . could more properly be termed a statute (*jus*) . . ." (TT-P, chap. 4, p. 101 [Latin, 2:134]). See also *Tractatus Politicus*, 2.19–22, pp. 298–299 [trans. Elwes]; *Ethics*, 3, prop. 2; 4, prop. 37, schol. 2. Cf. *Ethics*, 1, prop. 15.

35. Thus I do not think Spinoza was speaking altogether pejoratively when he wrote: "Now it is important to note here that the Jews never make mention of intermediate or particular causes nor pay any heed to them, but to serve religion and piety . . . they refer everything to God" (TT-P, chap. 1, p. 60).

36. In *Tractatus Politicus*, 3.10 [Latin, 2:17], Spinoza built upon this ancient Hebrew political fact and declared religion to be *quod viri privati officium est.*

37. TT-P, chap. 4, p. 103.

38. See *Guide of the Perplexed*, 2.40.

39. TT-P, chap. 4, pp. 102–103.

40. See *Guide of the Perplexed*, 2.35, 39; also, Novak 1983, p. 313, nn. 81–83.

41. See *Mishneh Torah: Mamrim*, chap. 1.

42. TT-P, chap. 4, p. 101 [Latin, 2:134].

43. TT-P, chap. 4, p. 104. See *Ethics*, 5, prop. 14.

44. TT-P, chap. 1, p. 60. Note also, "These dictates are revealed to us by God, speaking, as it were, within ourselves (*quasi in nobis ipsis loquente*), or else were revealed to prophets as laws" (*Tractatus Politicus*, 2.22, p. 299 [Latin, 2:12]). The word *lex* is applied to God's decrees only "by analogy" (*per translationem*) (TT-P, chap. 4, p. 102 [Latin, 2:135]). Thus God is the "author" of Scripture only metaphorically; see ibid., chap. 12, pp. 209–211.

45. See Zac 1965, pp. 208–209.

46. See Zac 1979, p. 204.

47. See TT-P, chap. 18, pp. 278–279; also, Feuer 1958, p. 130.

48. TT-P, chap. 4, p. 103 [Latin, 2:136].

49. TT-P, chap. 4, p. 105; *Ethics*, 5, prop. 42. As such, Spinoza's view of virtue for its own sake is quite close to Aristotle's notion of *arete* as choiceworthy for its own sake; see *Nicomachean Ethics*, 1176b8–9.

50. TT-P, pref., p. 55.

51. *Tractatus Politicus*, 2.22, p. 299.

52. See *Tractatus Politicus*, 2.20. Spinoza insists that the more rational an individual is the less is the need for submission to external authority; see Zac 1965, pp. 107ff.

53. See TT-P, pref. Note, "Thus the Hebrew nation was chosen by God before all others not by reason of its understanding nor of its spiritual qualities, but by reason of its social organisation and the good fortune whereby it achieved supremacy and retained it for so many years" (TT-P, chap. 3, p. 91).

54. Note, "For nobody knows by nature that he has any duty. Indeed, this knowledge cannot be attained by any process of reasoning; one can gain it only by revelation confirmed by signs" (TT-P, chap. 16, p. 246).

55. TT-P, chap. 17, pp. 255–256, 263 [Latin, 2:278, 281]. Spinoza means that individual rights are "God given" because they are natural, i.e., coequal with a human being's natural power (*conatus*). See ibid., chap. 16, p. 237. Moreover, by contracting with God rather than with any human potentate, the ancient Hebrews achieved *humani imperii libertas* (ibid., chap. 16 [Latin, 2:282]).

56. See Mishnah: *Yoma* 8.9.

57. See TT-P, chap. 3.

58. Spinoza speaks of man in "the eternal order of nature" as "an atom" (*particula*) (*Tractatus Politicus*, 2.8, p. 295 [Latin, 2:8]). Nevertheless, to be an "atom" of eternity is better than to be a transitory historical person, however important one is here and now.

59. TT-P, chap. 16, p. 237.

60. TT-P, chap. 16, p. 239.

61. TT-P, chap. 5, p. 112.

62. Novak 1983, pp. 407ff.

63. *Mishneh Torah: Melakhim*, 9.1.

64. See Novak 1983, passim; also Novak 1989, chapter 1.

65. Note, "If we want to testify, without any prejudgment, to the divinity of Scripture, it must be made evident to us from Scripture alone that it teaches true moral doctrine (*vera documenta moralia*); for it is on this basis alone that its divinity can be proved" (TT-P, chap. 7, p. 142 [Latin, 2:173]).

66. Da Costa speaks of the seven Noachide laws as *"qui ante Abrahamum fuerunt, hoc illis satis est ad salutem . . . secundum rectam rationem, quae vera norma est illius naturalis legis"* (*Exemplar Humanae Vitae* in *Die Schriften des Uriel da Costa*, ed. C. Gebhardt [Amsterdam, 1922], pp. 117–118).

67. TT-P, chap. 5, p. 122.

68. This question, of course, is at least as old as Plato. For discussion of it, see Novak 1975, pp. 29ff. Cf. Novak 1989, pp. 151ff.

69. See TT-P, chap. 1, p. 64; chap. 3, pp. 97–98; chap. 4, pp. 107–108; chap. 5, p. 113; chap. 11, p. 203; chap. 18, pp. 273–274. I think that is also why Spinoza usually has a higher opinion of the Sadducees than he does of the Pharisees. The Sadducees were minimalists, accepting only what was literally in Scripture as normative revelation. See ibid., chap. 12, p. 205.

70. TT-P, chap. 15, p. 233.

71. See, e.g., Thomas Aquinas, *Summa Theologiae*, 2/1, q. 100, a. 8; John Calvin, *Institutes of the Christian Religion*, 2.7.13.

72. See, e.g., *Summa Theologiae*, 2/1, q. 102, a. 2 and q. 103, a. 3 and a. 4; *Institutes*, 2.7.1.

73. See, e.g., *Summa Theologiae*, 2/1, q. 101, a. 1; *Institutes*, 2.7.10 and 4.20.16.

74. See *Summa Theologiae*, 2/1, q. 101, a. 1; *Institutes*, 2.8.11.

75. See TT-P, chap. 3, p. 100.

76. See *Tractatus Politicus*, 4.6.

77. TT-P, chap. 3, p. 100.

78. TT-P, pref., p. 54.

79. TT-P, chap. 19, p. 282.

80. See TT-P, chap. 5, p. 115.

81. See TT-P, chap. 3, p. 94.

82. See, e.g., B. *Kiddushin* 37a; also, Maimonides, *Mishneh Torah: Berakhot*, 11.2. Cf. Nachmanides, *Commentary on the Torah*: Deuteronomy 8:10.

83. TT-P, chap. 12, p. 206.

84. TT-P, chap. 3, p. 99.

85. TT-P, chap. 1, p. 70. See Yovel 1989, vol. 1, p. 181.

86. TT-P, chap. 3, p. 100 [Latin, 2:133].

87. For the modern Jewish attempt to reclaim Spinoza for Judaism, see, e.g., the collection of essays by Joseph Klausner, Nachum Sokolow, David Ben Gurion, et al. in Hessing 1962.

88. Note, "Spinoza is writing only a few years after the upheaval fomented by Sabbetai Zevi, the false Messiah. . . . Since all human affairs are transient, Spinoza says, the renewal of the Jewish kingdom is not inevitable; but if the return to Zion should take place, it will be because

of the immanent laws of nature and not by providential, divine revelation, or messianism" (Yovel 1989, vol. 1, p. 191). For the deep messianic longings connected with *l'affaire* Sabbatai Zevi in the Amsterdam of Spinoza's youth, see Scholem 1973, pp. 518ff.

    89.   TT-P, chap. 18, p. 272.
    90.   TT-P, chap. 19, p. 280.
    91.   See TT-P, chap. 11.
    92.   TT-P, pref., p. 54; chap. 12, pp. 208–209. See Strauss 1965, p. 258.
    93.   See, e.g., TT-P, chap. 19, pp. 280ff. For the significance of Spinoza making Jesus a paradigmatic philosopher, see Pines 1968, p. 22.
    94.   Strauss 1965, p. 17. Along these lines, see Schwartz 1985, pp. 58ff.
    95.   TT-P, chap. 18, p. 272.
    96.   Ibid. See McShea 1967, p. 163; cf. Schwartz 1985, p. 84, n. 88 (conclusion).
    97.   See Lucas 1927, p. 52; also Strauss 1965, pp. 164ff.
    98.   For the cogency of such a hermeneutical move, see Novak 1989, pp. 68ff.

REFERENCES

Alexander, S. 1921. *Spinoza and Time*. London: Allen and Unwin.
Allison, H. E. 1975. *Benedict de Spinoza*. Boston: Twayne Publishers.
Clark, R. W. 1971. *Einstein: The Life and Times*. New York: World Publishing Company.
Cohen, H. 1968. *Das Prinzip der Infinitesimalmethode*. Frankfurt am Main: Suhrkamp.
Feuer, L. S. 1958. *Spinoza and the Rise of Liberalism*. Boston: Beacon Press.
Gelhaar, S. S. 1987. *Prophetie und Gesetz bei Jehudah Halevi, Maimonides, und Spinoza*. Frankfurt am Main: Peter Lang.
Hampshire, S. 1987. *Spinoza*, rev. ed. Harmondsworth, Middlesex: Penguin Books.
Heschel, A. J. 1962. *The Prophets*. Philadelphia: Jewish Publication Society.
Hessing, S. (ed.). 1962. *Spinoza: Dreihundert Jahre Ewigkeit*, 2nd ed. The Hague: Nijhoff.
Levy, Z. 1989. *Baruch or Benedict: On Some Jewish Aspects of Spinoza's Philosophy*. New York: Peter Lang.
Lucas, J. M. 1927. *The Oldest Biography of Spinoza*, ed. A. Wolf. London: Allen and Unwin.

McShea, R. J. 1967. *The Political Philosophy of Spinoza*. New York: Columbia University Press.

Novak, D. 1975. *Suicide and Morality*. New York: Scholars Studies Press.

———. 1983. *The Image of the Non-Jew in Judaism: An Historical and Constructive Study of the Noahide Laws*. New York and Toronto: Edwin Mellen Press.

———. 1989. *Jewish-Christian Dialogue: A Jewish Justification*. New York: Oxford University Press.

Pines, S. 1968. "Spinoza's *Tractatus Theologico-Politicus*, Maimonides, and Kant." *Scripta Hierosolymitana* 20: 3–54.

Rawls, J. 1971. *A Theory of Justice*. Cambridge, Mass.: Harvard University Press.

Scholem, G. 1973. *Sabbatai Sevi: The Mystical Messiah*, trans. R. J. Z. Werblowsky. Princeton, N.J.: Princeton University Press.

Schwartz, J. 1985. "Liberalism and the Jewish Connection: A Study of Spinoza and the Young Marx." *Political Theory* 13: 58–84.

Spinoza, B. 1928. *The Correspondence of Spinoza*, ed. and trans. A. Wolf. London: Allen and Unwin.

———. 1951. *Tractatus Politicus*, trans. R. H. M. Elwes. New York: Dover Books.

———. 1985. *The Collected Works of Spinoza*, vol. 1, trans. E. Curley. Princeton, N.J.: Princeton University Press.

———. 1989. *Tractatus Theologico-Politicus*, trans. S. Shirley. Leiden and New York: Brill.

Strauss, L. 1965. *Spinoza's Critique of Religion*, trans. E. M. Sinclair. New York: Schocken Books.

———. 1979. "The Mutual Influence of Theology and Philosophy." *Independent Journal of Philosophy* 3: 111–118.

Wolfson, H. A. 1934. *The Philosophy of Spinoza*, 2 vols. Cambridge, Mass.: Harvard University Press.

Yovel, Y. 1989. *Spinoza and Other Heretics*, 2 vols. Princeton, N.J.: Princeton University Press.

Zac, S. 1965. *Spinoza et L'Interprétation de L'Écriture*. Paris: P.U.F.

———. 1978. "Spinoza et l'État Hebreux." In *Speculum Spinozanum: 1677–1977*, ed. S. Hessing. London: Routledge and Kegan Paul.

———. 1979. *Philosophie, Théologie, Politique dans L'Oeuvre de Spinoza*. Paris: Vrin.

Morality and War: A Critique of Bleich's Oracular Halakha

Noam J. Zohar

The renewal of a Jewish state has posed many unique challenges to the halakhic tradition; perhaps the most poignant of these is the confrontation of halakha with the realities of politics and warfare. A challenge of this sort is likely to bring out in sharp relief contrasting halakhic philosophies, which heretofore have lingered in silent—if uneasy—coexistence, behind a facade of accepted practices.

One such philosophy is founded on viewing halakha as a special medium for discerning God's inscrutable will. Believing that God's commands are distinct from ethics, adherents of this philosophy see halakhic discourse as a kind of formula for deciphering divine mysteries. This view presents a crucial question regarding the relation of the divine injunctions to ethical norms. Must halakhic teachings be minimally consistent with basic moral norms or are they rather to be completely divorced from morality?

A prominent contemporary spokesman for this approach is Rabbi J. David Bleich. A fine example of his philosophy of halakha is found in his essay "Preemptive War in Jewish Law."[1] This excellent essay is a pioneering compilation and systematic discussion of diverse rabbinic sources. Yet it seems to involve a deep ambiguity in the stance taken toward ethical imperatives, an ambiguity that, I shall argue, need not follow from traditional halakhic thinking. Let us begin by noting some of the problems in the halakhic tradition on war and Bleich's treatment of them.

THE MORAL PROBLEM OF "OPTIONAL WAR"

The halakhic tradition regarding warfare presents two basic moral difficulties: the "ban" (*cherem*) against Amalek and the seven Canaanite nations, and the category of "optional war" (*milchemet reshut*). In principle, the ban is the more objectionable, especially if read (in its stark formulation in Deut. 20:16–18) unmediated by rabbinic discourse: it prescribes wholesale extermination of populations. But the mainstream halakhic tradition has long rendered the *cherem* a thing of the past, with no present or future normative relevance. Analogous to the destruction of native peoples in North America, it burdens our collective memory, and is not held up as a standard for our political deliberations.

In terms of practical political morality, the halakhic category of "optional war" poses a greater problem. This contrasts with the category of "obligatory war," which in effect refers only to a defensive war, "to rescue Israel from an attacking enemy."[2] Although defending against aggression is plausibly defined as a moral imperative, how can an optional war—which, by its very definition, can be avoided—ever be permitted? The shedding of blood in a defensive war may be a necessary evil; but how can it be permissible to choose the bloody path of warfare if it is not an inescapable necessity?

A critical assessment of optional war should begin by examining the goals for which such a war could be waged. One goal explicitly specified by the Talmud is that of preemption: "to diminish the heathens lest they attack Israel." Somewhat more cryptically, the Talmud also classifies under this heading wars like those fought by King David for "well being" (*revacha*[3]). Strikingly, Maimonides, in *Mishneh Torah*, offers a sweeping monarchic agenda: A Jewish king may wage wars "to expand the Jewish realm or to enhance his glory and prestige."[4]

To gain a moral perspective, let us consider the comments of Shadal (R. Samuel David Luzzatto) on Deut. 20:10–11: "The text does not specify the cause for an optional war, or whether Israel may wage war without cause, merely to despoil and take booty, or to expand our domain. Now it seems to me that in the beginning of this section (20:1), in saying "When you go forth to battle against your enemy," Scripture is determining that we may

make war only against our enemies. The term *enemy* refers only
to one who wrongs us; hence Scripture is speaking only of an
invader who enters our domain in order to take our land or despoil us."

Shadal offers no account of how such a reaction differs from
an obligatory war of defense. The preceding talmudic formulation
offers a simple distinction, without renouncing the moral point
expressed by Shadal. Although suggesting a rather far-reaching
notion of preemption, it still implies that the war is justified by
the requirements of self-defense ("lest they attack Israel"). But
Maimonides's language seems clearly to allow waging war for conquest and glory. Within the halakhic framework of legal interpretation, this disparity is discussed first in terms of determining
Maimonides's source: Why did he leave out the talmudic statement
and what are the grounds for his own view?

R. Abraham di-Botan, in his commentary on Maimonides
(*Lechem Mishneh* ad loc.), seeks to answer both these questions
together by positing that the two goals are really the same. For the
kings' (legitimate) purpose in acquiring lands and glory is itself
prophylactic: Israel's military prowess will deter potential enemies
from attacking it. Is this interpretive move motivated by a similar
moral concern? This would depend on how *Lechem Mishneh*'s
fusion of the two rationales for optional war is itself interpreted.
For clearly it can be taken either (1) *restrictively,* the Maimonidean
goal may be pursued only to the extent required for deterring
actual enemies, or (2) *expansively,* any power play gains justification by reference to its deterrent function. Obviously, there are
other interpretive options, and Bleich compiles six different rabbinic
definitions of the terms for waging "discretionary ["optional"]
war." He proceeds to show why this entire category is excluded
from present application. But despite this, the notion of optional
war continues to have an impact on Bleich's analysis of contemporary guidance, both through a formal link he emphasizes explicitly
and through a particular philosophical orientation.

The formal link consists, according to Bleich, in a kind of
reverse reasoning: "Wars that are not to be categorized as designed
to 'diminish the heathens' would then be encompassed within the
category of war 'to deliver Israel from an enemy'—a *milchemet
mitzvah*" (p. 270). Thus, if any commentator has adopted an

extravagant view concerning optional war, this entails a correspondingly wide definition of "commanded war."

For example, the most extreme view on Bleich's list (that of *Lechem Mishneh,* which he understands in accordance with reading [2]) allows, under the category of optional war, "hostilities . . . designed to demonstrate military superiority in order to instill fear in potential aggressors." A preemptive move directed against any more concrete danger would be classified accordingly as "defensive," falling under the category of commanded war. In Bleich's exposition, the scope of defensive war is not circumscribed by substantive moral criteria; rather, it is defined as that which is less permissible than optional war.

This illustrates the moral difficulties associated with the very notion of optional war, even as a theoretical category, within the halakhic tradition. The only way to avoid moral vertigo is to grapple directly with the license for bloodshed, in the spirit of the rabbinic explanation of the two verbs used by the Torah (Gen. 32:8) to describe Jacob's trepidation before his confrontation with Esau (*"Then Jacob was greatly afraid and was distressed"*): R. Judah b. R. Ilai said: "Are not fear and distress identical? The meaning however is that he [Jacob] was afraid lest he should be slain, and was distressed lest he should slay [others]."[5]

Bleich commendably does not evade the inherent difficulties: A major part of his essay is devoted to the problem of justifying bloodshed in warfare. But to appreciate fully his argument, it is necessary to ask in what terms the prohibition on bloodshed is being defined. Is Bleich addressing the moral injunction against bloodshed or the halakhic pronouncement "You shall not kill"? And how separable are these two in his view?

Bleich's essay commences with a reference to "Jewish law and ethics"; these are immediately identified with halakha (p. 251). Indeed, several of Bleich's points read most plausibly as instances of moral discourse. The discussion is nowhere defined, in so many words, as purely halakhic, that is, as disclaiming all commitments to common morality.[6] Yet, as will be shown presently, some of Bleich's statements, in rendering earlier sources as well as in drawing contemporary conclusions, cannot easily be sustained as moral judgments.

BLEICH'S PRINCIPLE OF
"DIVINE SANCTION" FOR KILLING

Bleich points out that the conduct of (even defensive) warfare cannot be justified simply in terms of individual self-defense writ large. The problem, he says (pp. 275–278), is that arguing in terms of saving lives justifies far too little. For on the individual level, two major constraints apply: First, no permission is granted for taking the lives of innocent bystanders if this turns out to be entailed by stopping the attacker; and second, only imminent danger to life, as distinct from danger to property or to territorial integrity, can justify preventive killing.[7] Warfare—in which, according to Bleich, neither constraint applies—involves therefore some further, special license; it cannot be justified solely in terms of defending lives.

So how can warfare ever be justified? Bleich appropriately quotes a commentary by R. Naphtali Zvi Berlin (Netziv) on the verse that proclaims the divine prohibition against murder (Gen. 9:5). Because I shall contest part of Bleich's understanding of this text, I offer a translation of the entire paragraph:

"From the hand of a person's brother"—

> God specified that a person is culpable at a time when brotherly conduct is called for; not so in time of war and 'a time to hate' [following Qohelet 3:8]—then it is a time to kill, and there is no culpability whatever, for that is how the world was founded. Similarly we read in *Shevuot* 35: "A kingdom that kills [in warfare] one in six is not held culpable"; and even a king of Israel may wage an optional war, even though some Jews will be killed thereby.[8]

Clearly, Netziv is concerned about the moral status of soldiers and those who sent them into battle to kill and to be killed. Armies, he argues, do not expect "brotherly conduct" from each other; their killings are not ruptures in the moral fabric of human society, but rather a constant feature thereof. This distinction expresses the "war convention," under which soldiers killing enemy soldiers are not deemed murderers.[9]

Bleich finds here an indication for allowing the killing of bystanders, an inference that will be addressed later. What needs concern us here is what he makes of Netziv's rather elliptical explanation. For if indeed warfare is a situation where killing, at least of enemy soldiers, becomes permitted, how can we make moral sense of this permission?[10]

Netziv's language offers no more than a slight hint here, contained in the reference to the inescapable nature of things: "for that is how the world was founded." This is easily understandable with regard to defensive (obligatory) war: When attacked, it is our duty to resist, "to rescue Israel from an attacking enemy." But Netziv is referring explicitly also to optional wars, which seem obviously avoidable. Why should their conduct be considered a fixed feature of the world? The implicit picture of society is rather Hobbesian: Even beyond the necessities of immediate self-defense, states must regularly fight to survive. An optional war may leave more leeway as to its timing—and probably more room for negotiation and compromise—but it is finally also unavoidable.

I am not asserting with any certainty that this is what Netziv had in mind. In essence, all he does is to note that God recognized this convention when proclaiming that he would hold human beings responsible for bloodshed. In any case, offering a moral account of the war convention, that is, justifying the killing of enemy soldiers while maintaining the prohibition on killing noncombatants, is a difficult problem for moral philosophy.[11] What is noteworthy about Bleich's discussion is not that he fails to solve this problem, but that he appears to dismiss it.

Bleich argues that Genesis 9:5 should be construed as "excluding from the Halakhic prohibition against homicide the shedding of blood within the context of warfare provided that the war itself is legitimately undertaken, that is, *in situations in which the bonds of brotherhood have been severed in a manner sanctioned by Halakhah*" (p. 288, emphasis added). This exclusion refers to "the Halakhic prohibition" against homicide; Bleich's language suggests that this is perceived as wholly independent of the *moral* evil of murder. For the relevant situations are not defined by morally significant criteria, but by divine sanction; that is, proclaimed either through biblical revelation or through the oracular *urim ve-tumim*.

Thus actions that by plain reasoning are "homicide, pure and simple" (p. 277) are said to be "legitimize(d)" (p. 288) or "sanctioned" (p. 277) by divine decree. The "Halakhic prohibition" is conceived as belonging to a closed normative system, neither reflecting nor recognizing distinctly moral imperatives. This amoral conception of divine sanction is most clearly revealed in Bleich's account of the respective roles played by the Sanhedrin and by the *urim ve-tumim*, an account founded on a surprising reversal of their traditionally perceived functions.

PROCLAIMING WAR: TORAH VS. ORACLE

Bleich plausibly distinguishes between a defensive war, in which the normal condition of brotherhood is "shattered by the aggressor," and wars that we initiate, where it is we who break the peace. The halakhic tradition stipulates that the king gain prior approval from both the Sanhedrin (the supreme rabbinic court) and the oracular *urim ve-tumim*. At the outset (p. 282), Bleich rejects out of hand the possibility "that this tripartite requirement for declaration of war is designed to provide a system of checks and balances." [12] But are not checks and balances precisely what is needed in the face of so grievous a prospect as optional war? Perhaps Bleich believes that Jews do not need checks and balances. In any case, he proceeds to give an account of the specific function of each element. The king's role as political sovereign is uncomplicated, so we shall concentrate on the relation between the two religious institutions - the Sanhedrin vs. the *urim ve-tumim*.

Judging by their respective roles in other contexts, the division of labor between these two institutions seems straightforward enough. The *urim ve-tumim* were used, in biblical times, for enquiring of God about imminent prospects. [13] The great risks involved in initiating warfare surely warrant seeking a glimpse of the outcome; the venture's success is a necessary, though insufficient, condition for deciding to undertake it. The Sanhedrin, on the other hand, is the supreme teacher of Torah; it is the appropriate source for normative counsel, greatly needed for weighing any suggestion of initiating an optional war.

This understanding of the role of the Sanhedrin in declaring optional war is advocated, for example, by Rabbi Y. 'Amital, who cites, inter alia, a letter by Rav Kook. [14] R. 'Amital explicates the Sanhedrin's role in light of the basic postulate that there is a moral problem in initiating optional war. Indeed, he points out that, according to Chazon Ish, such war may be waged against only "outlaw" peoples, violators of the seven Noachide laws.[15] This involves, of course, collective judgment; but at least it is conceived as judgment, a quasi-punitive decision to be rendered by the supreme halakhic court.[16]

Instead, Bleich portrays the Sanhedrin here as a kind of executive body, requested to predict the outcome of the proposed military action. Though elders are appointed to the Sanhedrin by virtue of their erudition, piety, and excellence in normative reasoning, they are called upon to function like a national security council: "The Sanhedrin is charged with assessing the military, political and economic realia" (p. 285). For normative guidance, on the other hand, we are referred to an oracle: "In essence, the *urim ve-tumim* is required in order to legitimize military action that may cost the lives of innocent victims" (p. 288). Contrary to the traditional orientation of halakha,[17] divine will with respect to normative decisions is here not believed to be determined through study and debate, but rather through appeal to the divine spirit.

In effect, Bleich's interpretation moves the realm of Jewish statecraft away from the rabbinic ideal of living by the Torah, as applied by the learned teachers of the community. Crucial normative decisions are excluded from the reasoned debate of the Sanhedrin and subjected to inscrutable decrees from heaven.

Still, it would seem that Bleich's doctrine should have no contemporary impact, for, as he emphasizes, the oracle itself (as well as the Sanhedrin) is presently unavailable and thus "it would appear that, in our day, preemptive war 'to diminish the heathens' cannot be sanctioned by Jewish law" (p. 259). What crucially matters, however, is the basic principle that what is required is divine sanction rather than moral reason to allow war and bloodshed.

FORMALISM AND BLOODSHED: A CRITIQUE OF ORACULAR HALAKHA

For Bleich, the crucial normative factor regarding warfare is God's restriction of his prohibition against homicide to "brotherly situations." What distinguishes obligatory wars from optional wars is therefore not an essential difference in their moral character, but rather the mode whereby the divine license for bloodshed is determined. In a defensive war, God's will is known not through the *urim ve-tumim,* but by virtue of applying a formal halakhic category. Accordingly, the scope of the category of defensive war is extrinsically controlled, by minimal subtraction from authoritative definitions of optional war.

This means that if an enemy we wish to target for a preemptive strike can be provoked into any kind of action against us, we gain license to wage against it an all-out war. We attack first, in a limited way that halakhically does not constitute warfare; the enemy's counterattack "results in circumstances warranting [an obligatory war]" (p. 290). This account[18] focuses neither on the basic political circumstances nor on the war's true goals, but on the fulfillment of certain technical conditions.

In this mode of discourse, halakha itself has become an oracular device. Rather than promoting moral reasoning, the study of halakha produces formulas for divine decrees and dispensations. In Bleich's essay, the most distressing expression of this position is his rejection of noncombatant immunity.

Bleich supports this rejection by affirming that no contrary ruling is found in rabbinic sources, and that moreover "there exists no discussion in classical rabbinic sources that takes cognizance of the likelihood of causing civilian casualties in the course of hostilities legitimately undertaken as posing a halakhic or moral problem" (p. 277). Even if this were so,[19] such silence could not furnish any *moral* justification for harming noncombatants. For Bleich, however, a formal determination that the hostilities are "legitimately undertaken" evidently proclaims a divine license to pursue victory without regard for civilian casualties. This indicates that the ambiguity about the relation of halakha to morality has been resolved in a radical vein, isolating halakhic discourse from common morality.

Against this amoral view, let us conclude by citing an example of moral-halakhic discourse. The following discussion by R. Judah Löwe of Prague (Maharal) is clearly grounded in an alternative halakhic philosophy; that is, in an approach that seeks in God's word not an inscrutable oracular decree, but rather a clear moral teaching. The discussion consists of a refined analysis of the midrash quoted earlier about Jacob's distress over the possibility of killing Esau's men. Maharal points out that Jacob was preparing to act in self-defense; would he not then be perfectly justified in killing the oncoming company? He answers that, although this was obviously true with respect to the aggressive leader, Jacob had some doubts with respect to the men marching along with Esau:

> Perhaps they did not come to kill Jacob; although Esau brought them with him, they had come along under duress but without intending to kill. Now Jacob, since he did not know whether or not they had come to kill, was fearful lest he unlawfully kill them, and that is why he was distressed 'lest he kill others.' Against this, it might be claimed that we cannot have it both ways. If the law in such a case is that since they had come with one who was coming to kill, they were to be presumed to be like him—then he [Jacob] need not have been concerned: since they had come along, they had brought it upon themselves. If [on the other hand] the proper presumption is that they had come under duress, and that they would surely not do anything—then surely he would be forbidden to kill; there is no occasion for being "distressed," since it is forbidden to kill [them].—However, although they should be killed since they had come with Esau who was coming to kill, nevertheless he was afraid of incurring guilt, as it would be like an inadvertent sin. Jacob would have believed that they had come to kill while [in fact, perhaps,] they had not come to kill—so this is an inadvertent sin.[20]

It should be noted that a similar point is made by Rabbi E. Mizrahi, who explicitly refers to the prospective confrontation between Jacob and Esau as *war*, thus affirming moral continuity between everyday morality and the norms pertaining to warfare.[21]

Facing the challenges of a renewed Jewish polity, we ought to steer clear of the moral pitfalls entailed by an oracular halakhic philosophy. If the halakhic tradition is to be a source of inspiration for political thought in contemporary Israel, it must be guided by the classical eschewal of heavenly voices in favor of reasoned deliberation. This by no means implies that the study of Torah ought to be abandoned in favor of pervasive Western norms. Rather, it requires that we avoid using the forms of halakhic discourse as a medium for promulgating mysterious decrees. Instead, we must continue to carry on the enterprise of building a worthy moral universe from the rich and instructive resources of the halakhic tradition, "for this is your wisdom and your understanding."[22]

NOTES

I wish to thank the members of the Academy for Jewish Philosophy (especially J. D. Bleich, E. Dorff, and L. Goodman), as well as M. Walzer, for their instructive comments on earlier versions of this chapter.

1. Bleich 1989, pp. 251–292 (originally published in *Tradition* 21, no. 1 [1983], pp. 3–41).

2. The notion of *milchemet mitzvah*, a "commanded (obligatory) war," seems to suggest something like a "holy war" (Arabic, *jihad*). Yet Maimonides affirms that Jews are not to wield their sword to coerce conversion to Judaism. Admittedly, he holds that they should enforce by sword adherence to the seven Noachide laws; in this Maimonides is apparently opposed by most other halakhists, notably Nachmanides and Rabad. An analysis of this discussion is the subject of the comments by Chazon Ish cited in note 15.

3. BT *Sotah* 44b. By the biblical accounts, these can be variously understood as wars of liberation, as preemptive wars against belligerent neighbors, or as imperialist endeavors. The latter understanding is suggested in one rabbinic legend about David's realm. In response to complaints about insufficient sources of livelihood, David directs his people to "go forth in a band" (see *Sanhedrin* 16a–b). Yet even this text has been interpreted as referring to a basically defensive motivation; R. Re'uven Margaliyot writes: "King David, may he rest in peace, did not direct them to form bands and sally forth to collect booty! On the contrary, he advised them to attack the band [*note*: the Hebrew preposition *bet* can mean not only *in* but also *against*], for they were oppressed by the Amalekite bands who had been raiding the land and disrupting its economy. . . . Insecurity had pervaded the country because of infiltrating bands; thus the people were unable to make a living—whether through agriculture, since the bands looted the crops, or through international commerce. Therefore David directed them to attack that band, eradicating the looting Amalekite gangs, so that every person could peaceably make a living" (Margaliyot 1977, p. 34). The term *revacha* itself simply denotes improvement of a difficult situation and is therefore, by itself, too unspecific to draw any conclusion.

4. MT *Kings and Wars* 5:1.

5. *Genesis Rabbah* 76:2, p. 702.

6. For example, on p. 277 (Bleich 1989) it is asserted that, in rabbinic sources, harming civilians does not pose "a halakhic or moral problem."

7. Bleich notes a third difference as well: People can be *conscripted* for military action, but not for individual rescue operations. This is valid with regard to obligatory war; it does not, however, sufficiently recognize

the wide scope of exemptions applying to optional war, which make it dependent on what is, in effect, a volunteer army; see *Sifre* Deut. 194–198.

8. *Ha'ameq Davar* on Genesis 9:5.

9. See, e.g., Walzer 1977, pp. 36–37.

10. It has been argued by several writers that killing enemy soldiers can be justified purely in terms of self-defense. For Bleich, obviously, such a solution is not possible.

11. A striking moral account of the war convention has been offered by R. Shaul Yisra'eli in terms of universal consent, in his essay "The Kibbiya Incident in Halakhic Light" (originally published in *Ha-Torah ve-ha-Medinah* [*Torah and State: A Forum for Halakhic Studies in Matters of State in Israel*], vols. 5–6 (1954), pp. 71–113.

12. The sentence ends with another summary rejection: "or simply to render actual warfare halakhically difficult." Why should it be deemed "unlikely" to attribute such a purpose in a tradition that commonly defines itself as committed to peace, a definition reflected by the rabbinic quote by which Bleich aptly introduces his essay?

13. See, for example, 1 Samuel 23:6–13 (the ephod contained the breastplate of the *urim ve-tumim*). The talmudic discussion (*Yoma* 73 a–b and Yerushalmi *Yoma* 44c) suggests that asking the oracle merely what to do can be misleading: It is essential to focus the query on the prospects of success.

14. 'Amital 1987. R. Kook's letter, published in Kook 1985, vol. 1: 89 (pp. 92–101), consists of answers to a series of questions posed by M. Zeidel. One cluster of queries addressed halakhic traditions regarding warfare; the item pertinent to our issue evidently expressed puzzlement over Maimonides's teaching, that Israel should wage war against idolatrous nations to enforce abandonment of idol worship. R. Kook (ibid., p. 100) first insists that this goal is consistent with Israel's calling; but then he adds: "Obviously, it was nevertheless given to the court to examine the moral quality of the particular idolatry, and not all cases were the same."(My thanks to Professor A. Ravitsky for bringing these sources to my attention; cf. Ravitsky forthcoming)

15. The discussion by R. Y. Karelitz (Chazon Ish) is found in his comments to MT *Kings and Wars* 6:4. Throughout that discussion Chazon Ish speaks of nations who "commit themselves" ("*meqablin 'alehem*") to the Noachide code; this might be mistakenly taken as requiring a formal commitment. The context, however, shows that Chazon Ish is concerned with nations who heretofore had been violating the Noachide laws; he is arguing for allowing them to surrender and repent ("commit themselves"), thus escaping punishment for their prior crimes.

As R. 'Amital emphasizes, this usage should by no means be taken to exclude nations who simply abide by the Noachide code; these may certainly not be attacked, as stated explicitly in Chazon Ish's concluding sentence: "With regard to those, however, who have been observing (*"meqaymin"*) the seven commandments all along, we are not permitted to wage war against them."

16. Other rabbinic writers have conceived of the Sanhedrin here as representing the people, a kind of parliament whose consent is required for proclaiming war.

17. See, e.g., Berkovits 1983.

18. This seems tailored to suit the war in Lebanon, which was the occasion for Bleich's essay.

19. In rabbinic times, armies normally met on battlefields, separated from the civilians of either side, so the lack of discussion about problems like bombing a military installation located near civilians does not seem to indicate very much. The fate of civilians was, however, addressed in the context of siege warfare; see Artson 1987.

Bleich (1989, n. 39) cites Saul's warning to the Kenites, civilians who resided near the targeted Amalekites, as implying that "had the Kenites not heeded this admonition [to draw away], Saul might have slain them with impunity in the course of the battle against Amalek." Even if this is so, it by no means implies a blanket license for harming civilians, e.g., in circumstances where it is militarily impossible to issue a warning or where they cannot get away.

20. *Gur Aryeh*, Maharal's supercommentary to Rashi on Genesis 32:8.

21. Admittedly, regarding the actual norms of warfare, Maharal himself seems rather to share some of Bleich's operative conclusions. In another context (*Gur Aryeh* to Gen. 34:13), he endorses collective punishment in retributive wars, allowing the destruction of all civilians belonging to the offending nation. In this severe teaching Maharal explicitly differs from both Maimonides and Nachmanides (cf. Zohar 1993). Yet even then, he does not justify such deeds by reference to any amoral divine license; rather, Maharal believes this to be the prevailing norm in warfare, concluding with the assertion that "thus is it in all wars." Accordingly, he limits the liability to citizens of the offending nation; third party civilians retain their immunity, a distinction explicitly denied by Bleich, for whom homicide ceases to be a concern in the conduct of "divinely sanctioned" warfare.

22. Deut. 4:6; and cf. Maimonides, *Guide* 3:31.

REFERENCES

'Amital, Y. 1987. "Milchamot Yisrael 'al pi ha-Rambam" ["Israel's Wars According to Maimonides"]. *Techumin* 8: 454–461.

Artson, B. S. 1987. "The Siege and the Civilian." *Judaism* 36: 54–65.

Berkovits, E. 1983. *Not in Heaven: The Nature and Function of Halakha.* New York: Ktav.

Berlin, N. Z. Y. 1937. *Ha'ameq Davar* [Commentary on the Pentateuch], 2d ed. Jerusalem: Bamberger and Wahrman.

Bleich, J. D. 1989. *Contemporary Halakhic Problems,* vol. 3. New York: Ktav and Yeshiva University Press.

di-Botan, A. 1606. *Lechem Mishneh* [Commentary on Maimonides's *Mishneh Torah*].

Kook, A. Y. 1985. *Iggerot Re'iyah* [Collected Letters]. Jerusalem: Mossad ha-Rav Kook.

Löwe, Judah (of Prague). 1862 [1579]. *Gur Aryeh* [Supercommentary on Rashi's Torah commentary]. Warsaw [printed with E. Mizrahi's similar work].

Luzzatto, S. D. 1966 [1871–1876]. *Commentary on the Pentateuch.* Tel Aviv: Dvir.

Margaliyot, R. 1977. *Margaliyot ha-Yam on Sanhedrin.* Jerusalem: Mossad ha-Rav Kook.

Midrash Rabbah. 1939. *Genesis Rabbah,* trans. H. Freedman. London: Soncino.

Ravitsky, A. Forthcoming. "Prohibited War in the Jewish Tradition." In *The Ethics of War and Peace,* ed. T. Nardin. Princeton, N.J.: Princeton University Press.

Walzer, M. 1977. *Just and Unjust Wars.* New York: Basic Books.

Zohar, N. 1993. "Boycott, Crime and Sin: Ethical and Talmudic Responses to Injustice Abroad." *Ethics and International Affairs* 7: 39–53.

Response to Noam Zohar

J. David Bleich

The reader of Noam Zohar's critique of "Preemptive War in Jewish Law" should be aware of the issues that essay was designed to address. Those issues can be categorized as (1) the criteria of "defensive war" as variously defined by authoritative rabbinic scholars; (2) the permissibility of military action that incidentally and inadvertently results in loss of civilian lives; and (3) an analysis of the distinctive roles of the king, Sanhedrin, and *urim ve-tumim* in proclaiming an "optional war."

The first two goals were, I believe, discharged in a manner that more than satisfies the burden of proof imposed by halakhic dialectic and in a manner that any scholar trained in halakhic methodology would find unexceptionable for the simple reason that the exposition involves no *chiddush* whatsoever. To describe that task as "reportorial" is not to denigrate the significance of ferreting out sources, analysis, and presentation. The third issue, and its treatment, is "philosophical" in the sense that it is of absolutely no halakhic import. The thesis presented in my essay is analogous to a scientific hypothesis designed to explain certain empirical phenomena. In this case, it is a hypothesis designed to explain certain halakhic provisions. As is the case with scientific hypotheses, deductive "proof" is seldom, if ever, available. Alternative hypotheses designed to provide equally good or better explanations are certainly invited both in science and in the "philosophy" of Halakha.

I will, for the moment, pass over Zohar's incorrect and misleading description of that endeavor as "oracular halakha" and confine myself to pointing out a number of areas of gross misunderstanding.

First, Zohar is quite understandably troubled by the permission granted a monarch to engage in optional war: "how can an optional war—which, by its very definition, can be avoided—ever be permitted? . . . how can it be permissible to choose the bloody path of warfare if it is not an inescapable necessity?" Zohar's answer is, in effect, a confession of his inability to resolve the problem within the framework of Halakha. Shadal's comment that "Scripture is determining that we may make war only against our enemies" is simply incorrect as a matter of normative Halakha. The talmudic formulation of a "war to diminish the heathens lest they attack Israel" cannot be cited as support for "the moral point expressed by Shadal" for the simple reason that it is not the sole form of optional war sanctioned by the Talmud. Certainly, no halakhic authority has indicated that the category of optional war is limited in that manner. Little solace is to be found in the restrictive understanding of *Lechem Mishneh*'s reconstruction of Rambam's definition of *revacha*. The military action sanctioned by Rambam can hardly be described as a war against an "enemy." Moreover, in the final analysis, *Lechem Mishneh*'s comment represents but one commentator's opinion and is contrary to the position of so many others.

Be this as it may, Zohar's statement that "the notion of optional war continues to have an effect on Bleich's analysis of contemporary guidance" is an egregious misstatement. It is not the notion of optional war undertaken for territorial aggrandizement and the moral problems associated with such military action that have an impact upon contemporary guidance but the definition of *defensive war* that is of practical application. And, to quote Zohar, regrettable as even defensive war may be, "the shedding of blood in a defensive war may be a necessary evil."

The salient question is what degree of danger must be present to render shedding of blood halakhically permissible as a "necessary evil"? That, in turn, is contingent upon explication of the criteria of a "war to diminish the heathens" representing a response to a lower level of danger that can serve as justification only for an optional war and consequently constitutes a category of war that is not at all sanctioned in our historical epoch. The formal link is rather simple: On a continuum from the lowest level of danger to the highest, association of a level of danger with "war to diminish the heathens" implies that a greater danger may be regarded as grounds for a defensive war; otherwise, "war to diminish the heathens" would have been linked with a higher level of danger on the same continuum or, alternatively, that level of danger would have been identified by some other appellation as a form of optional war. Such an exercise is but deductive sleuthing enabling us to discover the criteria of danger recognized by the Sages as rendering war permissible as "defensive" in nature. Only after the halakhic criteria have been explicated can we meaningfully investigate the "substantive moral criteria" that inform the Halakha.

Second, Zohar does not seem to recognize the enormity of the halakhic problem involved in taking the life of a civilian even in a purely defensive war. A philosopher grappling with the problem of the bombing of Dresden or Hiroshima will carefully distinguish between the purposeful targeting of a civilian population and the incidental and unintentional killing of an innocent bystander. To the halakhist the former is virtually unthinkable; the halakhic permissibility of the latter is taken for granted despite Zohar's disclaimer. If, as Zohar seems to maintain, that is not the case, virtually no defensive action would find sanction in Halakha. Even in antiquity when armies met on the battlefield there were standard bearers and campfollowers who posed no threat to anyone. Moveover, even a cursory reading of 1 Samuel 15 reveals that the Kenites were innocent people but, had they not hearkened to the warning to remove themselves from the site of battle, they would have been annihilated together with Amalek. (Despite Zohar's response, now appended in a footnote, I am not aware that failure to heed a belligerent's order to remove oneself from danger constitutes a crime warranting capital punishment.)

It is incontrovertible that Halakha permits certain acts undertaken in the context of warfare that are not sanctioned when undertaken by an individual in the course of self-defense. "So," queries Zohar, "how can [such] warfare ever be justified?" Zohar again pays me a misplaced compliment in informing the reader that I "appropriately" quote a commentary by R. Naphtali Zvi Berlin (Netziv) in addressing that issue. He then proceeds to "contest part of Bleich's understanding of this text." In doing so he provides a pilpulistic analysis of the cited text having absolutely nothing to do with the import of Netziv's comment and simultaneously misrepresents my purpose in citing Netziv.

Netziv has absolutely nothing to say about the morality or immorality of war. The thrust of his comment is directed to halakhic justification of wars fought by non-Jews; his comment concerning "a king of Israel" is an aside. Contrary to the consensus of rabbinic authority, Netziv believes that Noachides enjoy a license to engage in warfare without incurring punishment for homicide. In the quoted paragraph he seeks to interpret scriptural passages in light of that thesis. Netziv intends no more and no less.

For my part, I cite Netziv's halakhic position neither with approval nor with disapproval. In point of fact, were any gentile to seek my halakhic guidance I would have no choice but to disclose that the weight of halakhic authority is contrary to the position of Netziv. In developing my hypothesis concerning the role of the Sanhedrin I borrowed Netziv's seminal thesis and applied it in a context entirely different from that contemplated by Netziv. "The words of Torah are poor in one place but rich in another place." Both my debt to Netziv and my extension of his remarkable insight are freely acknowledged. There is not the slightest attempt in the writing of Netziv, or in mine, to "justify" warfare. The exercise is limited to delineation of the parameters of the prohibition against homicide. Nor is there even the slightest hint of an attempt to "make moral sense" of permission to kill enemy soldiers. The enterprise is halakhically descriptive in nature; it is not at all a moral apologia. It is nothing more than the assertion that a *mattir* is required, that is, a halakhic mechanism rendering such actions permissible, and a description of that mechanism.

Third, it is indeed the case that, in some circumstances, the shedding of blood is "legitimized" or "sanctioned" by divine decree. That is manifestly apparent from biblical texts and halakhic codification of rules of warfare. This may well lead the philosopher to raise questions of theodicy. Those questions are raised on the assumption that God is just and that the task of the philosopher or of the theologian is to explain how and in what sense God's actions are just.

Divine will, at least at times, may indeed be determined through "study and debate." Yet, would anyone deny that it is also determined by means of prophecy, at least under appropriate circumstances? In his search for normative rules and moral justification,

Zohar has managed to miss the obvious. In all probability, the moral lesson to be derived from the halakhic provisions circumscribing warfare is that war, other than when undertaken in self-defense, can never be justified through "study and debate." Such decisions are far too weighty to be entrusted to human intellect. Hence the need for divine determination as revealed by the *urim ve-tumim*.

Fourth, Zohar erroneously credits me with not avoiding "moral vertigo" and grappling directly with the "license for bloodshed" involved in optional war. His kudo is undeserved; I do no such thing. Here, too, I do not in any way grapple with the moral or philosophical issue; my treatment is entirely halakhic and descriptive.

In line with that comment let me reiterate that optional war is certainly permitted as a matter of Halakha. Zohar's statement that "the only goal explicitly specified by the Talmud is that of pre-emption: 'to diminish the heathens lest they attack Israel'" is simply false. The Gemara, *Sotah* 44b, explicitly states: "The wars waged by the House of David for territorial expansion were optional in the opinion of all." The notion that optional wars are "quasi-punitive" is appealing but entirely erroneous. The statement attributed to Chazon Ish, on M.T. *Kings* 6:4, to the effect that optional war may be waged only against "outlaw peoples who systematically violate the seven Noachide laws" is an exaggerated and wishful reading of the source. Chazon Ish says only that war may not be waged against a *ger toshav* who has *formally* accepted the Noachide code. Since Rambam, M.T. *Kings* 8:10, rules that all gentiles must formally accept the seven Noachide laws upon pain of death, mere "fulfillment" could not logically confer immunity from optional war upon them. (See the very last page of R. Yitzhak Ze'ev ha-Levi Soloveitchik, *Chiddushei Maran Riz ha-Levi* [Jerusalem, 5723].) Moreover, but several lines earlier, Chazon Ish agrees that Rambam and Rabad require formal acceptance of the Noachide code. There is no reason to a posit a controversy between those authorities and Rambam with regard to this point. Chazon Ish's use of the term *meqaymin* must be understood as connoting fulfillment pursuant to formal acceptance.

Fifth, that the taking of human life in halakhically sanctioned warfare is excluded from the prohibition against homicide is perfectly obvious. The sole halakhic issue is establishment of the parameters of that exclusion. In optional wars the exclusion is triggered by the holy spirit as announced through the *urim ve-tumim*. It is clear that permission of the *urim ve-tumim* was a sine qua non of legitimate warfare. (Incidentally and contra Zohar, mere consultation of the *urim ve-tumim* was not an absolute guarantee of success. It is apparent from the discussion recorded in *Yoma* 73a–b that a query regarding a successful outcome was not integral to the mandated consultation.) That is indeed an oracular phenomenon, not a halakhic determination. Most emphatically, it does *not* involve a halakhic decision based on something beyond the human intellect any more than did God's command "Harass the Midianites and smite them" (Numbers 25:17), which was also post-Sinaitic in nature.

Exclusion from the commandment concerning homicide in defensive wars is halakhic, not oracular. It is halakhic because license for such activity was given at Sinai without further justification. The determination that a given set of circumstances constitutes a causus belli for a halakhically sanctionable defensive war is entirely a halakhic decision to be tendered in accordance with conventional canons of halakhic decision making.

Sixth, Zohar's most egregious error is his failure to distinguish between Halakha and ethics. The latter he endeavors to introduce with a citation from Maharal. Unfortunately, that citation is both inapt and inept. Maharal's expressed concern is entirely halakhic, and, in its own terms, predicated on the law of *rodef* rather than upon the halakhic category of war. No matter. Zohar could have cited numerous other sources expressing reservation and even censure with regard to warfare for which halakhic sanction exists.

Probably the most obvious source indicating an awareness of a moral problem over and above the technical concerns of Halakha is the comment of R. David Kimchi (Radak) on 1 Chronicles 22:8. King David is admonished: "But the word of the Lord came to me saying: Thou hast shed blood abundantly and hast made great wars; thou shalt not build a house unto My name because thou hast shed much blood upon the earth in My sight." The commentators are troubled by an obvious problem. Each of David's wars was either a "commanded war" or a divinely sanctioned "optional war." Why then should he be forbidden to build the Temple? Radak comments intra alia: "also among the blood of the gentiles that he spilled, it is possible that among those who were not combatants there were good and pious people. Even though [David] was not punished because of them since his intent was to annihilate the wicked . . . he was prevented from building the Temple which is for peace, expiation of sin and [the] crown of prayer." Radak certainly assumes that King David is held accountable only for the blood of innocent noncombatants. His accountability is assuredly solely in the form of *lifnim mi-shurat ha-din*, and, arguably, lesser mortals than he might not have been held accountable. Nevertheless, a degree of moral culpability exists despite halakhic sanction.

To state that a given act does not entail a violation of "Thou shalt not kill" is not to pronounce the act a mitzvah! There may be circumstances in which preemptive war would qualify as a "war of defense" but in which a military response would, nevertheless, be unwise, imprudent—and yes—immoral, but not murder.

Seventh, Zohar's statement ascribing to me the position that if an enemy "can be provoked into any kind of action against us, we gain license to wage against them an all-out war" is a canard. First of all, the position described is that of Chazon Ish—one for which I neither take credit nor suffer blame. Second, nowhere in the words of Chazon Ish, or in my own, do I find the slightest suggestion of license to provoke aggressive acts to fulfill "certain technical conditions" that render a preemptive strike permissible. An individual who provokes aggression to slay the aggressor in self-defense acts in a morally odious manner but nevertheless will avoid the death penalty. Once one is successful in one's provocation and becomes a victim of the aggressor one has no choice but to act in self-defence. Nothing in that scenario is exculpatory of the original act of provocation. What is true of the individual is true of the nation as well.

Eighth, both in his critique and in his own analysis Zohar flits back and forth between two distinct problems: the morality of optional war and the morality of causing casualties to noncombatants. Because the role of the Sanhedrin was consultative, it may well be argued that the Sanhedrin was consulted with regard to a variety of matters, such as the need for additional territory, assessment of risks involved, and proportionality of gain to the number of casualties likely to be incurred. Prior to consultation of the *urim ve-tumim* advice of the Sanhedrin may perhaps also be sought with regard to the moral propriety of the contemplated military incursion. Whether or not there is a role for the Sanhedrin in making a moral determination regarding an optional war that receives divine sanction through the medium of the *urim ve-tumim* and whether or not it makes sense to examine provisions of divine law through the spectacles of modern notions of checks and balances (and to subject the holy spirit as reflected in the *urim ve-tumim* to checks and balances, no less—although it might be argued that the *urim ve-tumim* served as a check upon the Sanhedrin), the Sanhedrin certainly was not the arbiter of the morality of causing the death of noncombatants. Those decisions were and are made in the course of combat; the role of the Sanhedrin was limited to declaration of war. No one would claim that any and all innocent blood is morally *hefqer* in war. By the same token, I have argued, the taking of *any* innocent life even in the course of warfare requires a *mattir* [formal suspension] of the prohibition against homicide.

Zohar tells us we must be guided by "the classical eschewal of heavenly voices in favor of reasoned deliberation." I know not how to eschew an unheard voice. I assuredly did not suggest consultation with a presently unavailable *urim ve-tumim*; nor, as I make abundantly clear, is such consultation at all appropriate with regard to defensive war. Moreover, Zohar seems unable to distinguish between "heavenly voices" and their respective roles. There exists no dichotomy between "heavenly voices" (read: *urim ve-tumim*, not *bat qol*) and "reasoned deliberation." Is there any believing Jew who does not pine for restoration of the Temple and, with it, of the *urim ve-tumim*? But, alas, for the present, the Temple and the *urim ve-tumim* simply do not exist. Neither has anyone suggested that halakhic discourse be used as a "medium for promulgating mysterious decrees." I am not aware of any "mysterious decree" that can conceivably be promulgated by means of halakhic discourse or otherwise. Zohar's final paragraph is confused and confusing. An amalgam of glib phrases does not an argument make.

Indeed, the point of Zohar's chapter eludes me. I find no challenge with regard to any point of Halakha. The thrust seems to be either that Halakha is deficient in its failure to coincide with commonly perceived moral norms or that proper attention has not been paid to the role of morality as a norm of halakhic decision making.

The response to the first point is best captured in an anecdote concerning a gentleman visiting the Louvre. He came upon a crowd of people gathered around the Mona Lisa. The gentleman looked at the painting, then at his fellow spectators and again at the painting. Finally, he remarked to the guard standing nearby, "Why are all these people spending so much time staring at this picture? The woman isn't at all beautiful." To this the guard relied, "My dear sir, it is not the Mona Lisa's value as a work of art that is subject to question; it is your ability to appreciate great art that is in question." Halakha is not on trial and, most assuredly, does not need my defense.

Zohar has inadvertently put his finger upon one significant issue: the relationship of ethics and Halakha and whether or not there is an ethic beyond Halakha. That question is hardly novel. It has been addressed by R. Aharon Lichtenstein in "Does Jewish Tradition Recognize an Ethic Independent of Halakha?" (Lichtenstein 1975) and, to a lesser extent, in my "Is There an Ethic Beyond Halakhah?" (Bleich 1987).

To this I would add that both Halakha and intellectual integrity are ill served by a revisionist reading, selection of non-normative views, and unrepresentative quotation of proof-texts. Halakha can be accepted, rejected, or ignored—but it should never be distorted or misrepresented in a misguided attempt to attract adherents. In some circles it has become fashionable to mold and sculpt halakhic sources to yield what is thought to be a more marketable product. Success in such endeavors does not represent even a Pyrrhic victory; it is a self-induced defeat. A Halakha that is not true to its own norms, principles, and canons is not the Halakha revealed at Sinai but the product of human self-deification.

REFERENCES

Bleich, J. D. 1987. "Is There an Ethic Beyond Halakhah?" In *Studies in Jewish Philosophy: Collected Essays of the Academy for Jewish Philosophy, 1980–1985*, ed. N. M. Samuelson, pp. 527–546. Lanham, Md., New York, and London: University Press of America.

Lichtenstein, A. 1975. "Does Jewish Tradition Recognize an Ethic Independent of Halakha?" In *Modern Jewish Ethics: Theory and Practice*, ed. M. Fox, pp. 62–88. Columbus, Ohio: Ohio State University Press. Reprinted in *Contemporary Jewish Ethics*, ed. M. M. Kellner, pp. 102–123. New York: Sanhedrin Press, 1978.

Reply to David Bleich

Noam J. Zohar

HALAKHA, ETHICS, AND THEODICY

In his sharp response to my critique, David Bleich writes: "It is indeed the case that, in some circumstances, the shedding of blood is 'legitimized' or 'sanctioned' by divine decree. That is *manifestly apparent* from biblical texts and halakhic codification of rules of war. This may well lead the philosopher to raise *questions of theodicy*" [third point, emphases added].

How, one wonders, is this effect of the divine decree "manifestly apparent" from biblical texts or from halakhic codifications? Bleich's idea appears to be this: Since the Bible presents divine commands to wage war, we must conclude that waging war (with the concomitant bloodshed) is rendered permissible by God's command; but this conclusion seems unwarranted. Let us think of God as a king. If our king commands us to wage war, is it this command that renders bloodshed permissible? On the contrary, the command itself can be appropriate only if we have prior grounds for allowing the activity of warfare.

Surely, God has compelling reasons for sending his people into battle. If a particular war (or a class of "commanded wars") seems unjustified, what is called for is hardly a "theodicy"; that is, a post facto attempt to justify God's deeds. For Bleich's concession that "[d]ivine will, at least at times, may indeed be determined through 'study and debate'" is a vast understatement. Rather, the basic premise of rabbinic Judaism is that God's words, unlike his deeds, are not an unyielding 'given,' but require interpretation and elaboration.[1] Therefore a command that, according to its plain meaning (*peshat*), appears immoral or even just unreasonable is to be (re)interpreted or qualified to become consistent with the rest of Torah.

The contrary portrayal of Halakha as a self-contained enterprise, which through its special "dialectic" and formal "mechanisms" yields morality-proof norms, is what I dubbed Bleich's *oracular halakha*. My point was that, although (as even I know) the *urim ve-tumim* oracle is nowadays unavailable, Bleich perceives all halakhic discourse as functionally equivalent to the oracle: It can furnish a "*mattir* [formal suspension] of the prohibition against homicide."[2]

Only when Halakha is viewed in this peculiar light is it possible to appreciate Bleich's definition of his essay's main goals: to produce an objective "report" of halakhic "facts."[3] That which Bleich considers "but deductive sleuthing" involves, in fact, modes of reasoning and background assumptions that are far from self-evident. I tried in my critique to show how this is so, and the reader must be the judge of whether I succeeded.

When writing about the relation between Halakha and ethics, I was well aware of the essays by Lichtenstein and Bleich, whose very titles seem to promise a head-on tackling of this fundamental issue. Anyone not yet familiar with these essays will certainly be rewarded by studying them, as they present and seriously analyze important sources. Still, they do not deal with the main issue of whether the forging or application of halakhic norms traditionally was—or indeed ought to be—insulated from the requirements of common morality.[4]

THREE DIFFERENCES IN READING TEXTS

In this section, I will discuss briefly three examples where Bleich's reading of halakhic texts differs from my own. This sample is not meant to be exhaustive, but rather to illustrate the tenuousness of his views.

First, Bleich asserts that my statement that the Talmud sanctions only preemption is "simply false." For, he says, "The Gemara, *Sotah* 44b, explicitly states: 'The wars waged by the House of David for territorial expansion were optional in the opinion of all'."

Whether this is "explicit" depends on how sure one is of the proffered translation. Bleich's "for territorial expansion" is hardly the literal equivalent of the Hebrew *lirevacha*. In modern Hebrew, following certain medieval rabbinic usages, *revacha* means "welfare," "well-being," or even "affluence"; this is probably the background for those interpretations that read here a license for wars of imperialist conquest. In rabbinic usage, however, *revacha* seems never to have this meaning. Rather, it is commonly the antonym of *tzara*,[5] "suffering" or "ordeal."[6] A translation more consistent with rabbinic usage would be, perhaps, "the wars waged . . . for relief." The precise nature of this "relief" would depend on the nature of the preceding *tzara*; therefore, I considered this text far from explicit.

Second, for a more explicit discussion of this same issue, I turned to prominent halakhic scholars of the twentieth century, citing Rabbis Karelitz (Chazon Ish) and Kook. As I noted, my interpretation of Chazon Ish's discussion, which Bleich considers "an exaggerated and wishful reading," is shared by Rabbi 'Amital, an eminent contemporary scholar. This in itself does not exclude the plausibility of Bleich's alternative reading (in my note 15, I indicated the textual grounds for that). Again, in the face of such disparate readings, it is difficult to maintain the image of halakhic discourse as a morally neutral exposition of God's will, revealed at Sinai.

Third, regarding the proper understanding of the texts by Netziv and by Maharal, I leave it to the reader to judge whether my own interpretation or that advanced by Bleich is to be preferred. Partly out of a wish to facilitate such judgement, I have offered in my chapter a full translation of each, translations whose accuracy Bleich seems to accept. Unlike the previous two examples, however, I suspect that the key to our differences in interpretation here will not be found in any detail of translation, nor in the weight assigned to any particular phrase. Rather, it lies in the different conceptual frameworks and presuppositions each of us brings to these texts. Whereas I freely acknowledge this, its denial seems central to Bleich's argument.

MARKETABILITY AND MORALITY

Can it be that there is an inherent connection between Bleich's lack of patience with alternative interpretations and his religious absolutism, that is, the claim that Halakha offers a univocal

representation of God's revealed will? Surely, nothing was further
from my mind than an effort to "mold and sculpt halakhic sources
to yield what is thought to be a more marketable product." So
what in my chapter ever suggested to Bleich a religious conscience
on the market?[7]

My uneasy hypothesis is that from the perspective of religious
absolutism this suggestion was found in the very presentation of
alternative texts and readings of the halakhic tradition. An abso-
lutist who is confronted with readings that deviate from what he
or she holds to be the true Halakha attributes them to ulterior
motives. After all, they are plainly wrong; why on earth would
anyone be promulgating them?

I will admit that my concern is not only theoretical; it involves
also a crucial issue of practical morality. Bleich tells us that "A
philosopher grappling with the problem of the bombing of Dresden
or Hiroshima will carefully distinguish between the purposeful
targeting of a civilian population and the incidental and unintentional killing of an innocent bystander. To the halakhist the former
is virtually unthinkable; the halakhic permissibility of the latter is
taken for granted despite Zohar's disclaimer. If, as Zohar seems to
maintain, that is not the case, virtually no defensive action would
find sanction in Halakha." Now some moral philosophers have
progressed a bit further in their analysis of these issues. The term
targeting carries a specific meaning, especially in discussions of
nuclear strikes: since the "target"—that is, the *aiming point*—can
be a military installation, it may be well known that many
noncombatants will be killed.[8] Does such a result come under the
definition of "incidental and unintentional," even though it is
clearly anticipated? And must such "incidental" deaths be "taken
for granted" in any defensive war, without regard for the scale
of the death toll or for the relative importance of the military
target?[9]

It seems to me that Bleich's primary focus on questions of
formal legitimacy tends to obscure the moral urgency of this
matter of proportionality. Far too easily, such formalism serves to
absolve military planners and fighting crews alike from the duty of
minimizing noncombatant casualties. My contrary insistence on
this duty is likely to be anything but "marketable," if we may
judge by popular support for the bombings of both Dresden and
Hiroshima. Yet even in war, it is worth remembering that "one

who rescues a single life—it is as though he had rescued an entire world" (Mishnah, *Sanhedrin* 4:5).

NOTES

1. The contrary belief, that God's will is inextricably bound to the text's plain meaning, is the kernel of the Karaitic position. The Karaites' denial of the authority of midrashic interpretations placed them outside the mainstream of traditional Judaism.

2. As I indicated, this portrayal of the oracle itself is at least debatable. See TB *Eruvin* 45a, and Rashi (s.v. "*I Shaarei*") who says that normative matters (*issur ve-heter*) are not to be put to the *urim ve-tumim*.

3. Obviously, even straightforward "reporting" about ancient (and often elliptical) texts, such as the talmudic literature, necessarily involves an exercise of judgment in choosing between alternative interpretations. See later for some examples regarding Bleich's interpretations as well as debatable translations.

4. For an illuminating debate on this issue, see Leibowitz 1992, pp. 6–7, 18–19, vs. Hartman 1985, pp. 89–108.

5. These two terms are literal antonyms as well: *tzara* means "narrow" and *revacha*, "spacious".

6. See, for example, *Genesis Rab.* 87:23; *Lament. Rab.* 3:41; Midrash Tehillim (Buber ed.) 22:7; the same holds in numerous other places.

7. This is, unfortunately, but one of several instances of incivility in Bleich's response (cf. Maimonides, MT, *Book of Knowledge, Foundations of the Torah* 5:11). My own critique is certainly far from perfect, but I never meant to cast doubt on Bleich's sincerity or on his basic competence in reading halakhic texts.

8. See Finnis, Boyle, and Grisez 1987, pp. 92ff.

9. For a detailed discussion, see Walzer 1977, chapter 9.

REFERENCES

Finnis, J., J. M. Boyle, and G. Grisez. 1987. *Nuclear Deterrence, Morality and Realism.* New York: Oxford University Press.

Hartman, D. 1985. *A Living Covenant.* New York: The Free Press.

Leibowitz, Y. 1992. *Judaism, Human Values and the Jewish State,* ed. E. Goldman. Cambridge, Mass.: Harvard University Press.

Walzer, M. 1977. *Just and Unjust Wars.* New York: Basic Books.

CONTRIBUTORS

J. David Bleich is the Herbert and Florence Tenzer Professor of Jewish Law and Ethics at Yeshiva University, where he also serves as Professor of Law in the Benjamin N. Cardozo School of Law and Professor of Talmud and Rosh Kollel le-Hora'a at the Rabbi Isaac Elchanan Theological Seminary. He is the author of *Contemporary Halakhic Problems* (3 vols., 1977–1989), editor of *With Perfect Faith: Foundations of Jewish Belief* (1983), and coeditor (with Fred Rosner) of *Jewish Bioethics: A Reader* (1979).

Aryeh Botwinick is Professor of Political Science at Temple University. He has written on Hume and Wittgenstein and is the author of *Postmodernism and Democratic Theory* (1993) and *Skepticism and Political Participation* (1990) and coauthor (with Peter Bachrach) of *Power and Empowerment: A Radical Theory of Participatory Democracy* (1992).

Elliot N. Dorff is Provost and Professor of Philosophy at the University of Judaism and Visiting Professor at the UCLA School of Law. He has written five books, including *Knowing God: Jewish Journeys to the Unknowable* (1993) and (with Arthur Rosett) *A Living Tree: The Roots and Growth of Jewish Law* (1988), and is coeditor (with Louis Newman) of *Contemporary Jewish Ethics and Morality: A Reader* (1995).

Daniel H. Frank is Associate Professor of Philosophy at the University of Kentucky. He has written in the areas of Greek philosophy and of medieval Islamic and Jewish philosophy. He is the editor of *A People Apart: Chosenness and Ritual in Jewish Philosophical*

Thought (1993) and *Autonomy and Judaism: The Individual and the Community in Jewish Philosophical Thought* (1992) and author of *The Arguments 'From the Sciences' in Aristotle's Peri Ideon* (1984).

Lenn E. Goodman is Professor of Philosophy at Vanderbilt University. A specialist in medieval Islamic and Jewish philosophy, he has published studies of most of the major Muslim philosophers as well as of such Jewish thinkers as Maimonides and Saadiah. His most recent books are *Avicenna* (1992), *On Justice: An Essay in Jewish Philosophy* (1991), and a translation with philosophical commentary of Saadiah Gaon's *Book of Theodicy* (1988).

Reuven Kimelman is Associate Professor of Near Eastern and Judaic Studies at Brandeis University. The author of articles on Jewish history, ethics, and liturgy, he is currently writing two books: *The Jewish Ethics of Power* and *The Liturgy as Literature: A Literary and Historical Commentary to the Jewish Prayerbook*.

Oliver Leaman is Reader in Philosophy at Liverpool John Moores University. He is the author of *Moses Maimonides* (1990), *Averroes and His Philosophy* (1988), and *An Introduction to Medieval Islamic Philosophy* (1985) and coeditor (with Seyyed Hossein Nasr) of *The Routledge History of Islamic Philosophy* (forthcoming) and (with Daniel Frank) of *The Routledge History of Jewish Philosophy* (forthcoming).

Abraham Melamed is Senior Lecturer in Jewish History and Thought at the University of Haifa. His research interests are in medieval and early modern Jewish intellectual history and political thought. He has written numerous articles on the history of Jewish political philosophy and his book, *The Philosopher King in Medieval and Renaissance Jewish Political Thought*, is forthcoming.

David Novak is the Edgar M. Bronfman Professor of Modern Judaic Studies at the University of Virginia. He has written numerous articles on Jewish philosophy and theology and is the author of eight books, among which are *The Theology of Nahmanides Systematically Presented* (1992), *Jewish Social Ethics* (1992),

Jewish-Christian Dialogue: A Jewish Justification (1989), and *The Image of the Non-Jew in Judaism* (1983).

Josef Stern is Associate Professor of Philosophy at the University of Chicago. His primary research interests are in medieval Jewish philosophy and in contemporary philosophy of language. He has written numerous essays in both areas, including "Maimonides on the Covenant of Circumcision and the Unity of God" (in *The Midrashic Imagination: Essays in Rabbinic Thought and Interpretation*, 1993) and "The Idea of a *Hoq* in Maimonides' Explanation of the Law" (in *Maimonides and Philosophy*, 1986).

Noam J. Zohar is Lecturer in Philosophy at Bar-Ilan University. His major research interests are in the philosophy of halakha and Jewish political philosophy and applied ethics. Among his publications are "Midrash: Amendment Through the Molding of Meaning" (in *Responding to Imperfection: New Approaches to the Problem of Constitutional Amendment*, 1994), "Collective War and Individualistic Ethics: Against the Conscription of 'Self-Defense'" (*Political Theory*, 1993), and "Artificial Insemination and Surrogate Motherhood: A Halakhic Perspective" (*S'vara*, 1991).

INDEX